Kill the Dragon; Get the Girl

A Commentary on the Book of Revelation

2nd Edition

By W.J. Sturm

Text copyright © 2018 William J Sturm

All Rights Reserved

Scripture quotations are generally taken from the King James Bible.

Some Scripture quotations in Revelation 5, 7, and 14 are taken from the New King James Version®, Copyright © 1982 by Thomas Nelson, Inc. (and those few out-of-sequence footnotes in those passages are particular footnotes retained from the NKJV.)

Table of Contents

Preface to 2nd Edition

Dedication

About the Author

Introduction

Chapter 1

Chapter 2

Chapter 3

Chapter 4

Chapter 5

Chapter 6

Chapter 7

Chapter 8

Chapter 9

Chapter 10

Chapter 11

Chapter 12

Chapter 13

Chapter 14

Chapter 15

Chapter 16

Chapter 19

Chapter 20

Chapter 21

Chapter 22

Appendices

APPENDIX 1: THE POST-TRIBULATIONAL RAPTURE

APPENDIX 2: JEHOVAH'S WITNESSES & THE 144,000

Preface to 2nd Edition

I like to think of this as a living and breathing project. I am always learning and always seeking to perfect what God has allowed me to do. My prayer is that you will find the summary of updates below helpful as you begin marking up your copy of this edition without needing to read the whole thing after you have already personalized your copy of the original edition.

1. Added to the introduction are:
 -- A word about Revelation's Theme
 -- A word about the Preterist perspective was added to the introduction
 -- A word about Amillennialism
 -- Additional Discussion about "Why Another Revelation Commentary"

2. Commentary added on Revelation 2:10

3. Adjusted commentary on Revelation 3:10-11

4. Adjusted commentary on Revelation 4:3

5. Additional commentary added in Revelation 5

6. Additional commentary on Revelation 7:9-15

7. Adjusted commentary on Revelation 12:1-5

8. Additional commentary on Revelation 14:1-5

9. Additional commentary on Revelation 14:14

10. Adjusted commentary on Revelation 20:1-2

11. Additional commentary on Revelation 20:4-6

12. Additional commentary on Revelation 21:1

13. Table comparing Revelation 21 and the book of Isaiah added

14. An appendix with a defense of the post-tribulational rapture added

15. An appendix with the 144,000 and the Jehovah's Witnesses added

The overall theme?

I still do think a great theme in Revelation is the "Ultimate Exodus"…but what if the main theme is different? What?!?! Yes, we all know there is a comparison between Exodus and Revelation that is above 30 in number (later in this book), but when we see the thing known as a chiasm (opening of the theme in the beginning of a body of literature and the closing of the theme in the same book) it becomes apparent that there is a Bible-wide drama of God and His wife. So the theme of Revelation could simply be "Kill the Dragon; Get the Girl." John would not have struggled to see this theme having hung out with Matthew—hearing what Matthew had heard from Jesus in his Gospel, chapters 9, 22, 25 and John's Gospel, chapters 2 and 3.

"This guy changed his mind?!"

I think so. Take a look and see what you think: The book begins with the overview of the book: a wedding procession (Revelation 1:7) continues with the groom's eyes of fire (jealousy?) (Revelation 1:14); goes on with his irritation with her flirting (Revelation 2:20); gives a teaser of "access to the king" [a la Song of Solomon (Song of Solomon 2:4) or (Queen of Sheba, 1 Kings 10); Revelation 3:7]; a sort of invitation for intimacy with the king [more reflection on Song of Solomon (Song of Solomon 5:2); Revelation 3:20]; destruction of a counterfeit bride (Revelation 17-18) and counterfeit bridegroom (Revelation 19:20); pronouncement of the marriage feast (Revelation 19:6-9); killing of the bully/ravager (Revelation 20:1-3; 10); unveiling of the bridal chamber (Revelation 21-22); the wedding license/certificate (Revelation 21:23-27); and closing with the invitation from the bride to attend (Revelation 22:15-

21). I guess that is why I say the theme of Revelation could simply be "Kill the Dragon; Get the Girl." Here's an outline of this understanding.

1. There are other hints within this book that lead the reader to see the marriage motif.
    a. presentation of those in "white" (3:5; 16:15; 19:11ff)
    b. unveiling of the bridal chamber (Revelation 21-22)
    c. A closing invitation from the bride to attend (Revelation 22:15-21).

2. There are other hints within this book that lead the reader to see the marriage motif.
    a. a wedding procession (Revelation 1:7)
    b. the groom's eyes of fire (jealousy?) (Revelation 1:14)
    c. irritation with her flirting (Revelation 2:20)
    d. gives a teaser of "access to the king" (Revelation 3:7)
    e. a sort of invitation at the door for intimacy with the king (Revelation 3:20)
    f. A bride price is paid by the groom (Revelation 5:9-10)[1]
    g. destruction of a counterfeit bride (Revelation 17-18)
    h. counterfeit bridegroom (Revelation 19:20)
    i. the wedding license/certificate (Revelation 21:23-27)

3. There is further assistance from a little suspected book in Old Testament (in addition to places like Isaiah 5:1-5). See my commentary on Song of Solomon (5th chapter) for more.

The Biggest Issue With Preterism

If you're not sure what this is, please go to the next section. If

---

[1] Amazing, really: God's redistribution of wealth takes place here. Pastor Jonathan Andrews pointed this obvious principle out here. God uses marriage to even the field. He pointed this out to me after I explained the difference between a dowry and a bride price. The "dowry" is paid by the father of the bride to a poorer son in law who would not otherwise find it financially helpful to marry the woman while the "bride price" is paid by the son in law to the father of the bride who would otherwise miss the extra income earner in the home.

you are wondering why I do not believe this perspective should be that through which one views Revelation, the answer is not "Because Revelation was written after A.D. 70." It may not have been, quite frankly. The biggest problem, in my view is with the notion that the climax—having to do with the Beast and the False Prophet and 1260 days of trouble from the dragon are to be found in Jerusalem—are enough to trouble the whole world…primarily those in 7 local churches in Turkey!

The Biggest Issue With Amillennialism

If you want to know why I reject this view, it all comes down to one dominating issue: The First & Second Resurrections of Revelation 20:4-6. If the "first resurrection" is "the new birth," one must ask how those who take part in the second resurrection "live again after the 1000 years are finished" (20:5-6)? One must be a universalist if they wish to be exegetically consistent and believe this is the "new birth."

Dedication

In addition to the regular lavishing of praises I wish to do to God for the work of His Holy Spirit and the sacrifice of His Son, I would also thank my dear wife, Nikki, and our children Bethany, Jacob, and Leah for understanding that their dad does not have a work shop or hobby; he has a love to understand and illustrate Scripture; he has a love to invite pest controllers, roofers, carpet installers, electricians, drawlers, and landscapers to his home so that he can witness to them. When one sees 100's of hours exhausted for the culmination of a meager work as this, they see a patient family behind the author.

About the Author

Previous to Sandy Ridge Baptist Church, Bill Sturm served as the Associate Pastor of Berean Baptist Church in Fayetteville, NC following almost nine years on active duty in the United States Army. He otherwise specializes in Chaplaincy, World Religions, and Church History. His most recent formal education was the completion of his Th.M. from Liberty Baptist Theological Seminary (2014). He was saved out of a life of "Sinner's Prayer"-ism and placed his faith in the finished work of Christ alone in 1999. Bill has felt the call to ministry most of his life, having preached as a 5th grader to his peers in childrens' church. He is a student of Scripture, a student of his family, a student of people, and enjoys theological reasoning, ethics, and the game of soccer. He currently serves as a Chaplain in the United States Army Reserve. His greatest challenge is his prayer life. Preaching Christ and His cross are Bill's passion. He is happily married to Nikki--his wife of 20 years, and they have three children. Contact Bill at pastorbillsrbc@gmail.com

Introduction

Why Another Commentary on Revelation?

A different approach

    a. The reader will notice an overriding theme throughout this commentary on the parallels between the book of Exodus and the book of Revelation. That is to say that Revelation conveys the ultimate Exodus of God's people from Egypt.

    b. The reader will notice that there is <u>absolutely no affirmation to a pre-tribulation</u> <u>rapture</u>. This is unusual today. Later into the book you may be tempted to ask "Well, will there be Christians on the earth at the time?" I have every reason, because of this book of Revelation, to say "yes." Again, other than the seventh trumpet in chapter 11, I don't see any signal for any kind of rapture at all. We're convinced that somehow we leave. Okay, if you want to believe that, fine, but the burden of proof is on the person who wants to find it in the book of Revelation. I taught this to a class for over a year and offered opportunity—in either formal or informal settings—to hear arguments for a pretribulation rapture. Here are some questions for the reader:

1. Strange, isn't it, that a book explaining Daniel's 70th week—a week having nothing to do with Gentile Christians—is written in detail to....Gentile Christians in 7 different locations outside of Israel?

2. Strange, isn't it that He tells these 7 churches that there are promises to them if they will overcome; there are those who are lauded who overcome the dragon in chapter 12 and the beast in chapter 15; and yet, somehow there are those who insist that there is no connection between the promises to the overcomer within the 7 churches and those later in the book who overcome? No, rather, they propose to you that these who are promised wonderful things if they overcome are removed before they must overcome anything—thereby making the remainder of the book up until chapter 19 basically meaningless?

3. Strange, isn't it that the first scene of thousands and thousands of saints—perhaps millions of saints is in Revelation 7, not Revelation 4 and they are described as those who "come out of Great Tribulation?"

4. Strange isn't it, that in the middle of the visions of the beast and the false prophet in chapter 13, the Scripture says something that it hasn't said in 10 chapters when it said it to each of the 7 churches: "He that hath an ear, let him hear what the spirit saith unto the churches."

5. Strange, isn't it, that it is in the middle of the vials, chapter 16, when the reader, which is the members of seven local churches made up of Gentile believers are told to "watch for the thief lest they be caught unaware?" More on this, we find that this chapter contains one of the seven "blessed statements" found throughout the book. We would expect the "reader who won't be here between chapters 4 and 19" to not find such precious promises in these same chapters.

Am I sure about everything we are going to interpret?

We know "opaque" means no light travels through. "Transparent" means you can see through it like glass so if I went and stood on the other side of that window, you could tell it is definitely Bill Sturm and his head. So, if we took that covering and put it over the window and I went and stood outside, you'd say, "Well, he looks bald like that knuckle-head but we're not sure if it's him." So "translucence" means that you can tell a silhouette, you can tell that there is the form of a man out there but you're not exactly sure who it is. "Transparency" means you can see clearly who it is.

Now, let me just tell you that Bible prophecy is a lot like that. Do you remember when the wise men came to Jerusalem and they said, "We're looking for the king of the Jews," and they told that to King

Herod. Do you remember that? King Herod called some of his wise men together and what did they do to determine where the child would be born? They searched the Scripture; they found a verse in Micah 5:2 which said very clearly he would be born in Bethlehem. Very clear. That would be called a transparent prophecy. You look, "Oh, that's obvious. Bethlehem, it says so. It's very clear."

And then there are some prophecies in the Old Testament that are not transparent at all—they are translucent which means, "Here's a good guess at what it means but we're really not going to know until it is fulfilled." For instance, Psalm 16 says that David was writing and he said, "You will not suffer your holy one to see corruption or leave my soul in hell." Well, that's interesting. How in the world is David going to die but not be dead long enough to see corruption? So, there must be some kind of mystical meaning there. Until, Peter gets up after Jesus died, rose again, went to heaven, 50 days after the resurrection of Christ, there's Pentecost. When Peter preaches in Acts 2 and says, "Hey, Psalm 16 was about Jesus." Well, that wasn't obvious by reading Psalm 16 until after the fulfillment.

Date & Geography: It has been generally accepted that the book of Revelation was written about 95 AD. Revelation is written to seven churches here in what is known as Asia Minor in the book of Revelation and this is also called just plain old Asia in the book of Acts, so Asia or Asia Minor. So Asia wasn't necessarily known as a continent back in the first century, this was know as both Asia in the book of 1 Peter, for instance, and it's also known as Asia Minor. So maybe, by the time Revelation was written, it became known as the small Asia or Asia Minor. So people became aware of the geography, maybe there was a continent, a greater part of the world known as Asia and so this became small Asia or Asia Minor by the end of the first century. But the book of Revelation is a letter much like most of the New Testament is a letter and it's a letter to seven different churches. And you say, "How do you know that?" Well, you'll see.

Additional Information

Throughout this commentary, the reader will notice comparisons of a couple of different aspects throughout Scripture.

The comparison of "Exodus" with Revelation will be one of these tables. Please notice the highlighted portion of these successively updated tables which show that John had, on his mind, the final exodus—the Ultimate Exodus—of God's people from the ultimate Egypt, a godless earth. Use this table as your guide:

Theme	Exodus	Revelation
1. A Book of Life out of which to blot	32:32-33	3:5
2. Saints' Protection	8:22;	3:10
3. The Lamb	12:4	5:5-9; 12:11
4. A contest for the earth	9:29	5:9; 20:1-6
5. Darkness over wicked	10:21	6:12
6. Anti-Christ Figure	Pharaoh	Beast
7. An Exodus	12-14	7:14
8. The Sinai-like response	19:16-18	8:5; 11:19
9. Hail Judgment	9:13	8:7
10. Water becoming blood	7:14	8:8; 11:6; 16:3-7
11. "Bitter waters" for idolaters	32:20	8:11
12. Darkness judgment	10:21	6:11; 8:12; 9:2; 16:10
13. Locusts judgment	10:1	9:3
14. "Destroyer"	12:23	9:11
15. Judgment from "waters"	13-14	9:14
16. Those judged harden their hearts	9:34	9:21; 16:9-11
17. Fiery Manifestation of God.	24:11	10:1
18. God's voice sounds like thunder	19:19	10:3
19. The realm of God's creation	20:4	10:5-6

20. Lots of temple talk	25-31	3-15
21. Fed in wilderness	16	12
22. Leaving Egypt	12-13	11:8; 12:6
23. Into wilderness on eagles' wings	19:1-4	12:14
24. "Earth" swallowing the armies of Egypt	15:12	12:16
25. The miracle worker has a prophet	5-8	13
26. Led to a mountain	15:17	14:1
27. Redeemed	15:13	14:4
28. Firstfruits brought to House of God	23:19	14:4
29. The "Song of Moses" by a "sea."	15:3	15:3
30. "All the earth" is the prize	9:14	15:4
31. Unable to enter temple because of	40:35	15:8
32. Hail upon enemies of God.	9:8-12	16:2
33. "Eating with God"	24:10-11	19:9; 21:3
34. God dwelling among His people	29:45-46	21:3
35. 12 Precious Gems in God's dwelling place	28:17-21	21:14-20
36. Tree of life language[2]	25:31-40	22:2

There is also a comparison of "Mystery Babylon" and the "New Jerusalem." You'll see this in Revelation 21 and 22 as you see the New Jerusalem introduced and it will be pretty clear to you that this is probably another intended thematic comparison by John the Apostle—especially when this commentary holds that Jerusalem is "Mystery Babylon." Use the following table as your guide:

	Mystery Babylon	New Jerusalem

---

[2]Learned this from this great source: Allen P. Ross *Recalling the Hope of Glory* (Grand Rapids: Kregel Publications, 2006), 100-101.

Introduced by 1 of 7 vial-angels	17:1	21:9
The whore/the bride	17:1³	21:9
Kings of Earth	Fornication with her (17:2)	Bring their glory to her (21:24)
Carried away	Into the wilderness (17:3-5)	Into a high mountain (21:10)
On foreheads	"Mystery Babylon" (17:3-5)	name of God (22:3-4)
Kings of Earth	Fornication with her	Bring their glory to
Carried away	Into the wilderness	Into a High Mountain
Ascending/Descend	Beast from bottomless	New Jerusalem from
"Great City"	17:18	21:10
"death and mourning"	18:8	none, 21:4
"precious stones"	18:16	21:19
"gold"	18:16	21:21
"pearl"	18:16	21:21

Another comparison is how things develop in Genesis and find their resolution in Revelation. As such, in chapter 14 you will notice another table develop to show how these "problems" are "resolved." Use the following table as your guide:

	Genesis	Revelation
Babel/Babylon	Rise of (10-11)	Fall of (14, 16-19)
God comes looking toward His people	Hiding (3:8)	Unashamed (16:15)

---

³It should be pointed out that while the "whore" of Revelation 17-18 is usually identified as "Jerusalem" in the Old Testament (Ezekiel and Jeremiah), the church is here identified with "New Jerusalem" (Revelation 21:9-10).

God comes to see those gathered	Gathered (11:1-6)	Gathered (19:17-18)
Toppling of god-	Nimrod (10:9-10)	Antichrist (19:20)
Sea	Covers the earth (1:2)	No Sea (21:1)
Tree of Life	Removed (3:22)	Restored (22:2)
Nations	Fracture/Begin (10-11)	Heal under Christ (21:24; 22:2)
Curse	Results (3:17)	Removed (22:3)
Rulership	Man, with God's Permission (1:26)	God, with Man's Permission (22:3)
Service to God	Begun (2:15)	Continued (22:3)
Disposition	Ashamed (3:9)	See His Face (22:4)
Light	Source Given (1:14)	Source Removed (21:23; 22:5)
The Word	Gave life (1:1-29; John 1:1-3, 14)	Here to Recreate (19:13; 21:5)

Chapter 1

1:1

The Revelation of Jesus Christ. Please notice: it is singular. So, now you know more than most of your friends. It is not the "book of the revelations." It is the book of the Revelation. It is *the* Revelation. So, now we know that the book of Revelation is about one revelation. Therefore, the book of Revelation is to show us the revealing of something or somebody.

these things are going to shortly come to pass. Yeah, what do you consider shortly? It's been a long time since this was written. We're talking about more than 1,900 years since it's been written. What's taking so long? I thought this was shortly going to come to pass? It doesn't say in the book of Revelation that the rapture is shortly going to come to pass. Do you see that? John said the whole book could happen any day.

So we're talking about what must surely come to pass is the beginning of things to get things moving. More will follow in verse 3.

he sent and signified it by his angel unto his servant John. Matthew 10 says this is the son of Zebedee and the brother of James.

1:2

Who bare record of the word of God, and of the testimony of Jesus Christ, and of all things that he saw. He sent and signified it by this angel to John and most of this signification or signs that John saw through this angel were just simply visions. He saw them. The last book in the Bible, written by John, is his testimony, his personal revelation that he received from an angel, from Jesus, from God the Father. So, that's an important relation there. The same words are used again later on:

> *Revelation 1:9 I John, who also am your brother, and companion in tribulation, and in the kingdom and patience of Jesus Christ, was in the isle that is called Patmos,* ***for the word of***

God, and for the testimony of Jesus Christ.

*Revelation 6:9 ...**for the word of God, and for the testimony which they held**....*

*Revelation 12:11 And they overcame him by the blood of the Lamb, and **by the word of their testimony**.*

You're going to find that most of what you read in the book of Revelation is found in a prophet in the Old Testament. So, I could pull out a Study Bible and I could just tell you what the dude says or we could interpret it through the Old Testament because that is, by the way, what kind of language we're dealing with here. Revelation is much Old Testament language and the reason most of us are not aware of that is because many of us have not read the Old Testament. You have to be familiar with how the Old Testament prophets spoke.

Now, how is it given **through an angel**? Here's what Stephen (Acts 7:53), here's what the writer of Hebrews (Hebrews 2:2), here's what Paul (Galatians 3) said—they all said that angels gave the law to Moses and now here we're told in the book of Rev- elation that an angel gave this book to John. So this is nothing new.

1:3

Blessed are they that keep the words of this book of Revelation. If you do a simple word search, you'll find there are seven of these "blessings" for the reader, found throughout the book.

for the time is at hand. It's right upon us. See this again in the last chapter, "And he said unto me, These sayings are faithful and true: and the Lord God of the holy prophets sent his angel to shew unto his servants the things which must shortly be done." So he says it twice. These things are going to be done shortly. Okay, so it is definitely a theme that these things are going to be shortly done. Now, please understand that he is taking the book of Revelation as a group and he says,

"These things must shortly be done."

I'm not telling you, "Here's exactly what it means." I'm telling you: here's our options: either it means that it all had to be done in the first century and all of it has been fulfilled and yes, there is a group of people who believe that the book of Revelation has all been fulfilled. Yes, there are. They're called Preterists. "Well, why is it crazy?" Well, because of what's included in the end of the book of Revelation. Like say, Armageddon. Like say, the Second Coming, the revelation of Jesus Christ. Like say, the new heaven and the new earth. All of that is nothing but allegorized and sign and just picture to them.

Option 2: we can say that it was truly to build vigilance because in chapter 22, verse 20, "He which testifieth these things saith, Surely I come quickly. Amen. Even so, come, Lord Jesus." So we're not comfortable as 2014, English speaking Americans reading our Bibles sitting in comfortable chairs hearing that something that was sup- posed to be done quickly hasn't been done yet. But please understand that to people who are living the life that John is living, this was of great comfort to know that these things could quickly come to pass, to include the Second Coming of Christ.

Thirdly, It could be that once it starts, it happens quickly. In other words, if the book of Revelation was about to be unfolded like John said in Revelation 1, then Christ really was coming quickly once these things start to happen in Revelation 22. This also occurs in Luke 21:28.

1:4

John to the seven churches which are in Asia: Grace be unto you, and peace, from him which is, and which was, and which is to come; and from the seven Spirits which are before his throne; I would argue that the Bible uses the number seven more often for completeness than proposed "perfection." say "completeness" because it's when things are done. All the way back on the first seven days of creation, the seventh day he rested because he was done. Not because he was tired, but because he was done. The seventh day is the Sabbath. The seventh time that they marched around Jericho was when the walls fell. Seven times Namaan dipped in the Jordan River to get himself healed of leprosy; seven years of plenty in Egypt; seven years of famine followed that (in Joseph's time); seven years of Nebuchadnezzar when he went insane in the wilderness; seven petitions in the Lord's prayer; seven parables in Matthew 13 that are told by Jesus; seven loaves of bread that fed the multitudes as one of Jesus' miracles; and seven sayings of Jesus on the cross.

There are **seven churches**; **seven Spirits** in this verse with **seven** stars, **seven** lamps, **seven** seals, and **seven** horns are to be found in this book. .

1:5

Unto him that loved us, and washed us from our sins in his own blood. This phrase is a part of a description of Jesus Christ. Please look with me there. One might notice in other translations of the Bible that there is a different terminology. Unto Him that "loved us and freed us from our sins…" Why the difference? It's really simple. The word "freed" and the word "washed" are different in one vowel. "Freed" has one less "upsilon." Probably, once upon a time, a scribe accidently dropped the vowel while copying. When I say "scribe," I am talking about anybody who may have been copying the manuscript at that time—it need not mean a professional guildsmen. Moreover, it seems more likely than the alternative which would be that somebody accidentally added a vowel to get "washed." **And from Jesus Christ, who is the faithful witness, First begotten of the dead, Prince of the kings of the earth.** John said "**unto him**," and he starts talking about Jesus and he gets carried away. He says, "**unto him that loved us and washed us from our sins in his own blood. And hath made us kings and priests.**" He hasn't stopped with his doxology. **And hath made us kings and priests unto God and his Father.** Now he's done describing Jesus and he says **to him be glory and dominion forever and ever. Amen.**

This should surprise us because that's not how John was taught to pray. That was something he was told only to talk to the Father about. "For thine is the kingdom and the power and the glory forever. Amen" (Matthew 6). But here he is taking one person of the Trinity and it's not the Father and he gives to the Son all honor and glory because **he has loved us and washed us from our sins in his own blood.** And think about the description he's giving here. Think of all the things that John could've said about the one he wants to give, in verse 6, **dominion and glory**. He could've said, "Unto him that made the earth. Unto him that became God in the flesh. Unto him that became the one who spread out the stars in creation week and created Lucifer, of all things. He created everything. The angels," he said, "I could describe them that way, but I'm going to describe him this way. He's the one that loved me and washed me from my sins in his own blood." This is that same Jesus that Paul talks about where he says

> *2 Corinthians 5:14-15,* **the love of Christ** *constrains us, because if* <u>one</u> <u>died for all</u>, *then we're all dead.*

> *Galatians 2:20,* ***[Jesus] loved me*** *and* <u>gave himself</u> *for me.*

> *Ephesians 5:2, And walk in love as* **Christ also hath loved** *us* <u>and given</u> <u>himself</u> *to us an offering to God for sweet smelling savor."*

> *Ephesians 5:25 Husbands love your wives as* **Christ loved the church** *and* <u>gave himself for it</u>.

John said, "I can describe him in many ways but here is how I'm going to describe him, I'm going to describe Jesus in terms of how he affects me. He loves me and he washed me from my sins in his own blood."

And now, this is the first of four times in the book of Revelation where John describes Jesus as one who does things with his blood; Chapter 5:9 it says that the 24 elders said that he "redeemed them by his blood"; Chapter 7:14, saints that came out of great tribulation made their "robes white in the blood of the Lamb"; Chapter 12:11, they overcame him "by the blood of the Lamb."

Unto Him that loved us and washed us from our sins in His own blood is just a part of the benefit to us. **And made us kings and priest unto God and his Father.** Three actions here: he loved us; he washed us; he made us. The two first actions "loved us" and "washed us" are participial phrases, verbals. That means that they look like verbs in the English but they are actually adjectives, they are adverbs. And so, we could read it as such: while loving us and while washing us from our sins in his own blood, **he made us kings and priests**. Therefore, the whole while that he made us kings and priests, he was washing us from our sins and the whole while that he was washing us from our sins, he was loving us.

"A **king** and a **priest**?" John is a slave of Rome, practically imprisoned. All the other Apostles are dead. How do we go from being slaves to sin to being kings in Christ? Look at chapter 1:1. Notice to whom the book is written. It's **the Revelation of Jesus Christ which God gave to him to show unto his servants.** This is just a paradox. How do you get to be a **king** with Christ? By being a **servant**. That's how he was exalted with the Father, by being a servant. We remain **priests**. "John, you're ridiculous. What temple are you serving in on the isle of Patmos? Where is the glory in your temple." "Oh, the glory is in this temple."

1:6

made us kings and priests. This is a theme that is carried on through the New Testament so many times that it would almost overwhelm me to bring them up.

> *1 Peter 2, we offer up spiritual sacrifices. Romans 12, we offer up reasonable sacrifices. Hebrews 13, we offer up sacrifices of praise.*

1:7

He cometh with clouds. This implies a resurrection of the One Who died in verse 5. We're talking about the same resurrected Christ who in Acts 1:13 went up to heaven as his observers were promised that "the same Jesus who went up is coming down just like he went up." And you read Zechariah 14, it says, when he comes again he's going to put his feet on the Mount of Olives. That's where he left from in Acts 1.

Behold, he cometh with clouds; and every eye shall see him, and they also which pierced him: and all kindreds of the earth shall wail because of him. Even so, Amen. Please notice that the main point of the book of Revelation, the main point of John, is not a secret rapture that happens sometimes before a seven year tribulation period. The main point of John in the book of Revelation, the thing he's going to be most explicit about, is the revelation or the revealing of Jesus Christ and he says, "Here's when it is and here's what it is," in verse 7. It is a time in which **every eye will see him** when **he comes with the clouds.** That is **the revelation of Jesus Christ.** When is Christ revealed from heaven? Chapter 19, and that is what the entirety of the book, for the most part other than the epilogue in chapters 20-22, all are leading to. So, the book of Revelation is not leading to, "Oh, I can't wait until we get snatched out of here." That is not John's goal in writing this letter.

Now, take a look at Daniel 7:9 (and following).

Did you notice, that in this passage in the book of Daniel, you have two figures: the Son of Man (verse 13) and the Ancient of days (verse 9). John is caught up to the throne room in heaven, Revelation 4. He sees one sitting on the throne and there's only one worthy to take the book from the One on the throne.

"All nations." How about verse 14? All nations. So, this is a worldwide thing. Now, this all looks very much Revelation-like, doesn't it? I mean, you've got books being opened in Revelation 20:12, "and the books were opened: and another book was opened, which is the book of life: and the dead were judged out of those things which were written in the books." You have worldwide influence. How about Revela- tion 5:9, "And they said, Thou art worthy, O Lord, for thou hast redeemed us by thy blood out of every kindred, tribe, people and nation." How about the beast and the fire thing. Did you know that that actually takes place in Revelation 19? Everlasting Kingdom: you'll see that in chapter 12:10-11.

We're seeing that none of the stuff that we see in Revelation is new.

He cometh with clouds. Consider Psalm 104:3, Matthew 26:64, and Luke 21:26-28 as well.

So, who are **the clouds**? It says in Revelation 19, "I saw heaven opened and one came on a white horse and the armies of heaven followed after." If the **clouds** are the same clouds as in Daniel 7, the same clouds as in Joel 2, they're probably not moisture-type clouds; they're probably known as "the armies of heaven."

Every eye shall see him. That means that the secret snatching away of the church is not the point of this book. I am saying, if you're hoping to find a secret snatching away in the book of Revelation, where the church disappears out of here before the tribulation, then you're going to be real disappointed with the lack of evidence.

and they also which pierced him

> *Zechariah 12:10. And I will pour upon the house of David, and upon the inhabitants of Jerusalem, the spirit of grace and of supplications:* ***and they shall look upon me whom they have pierced.***

Who pierced him? There is no need to get nervous saying the Jews killed him. Paul says the Jews killed him. Peter says the Jews killed him. The Jews said the Jews killed him, "his blood be upon us and on our children" (Matthew 26). Peter said, in Acts 2, "You killed the one that God has made both Lord and Christ." Paul says it was the Jews (1 Thessalonians 2). Peter says it was the Jews. The Jews said it was the Jews. Effectively, God did:

> *Isaiah 53:10 It pleased the Lord to bruise him.*
>
> *Matthew 26 **I will smite the shepherd** and the sheep will be scattered.*

Who pierced him? There is no need to get nervous saying the Jews killed him. Paul says the Jews killed him. Peter says the Jews killed him (Acts 2). The Jews said the Jews killed him, "his blood be upon us and on our children" (Matthew 26). Paul says it was the Jews (1 Thessalonians 2).

1:8

Alpha and Omega…the Almighty This refers to the Father and 1:16-18 refer to the Son. These point to the equality of the Father and the Son Who Both claim to be "The First and the Last." Revelation 4:8 keeps that title "Almighty," utilized for the Father in 1:8, and applies it to the "One on the throne." The Lamb, distinguished from the One on the throne, does not even come into view until Revelation 5 of that two-chapter, throne room overview. Later in Revelation 21:22, the Lamb and the Almighty are mentioned in tandem, thus confirming that the Lamb—the Son—is to be distinguished from the One Who is identified as the "Almighty."

1:9

I John, who also am your brother, and companion in tribulation. Remember the words of Jesus:

> *John 16:33, These things have I spoken unto you that in me you might have peace. In the world, **you shall have tribulation** but be of good cheer I have overcome the world.*

This happened about 60 years before John wrote the book of

Revelation and so John was not caught off guard when it happened. **And in the kingdom and patience of Jesus Christ,** and we'll see that this is really a structure for the book of Revelation but look at the end of the verse: **was in the isle that is called Patmos, for the word of God, and for the testimony of Jesus Christ.** Where have you already seen this in this passage? Verse 2: **Who bare record of the word of God, and of the testimony of Jesus Christ and of all things that he saw.** John says, "You need to know that I am here and I am here for two reasons: because of the testimony of Christ that I've already borne witness to and because of the testimony of Christ that I'm about to write about."

1:10

I was in the Spirit on the Lord's day, and heard behind me a great voice, as of a trumpet, saying, I am Alpha and Omega, the first and the last. Alright, who's talking? Look at verse 12, "I turned to see the voice that spake with me. And being turned, I saw seven golden candlesticks; and in the midst of the seven candlesticks one like unto," who? "The Son of man." Who is that according to the rest of the New Testament? Jesus. So, Jesus is the Almighty? Revelation is not new material. It is mate- rial that has been spoken about throughout the New Testament and throughout the Old Testament. This is old material. And so, when we read the Revelation at the end of the New Testament, we treat it like it's new material but it's not. See Joel 2:1-10 to prove this.

    We're going to find out that we have a Day of the Lord. In verse 2, it is "a day of clouds." A Day of the Lord is the "day of clouds." And he goes on to talk about them, they, them, them, them, they, they, they, they, they, them, they, them, they, them, they, them, they, them, them, all the way through verse 10 and it says in verse 11, that we're talking about the army of the Lord.

    When God judges Israel it is always called "the Day of the Lord." For the most part, we see a two fulfillment idea from the Day of the Lord. Now, at first, it sounds kind of far-fetched but I need to show you this in the text. We see the Day of the Lord talked about in

Joel 1:1-11, and in Joel 1:4 and 2:25 the army of the Lord is identified as these clouds of locusts. When they approach a camp, it looks like a cloud. Have you ever seen one? So, we have these clouds of locusts and they are coming into the people of God and they are devouring their land, they're eating all the crops and God calls it the Day of the Lord. Indeed, when Israel was judged by God in the Old Testament, they were judged through things like famine and it was known as the Day of the Lord.

After he restores the years that the cankerworm has eaten, look at verse 28, "And it shall come to pass afterward, that I will pour out my spirit upon all flesh; and your sons and your daughters shall prophesy, your old men shall dream dreams, your young men shall see visions." When was that fulfilled? Acts 2, day of Pentecost. Peter gets up and says "this is that which Joel prophesied." So, Joel 2:28 has been fulfilled.

It might be fulfilled again later on at the beginning of the millennium but it has been fulfilled already.

> *Joel 2:29 And also upon the servants and upon the handmaids in those days will I pour out my spirit. And I will shew wonders in the heavens and in the earth, blood, and fire, and pillars of smoke. The sun shall be turned into darkness, and the moon into blood, before the great and the terrible day of the LORD come.*

Everything we just read is in the book of Revelation, chapter 6, but I also want you to notice that even though the Day of the Lord had passed, it's still coming. Look in verse 31, there is a "great and terrible day of the Lord" still coming. And the armies, as you'll see from the book of Revelation, are quite literal.

So the first fulfillment which took place with Israel's being judged by God in the Old Testament was nothing but a foreshadow through the clouds of locusts, there will be nothing but a foreshadow of what happens at the Day of the Lord that is the great and terrible and still coming in the future in which there will be a cloud from the armies of heaven coming with the Christ when he descends.

Has the Day of the Lord passed? Yes. The Day of the Lord still coming? Yes. Carbon copies of each other? No, one foreshadows the other. If you're approaching the Rocky Mountains in Colorado and you say, "Okay, there is just one range." When you get up over that first ridge, you're going to see that there are miles and miles and miles between two or more different ridges. And in the eyes of the prophets, this was just one fulfillment but once you got over that first bump, it's New Testament days. Pentecost has come and gone and you see there is still yet a great and terrible Day of the Lord coming. So, they're not the same mountain ridge, they just look like it from a distance.

This is explained, somewhat, in Zephaniah 1:14-17. Was this fulfilled by the Assyrians and the Babylonians or will it happen in the book of Revelation? The answer is: both. The point of Revelation was to show you that you haven't crossed the entire mountain range, you're in the valley right now between the fulfillments. That's the whole point of the book of Revelation. There is still a great and terrible Day of the Lord coming.

Now, Joel talks about the Day of the Lord. Zephaniah talks about the Day of the Lord. What has John seen in his vision? **The Lord's day**. John has seen what Daniel saw. John has seen what Joel saw. John has seen what Zephaniah. And he's adding more detail to it for us. That is the purpose of this great passage. Some are troubled that John uses the phrase "Lord's Day" instead of the often used "Day of the Lord." Sometimes it is suggested that this is a reference, not to a future time period, but rather that it is a reference to Sunday. Given the apocalyptic nature of the book along with the frequent references to the Old Testament, one should excuse the fact that John never uses "Day of the Lord" in any of his five books in the New Testament and his "Lord's Day" should be seen as his equivalent to that phrase.

I was in the Spirit on the Lord's day, and heard behind me a great voice, as of a trumpet. It is prophetic language to say "the Day of the Lord," and so here John says, "You need to know that I was whisked away to a future period known as the Day of the Lord and it happened here on this island called Patmos." Remember, when we're dealing with a Scripture passage, we're concerned primarily with two things: what did the author intend and what did the audience understand? Now, remember, the Day of the Lord can be found in every prophet of the Old Testament. The Day of the Lord is mentioned in every prophetic book so when John says, "I was in the Spirit during the Day of the Lord," then we have to trust that, okay, John is now expanding on something the Old Testament prophets wrote about. **And I heard behind me a great voice as of a trumpet, saying , I am Alpha and Omega, the first and the last:** Immediately, one should reference Isaiah 48:12 and see that the Son of Man is claim- ing that which Jehovah God uses to describe Himself. That's outlandish!...unless the Son of Man is somehow Jehovah! **and, What thou seest, write in a book, and send it unto the seven churches which are in Asia; unto Ephesus, and unto Smyrna, and unto Pergamos, and unto Thyatira, and unto Sardis, and unto Philadelphia, and unto Laodicea. And I turned to see the voice that spake with me. And being turned, I saw seven golden candlesticks; and in the midst of the seven candlesticks one like unto the Son of man.** If you're reading the book of Revelation, you're one of the believers in one of these seven churches, what are you immediately going to think about when you see this terminology of "Son of Man?" Probably the Psalms and probably the prophets. Which prophet in particular? Daniel. Ezekiel also talks about the Son of Man. Remember, now, they are going to think about what they've already heard, what they've been hearing in synagogue every Sabbath day until the time they switched over to worshipping on the first day of the week with the church.

1:11-12

I am Alpha and Omega, the first and the last. 12. I turned to see the voice that spake with me. And being turned, I saw seven golden candlesticks; See 1:20 notes. **And in the midst of the seven candlesticks one like unto the Son of man.** Didn't we see the Son of man in Daniel 7? Yes, we did. **Clothed with a garment down to the**

foot, and girt about the paps with a golden girdle. His head and his hairs were white like wool, as white as snow. Did you see that in Daniel 7? Yes. You are seeing in Revelation 1 a rehearsal of what was already seen in Daniel 7.

Notice how much Daniel and John have in common. When Daniel spoke and wrote, he was moved by the Holy Ghost, that's 2 Peter 1:21. It's a nautical term. The idea there is that the prophets were carried about like they were sailboats and the wind was the Holy Spirit. Revelation 1:10 and see **I was in the Spirit on the Lord's day, and heard behind me a great voice, as of a trumpet.** So, how did John get this great revelation? **He was in the Spirit.** The Holy Spirit moved him just like he moved the Old Testament prophets of 2 Peter 1:21. What is the Holy Spirit, the writer of the book of Revelation, making sure you know? The New Testament prophet, John, is just as dependable as the Old Testament prophet, Daniel, because both were in the Spirit.

1:13

One like unto the Son of man, clothed with a garment down to the foot, and girt about the paps with a golden girdle. John's point is to connect the dots between Daniel 7 and Revelation 1.

> *Psalm 80:17 "Let thy hand be upon **the man of thy right hand, upon the son of man** whom thou madest strong for thyself."*

Asaph probably didn't know exactly what he was writing but he was prophesying of Jesus here, the Son of Man, who is at God's right hand. So, when you talk about the Son of Man in the New Testament, please understand that if you've heard teach- ing in your life that Jesus is the Son of Man and that is a reference to his humanity, that is partially correct. New Testament believers had a Bible, right? It just had 27 less books than ours; it was the Old Testament. So, when we read the book of Revelation, we need to remember that the readers of this letter of the book of Revelation were people that knew primarily and almost only, the Old Testament and so when we see things like what we're going to see in Revelation 1 talking about the Son of Man, it is not, "Oh, it just means that he's human too." Sort of. It really means that he is the one who is at the right hand of God. You see it here in Psalm 80:17 as you remember Daniel 7:9-14.

1:14

His head and his hairs were white like wool, as white as snow; and his eyes were as a flame of fire. You'll hear a teacher that will take you off into 1 Corinthians 3 and say, "See, it says your works will be tried by fire; so this must be Jesus judging with His eyes" Maybe so, but you've John writing in AD 95, you've got Paul writing Corinthians in 40s AD, two writers separated by 50 years. Do I think they both had each other in mind when they were writing this? Not really, I know God wrote the entire Scripture but there's also that human fingerprint.

But what if, this is the eyes of jealousy towards his bride and represented in these seven churches? Remember, the bride that is gathered in the New Jerusalem is the bride that is present in local churches. Show me a Christian that doesn't belong to a church and I'll show you something that doesn't exist in the New Testament. Every letter was written to a church member.

1:15

And his feet like unto fine brass, as if they burned in a furnace. I wonder why they looked like they were burned in a furnace? Because everything about him looked like it was on fire. You saw the description in Daniel 7. **And his voice as the sound of many waters.**

> *Ezekiel 1:24 And when they went, I heard the noise of their wings **like the noise of great waters, as the voice of the Almighty.***

Revelation 1:15 describes the voice of who? The Almighty. It doesn't say the Almighty, though. The Son of Man who in verse 18 is who? Jesus, the one who was dead and is now living. Right? So, Jesus' voice is as the sound of many waters. John is taking some of the material that Ezekiel wrote by aid of the Holy Spirit and writing more upon it. When we find out that the one whose voice is like great waters is the Almighty. So, three times in the book of Revelation 1 we find Jesus being called God. So, why is that here? To show you that Jesus is God.

1:16

And he had in his right hand seven stars. See Verse 20. **And out of his mouth went a sharp twoedged sword:** What we need to ask ourselves is: when John saw Jesus did he see this huge battle sword coming out of his mouth? What did the prophets say that will help me understand what the Apostle said? Here's a prophet from the Old Testament,

> *Isaiah 49:2, "And he hath made **my mouth like a sharp sword.**"*

You know, that is a comparison of a prophet's tongue. I know we could jump to another New Testament book. I am fully aware of that. Hebrews 4:12, but is that what the author intended here? I would say to you that the author intended for you to know what the Old Testament said about it, and the Old Testament says that Jesus has the mouth of a ready prophet in Revelation 1:16.

Those returning with Christ in Revelation 19 are those that make up the church. You don't see a sharp battle sword coming out of our mouths. As a matter of fact, here's what Scripture says about that sword coming out of Jesus' mouth in Revelation 19, it says, "**I saw out of his mouth a sharp twoedged sword,**" and in 2 Thessalonians 2, listen to this Scripture, it says, "He will consume the wicked with the spirit of his mouth and with the brightness of his coming." He said, "I gave you life by speak- ing and I'm going to take it away by speaking." He said, "I'm the Alpha and I'm the Omega. If I created this thing in Genesis 1, I'll wrap it up and throw it out of here in Revelation 20." And that's exactly what he does.

And when I saw him, I fell at his feet as dead. And he laid his right hand upon me, saying unto me, Fear not. I am the first and the last. Well, I want to know who it is. We already know it's the Son of Man. Who is the first and the last? Who is the Alpha and Omega? Who is the Son of Man? And you say, "Well, I already know." Yeah, but the reader didn't. Become the audience. See verse 18 for the answer.

I am Alpha and Omega, the first and the last, Notice that it looks a lot like verse 8 except that we see in verse 12, John turns to see who it is that is speaking and in verse 13 it's the Son of Man and the Son of Man according to verse 18 is Jesus, the one who died and rose again. So, Jesus is God.

1:17

And when I saw him, I fell at his feet as dead. Although John fell at his feet as dead, it may not be a picture of how we will be in the presence of Christ. It is certainly indicative of the fact that our first moment in Heaven will not be about mama or about not having any more back pains. It will be about being before Jesus. We have got to thinking about the fact that when we are in our glorified bodies we will, as a matter of fact, not die. John had a typical response that Moses was told he would have in Exodus 34 when God meets with him on Mt. Sinai and God allows him to stay alive after only seeing his hinder parts. I would like to say that there's a lot in Scripture about our bodies being changed. Certainly Christ's body was changed in His resurrection. Consider 1 Corinthians 15:51 'We shall not all sleep, but we shall all be changed in the moment in the twinkling if an eye, for this corruption must put on incorruptible, and this mortal shall put on immortality.'

We're going to be changed. Philippians 3:21 says, "He'll change our vile body and fashion it like his glorious body." Well John's first moment before the glorified Christ in Revelation chapter 1 had been the first time He had seen Jesus in over 60 years. Now, this time, he sees him in his glorified sense. Was Christ's body glorified at the resurrection three days after his crucifixion? Well, it was certainly a glorious body, but glorified? I would say not. John was still looking at Christ in his very unglorified, human sense. So Christ was not only glorious in his body, but he had a glorified body and John had neither. So, he could've been expected to fall basically with a heart attack perhaps, in Revelation 1. So, this same author, John, said in 1 John 3:1-2 "Behold what manner of love the father hath bestowed upon us that we should be called the sons of God, therefore the world knoweth us not because they knew him not. Now are we the sons of God and it doth not yet appear what we shall be but he shall appear and we shall be like him and see him as he is." John said, around about the time of the writing of Revelation, "I'll be able to stare at Jesus, and I'll be able to stare at him for a while, and I'll be able to stare at him for a long time, and I'll be able to stare at him for eternity." Why? "Because I'll be just like him." So in our resurrected bodies which will be glorified and fit for Heaven, we'll be able to look at Jesus, and unlike John in Revelation 1, I'll be able to keep looking. Our bodies will not fail us, our eyes will not fail us; our first moment in Heaven will be about Jesus and every moment that we have pursuing every nook and cranny of that golden city, the new Jerusalem, it will still be with Jesus in our minds. We will see Him as He is and so we will be made alive because we will be like Him. 1 John 3:3 says 'and every man that hath this hope in him purifieth himself, even as [Christ] is pure.'

1:18

I am he that liveth, and was dead; and, behold, I am alive for evermore, Amen; and have the keys of hell and of death. You can write in your Bible next to Revela- tion 1:18, Colossians 2:12-14 where it says that he was raised above principalities and powers and spoiled them, making an open show of them. When did he do that? And what did he take? He spoiled them. That's a military term for you went into their camp and yanked the precious stuff out of their tents. Well, he took something. We find out in Matthew 16:18, "the gates of hell will not prevail against the church." Why will they not prevail against the church? Because the head of the church has the keys. You can't be held in a house to which you have the keys. Death and hell show up as twins all throughout the book but at the beginning, Jesus says, "John, don't worry about that. I have the keys."

I am alive for evermore. God has been preaching the gospel for a mighty long time. Right there you have the gospel. Jesus Christ preaching the gospel. "I died for you and I'm alive now." It says in Acts 2 that it was not possible for him to be held in death. You get a good picture what that's like in the book of Jonah. Think about this now, chapter 2, you have Jonah praying to God out of the belly of a whale. It says that God spoke to the fish and it spewed Jonah up on the beach. Jesus said in Matthew 12:40.

> *As Jonah was three days and three nights in the whale's belly, so also shall the Son of Man be three days and three nights in the heart of the earth.*

So, we already know that Jonah being in the belly of the whale for three days and three nights is a picture of Christ being in the heart of the earth for three days and three nights and so when that whale spits Jonah up on the beach, the whale couldn't keep Jonah. God gave that whale so much indigestion he was going to get rid of Jonah one way or the other, he spewed him out and that was a picture of death not being able to hold Christ once God raised Jesus from the dead. He put His Spirit into the body of Christ and that's why Jesus is actually the one speaking in Psalm 16. Jesus is actually the one praying we find out because when David wrote it, Peter said he was speaking of Christ when the Psalmist said, "You will not leave my soul in hell or suffer your holy one to see corruption." So, Christ couldn't be held by death.

1:19

Write the things which thou hast seen, and the things which are, and the things which shall be hereafter. Alright, so if you wanted to, you could circle "the things which you have seen," that's past; "the things which are," that's present; "the things which shall be hereafter," that's future. So, you've got past, present, future and that's okay. We're not worried about that. Why are we not fearing? Because we see in chapter

1:8 the one who is giving John the message is the one who is, was and is to come. There's not a place on the timeline where you can't find God. He was and is and is to come and, "John, you need to write on what you've seen, what is and what will be hereafter." We find that this letter is to "angels" of 7 church (2:1; 2:8; 2:12; 2:18; 3:1; 3:7; 3:14).

Here in Patmos we have John writing this letter of the Revelation to seven churches. Seven churches in western Turkey—formerly known as Asia and before that, Asia Minor—in the late first century.

Out of all the things that could have been written about, out of all the things about which John could have written, why did he pick this? **Please notice the command given to him in verse 19.** Remember, this is the Son of Man, Jesus Christ, talking to John saying, **Write the things which thou hast seen, the things which are and the things which shall be hereafter.** This would be what John had seen so far in the Book of Revelation.

Then he says, **Write the things which are.** So, we're supposed to talk about the things that are going on right now and then, please notice the last thing he's supposed to write about, **the things which shall be hereafter.** So, "John, I want you to write about the past, the present, the future."

Let's talk about the past. He's already done that, he recorded that for us in chapter 1. Let's talk about the present. If we're going to talk about the present, **write the things which are,** he could have written about a number of amazing things in Rome. He could have written about anything happening in the government of the day but he didn't. What did he write about? Churches. The fact that he could have written about anything but Christ has him write about churches. What does that mean to us today? The church is not just important, it's all that matters. He says, "Alright, let me tell you what's going on today," and he talks about seven churches.

1:20

The mystery of the seven stars which thou sawest in my right hand, and the seven golden candlesticks. Here you are, I'm going to tell you what they are so you don't have to guess: **The seven stars are the angels of the seven churches: and the seven candlesticks which thou sawest are the seven churches.** So, now you know when you look at verse 16 what the stars are and you know in verse 12 when you see golden candlesticks you see what they are. The candlesticks are the churches that he's writing to and the stars are the messengers to those churches. As we get into the seven churches—the recipients of this letter—I wanted to provide a chart to follow:

Chapter 2

	Arch Enemies	Old Testament References from Jesus	Promised Reward shows up in end of book
Ephesus	Apostasy	"Tree of Life" (Genesis 2-3)	"Tree of life in the midst of the paradise of God" (22:2; 22:14)
Smyrna	Persecution	"ten days of testing" (Dan 1)	"Will not be hurt of the second death" (20:6; 20:14; 21:8)
Pergamos	Apostasy and Persecution	"Manna" (Exodus 12)	"a new name written" (19:12)
Thyatira	Compromise	"Jezebel" (1 Kings 17-21)	"power over the nations; ruling them with a rod of iron" (19:15); "morning star" (22:16)
Sardis	Self Deception	"seven spirits" (Zechariah 6)	"clothed in white raiment" (19:14); "name in the book of life" (20:12-15; 21:27); "name confessed before God and angels"
Philadelphia	Persecution	"key of David" (Isaiah 22:22)	"will be a pillar in the temple; go no more out" (7:15-17; 21:22); "name of God upon them" (22:4); "a new name" (19:12)
Laodicea	Self Sufficiency	"rebuking" His children" (Proverbs 3:11)	"sit with Christ is His throne as He sits with the Father" (22:1-3)

2:1

These things saith he, Unto the angel of the church of Ephesus write; These things saith he that holdeth the seven stars in his right hand, who walketh in the midst of the seven golden candlesticks. Remember 1:20? Look there for the meaning of "stars" and "candlesticks." Jesus says, "Here is how I describe myself to you: I hold the angels to the seven churches right here in my right hand." Probably, the likely answer is that these angels are the pastors of those churches because "angel" is a Greek word. So, the English word "angel" comes from the Greek word *angelos* which means "messenger." So, if you wanted to translate the word instead of transliterate the word, you would say this, chapter 2:1, "These things saith he that holdeth the seven messengers in his right hand."

I walk in the midst of the seven golden candlesticks. How do we know that they are the churches? Chapter 1:20. This is how Jesus introduces himself to the church at Ephesus, "I am the one who walks amongst the churches and I am the one who holds their messengers in my hand. I hold your messenger in my right hand." Why does he say that? As stated in chapter 1, Psalm 80:17 speaks of the "right hand" being a place of authority. "I have your messengers right here in a place of power." How does Christ see your pastor? And the answer is: he sees your pastor or pastors as being right here in his right hand as he walks in the midst of the church. Think about what that symbolism says. A good, well functioning church, you have a pastor or pastors who are in touch with the head of the church, Jesus Christ, and you sense his presence in your church because he's walking in it. If you don't sense Christ's presence in your church, perhaps one of the reasons is because he is not holding your messenger in his right hand.

> *Leviticus 26:12 I will walk among you.*

2:2

I know thy works, and thy labour, The only two of the seven churches that don't get commended for something are Sardis and Laodicea (2:9; 2:13;

2:19; 3:10)

and thy patience and how thou canst not bear them which are evil: What does this church, this Ephesian church, have in common with John? Consider 1:9, in particular, to get an idea what this church has in common with this Apostle. Patience. **I John, who also am your brother, and companion in tribulation, and in the kingdom and patience.** Patience is one of the over-riding themes in the book of Revelation. Patience is a big deal to God. John says, "You know, I feel real close with this church at Ephesus because we're both enduring things for the testimony of Jesus."

And thou hast tried them which say they are apostles, and are not, and hast found them liars. Here is a church full of people who understood, "You don't belong here if you don't serve Christ." If you want to be religious and check your little box, hit the road. There are other churches you can do that at. We could throw a stone from the steeple and hit seventeen Baptist churches. You can find one that can bare those who are evil and they'll let you be a deacon.

2:3

And hast borne, and hast patience, and for my name's sake hast laboured, and hast not fainted. Look, he's said "you have patience" twice.

2:4

Nevertheless I have somewhat against thee, because thou hast left thy first love.

> *Jeremiah 2:1, "Moreover the word of the LORD came to me, saying, Go and cry in the ears of Jerusalem, saying, Thus saith the LORD; I remem- ber thee, the **kindness of thy youth, the love of thine espousals**, when thou wentest after me in the wilderness, in a land that was not sown.*

He said, "I remember Israel. I remember when we were engaged and you loved me." He says, "You've lost that little honeymoon sort of puppy love for me." God says, "I've already talked about this. And do you want to know what it means for me to walk among the church? Look in Leviticus. Do you want to know what it means for someone to have a first love? Look in Jeremiah." God comments the best on his own Word. So, I would write Jeremiah 2:2 next to Revelation 2:4 in your Bible.

Christ says to the church at Ephesus, "You do this great. You have church discipline. You don't let the phony preachers preach in your pulpits. You don't let them lead your Bible studies. You don't let fornicators and adulterers and idolaters worship with you. You found them that are evil. You can't bear with them. You don't let drunks hang out in your church without you rebuking them for their sin." Now, some of you think that that is not love, but God said that is good church stuff.

He says, "But here's what I have problem with: you don't love me like you used to. Back when we first met, back when we were engaged, back when you were trying to pursue me, you don't love me like that anymore."

2:5

Remember therefore from whence thou art fallen, and repent, and do the first works. The first works has that same idea: do what you did to get God's attention at the beginning. Some of us think that repentance is only for unbelievers. "I don't want to go to hell anymore so I'm going to believe on Jesus." No, it's for believers also. Repent, change your mind about this thing. You need to turn around and head back.

I will come to you. Four of 7 churches have this threat (2:16; 2:25; 3:3). [4]

---

[4] It is not assumed that all these are His 2nd coming, but may be, as in this place, rather a coming to remove the candlestick. This is discussed in my commentary on Matthew (10:23). Some are; some are not.

Or else I will remove thy candlestick. So, one of those seven candlesticks/menorahs and each one probably represented each of the seven churches. And Jesus says, "Repent and love me like you did at first or I'm going to take your candlestick out of my presence." This Ephesian church had a particular function, a particular place to fill and Jesus says, "You love me like you did at the beginning or I'm going to take you out of your place." What does that mean? It means it might say "church" on the sign and you might have someone you call the pastor, but you are not a church. You are an organization that meets on a regular basis and you talk about super-duper things.

2:6

But this thou hast, that thou hatest the deeds of the Nicolaitans which I also hate. He says that he hates the works of the Nicolaitans. It comes from two words which mean "conquering the laity" or conquering the church members. So, there was a par- ticular group of people out there that set the pastors way up here and the members way down there.

2:7

He that hath an ear, let him hear what the Spirit saith unto the churches; To him that overcometh will I give to eat of the tree of life, which is in the midst of the paradise of God. What does an overcomer overcome? Chapter 12:11 talks about these people overcoming the dragon, who is Satan. In chapter 15:2 it talks about them overcoming the beast which we will find out later is known as the antichrist. So, please know that this is not a proof text for smoking cigarettes or getting tattoos. Many people say, "If you don't overcome particular sins in your life you're not saved. It says so right here." No, because in the book of Revelation, we have this wonderful thing known as context and in context, in chapter 12:11, it says, "And they overcome him by the blood of the Lamb and by the word of their testimony and they loved not their own life even to death," talking about the dragon. In chapter 15:2, it talks about these overcomers overcoming the beast and the false prophet.

2:10-12

Do not fear any of those things which you are about to suffer. Indeed, the devil is about to throw some of you into prison, that you may be tested, and you will have tribulation ten days. What a great encouragement! Perhaps this is reminiscent of the book of Daniel. This would not be new as chapter 1 is replete with references to Daniel 7 and Revelation is continually looking at Daniel. Again, look at this commentary in chapters 1 or 10 or 20 for starters. As Daniel and the three Hebrew children were placed in ward for 10 days of testing with their proposed diet before the king, so also we have a very clear understanding that these believers, in the beginning of this book, are being led to step up to the walk of those before them. I know feeling sure about this may seem presumptuous to some…

Be faithful until death, and I will give you the crown of life. Is this a piece of jew- elry? An ornament known as "the crown of life" that sits upon one's head? Perhaps, but neither the Old Testament (Psalm 103:4) nor New Testament (1 Thessalonians 2:19-20) require this stringent literalism. It is probable that this means that those who are faithful will be adorned with "life."

12. And to the angel of the church in Pergamos write; That is the letter to the third church. This is the order in which he would've traveled in this u-shaped path is the order in which the churches are addressed. And the reason they're addressed that way is because the letters would have been dropped off or delivered in the order in which he would've gone to visit those places.

These things saith he which hath the sharp sword with two edges; First of all: notice, please, that Jesus refers back to chapter 1 when he introduces himself. Do you remember, the church at Ephesus? He says, "I am the one who hold the stars in my right hand and I'm the one who walks amidst the seven candlesticks." And that is how he is described in chapter 1. Do you remember that vision of the Son of Man? To Smyrna, he introduces himself as "the first and the last and the living one who was dead." Do you remember that from chapter 1? Then the church of Pergamos, notice how he introduces himself in verse 12, "These things saith he which hath the sharp sword with two edges." So, here's the question: why did Jesus describe himself this way? Look at chapter 1:16, "And he had in his right hand seven stars: and out of his mouth went a sharp twoedged sword." **2:16 Repent; or else I will come unto thee quickly, and will fight against them with the sword of my mouth.** Whatever that meant to them in that culture, we know that it meant something in particular to them in this book. So, the entire book is about the revelation of Jesus Christ. It says so in the very first verse of the very first chapter that the title of the book is "The Revelation of Jesus Christ." It's forecast in chapter 1:7; it's recorded in chapter 19. When you're reading this as a member of the church of Pergamos, what do you feel like you're being warned about? Punishment. When? When Christ returns. He says it twice. We're supposed to be able to put the twoedged sword coming out of his mouth with the Second Coming and this church is warned about it twice.

> *1 Peter 4:17 For the time is come that **judgment must begin at the house of God**: and if it first begin at us, what shall the end be of them that obey not the gospel of God? And if the righteous scarcely be saved, where shall the ungodly and the sinner appear?*

The church of God was also to fear the day of the Coming of Christ.

> *1st Peter 1:13 Gird up the loins of your mind, be sober, and hope to the end for the grace that is to be brought unto you **at the revelation of Jesus Christ.** 16. It is written, Be ye holy; for I am holy. And if ye call on the Father, who without respect of persons judgeth according to every man's work, **pass the time of your sojourning in fear.***

The church needs to be aware that the one with the twoedged

sword is coming and they need to prepare themselves.

These things saith he which hath the sharp sword with two edges. Revelation 1:16, says, "I saw going out of his mouth a sharp twoedged sword." So, I need us to understand that Jesus, who is addressing these seven churches through John, is introducing himself, referring back to chapter 1 in ways in which he was described. In six of the seven churches, Jesus introduces himself to them in a way that refers back to the first chapter. So the question is, really: why did Jesus introduce himself to the church of Pergamos in this way. First, we need to understand what the sharp two-edged sword represents.

If you're John living in that day, what does that communicate? You already know that the symbol of the Roman Senate is a sword. Who comes out on top in this little comparison? Jesus. Jesus says, "If you want to fear someone, fear me." And you say, "Well, wait a minute, he tells John not to fear him." Yes, but we have two possibilities. When you are afraid of something, you just need to find something you fear more. So, don't be afraid of the Roman government, fear the one with the sharp twoedged sword coming out of his mouth. Jesus says, "Don't fear the Romans." "Oh God, how am I not to fear the Romans? I'm marooned on an island. How am I not going to fear the Romans?" "Because I'm going to give you something greater to fear. The one with the sharp twoedged sword coming out of his mouth."

2:13

I know thy works, and where thou dwellest, even where Satan's seat is: The is the Altar of Zeus in Pergamos looked like a throne and that's why the church called it "Satan's seat" because it looked like the throne of Satan. As a matter of fact, there are other guesses. I would be remiss if I were to tell you that there weren't other guesses. There was also a temple of the god of healing that looked like a throne of Satan. The fact is, Pergamos was an interesting city. It had the second largest library in the known world behind Alexandria. It had 200,000 volumes which might not sound like a big deal for a huge library but how about when every book is copied by hand? Pergamos also had the second largest amount of gods and temples. So, the fact that it describes Pergamos twice as the place where Satan lives, at the beginning of verse 13, the place **where Satan's seat is** and the last part of verse 13, this is **where Satan dwells**, is prob- ably a reference to the temple or the altar of Zeus.

and thou holdest fast my name, and hast not denied my faith, Jesus said, "You guys don't ever deny me. It's my faith. It's my body of doctrine." If you didn't get it from Jesus, it doesn't matter if you got it from Joseph Smith or C.T. Russell, it's wrong. The real faith comes from Jesus. **even in those days wherein Antipas was my faithful martyr, who was slain among you, where Satan dwelleth.** "You held my faith even in those days wherein Antipas was my faithful martyr." So, Antipas, according to Tatford and his "Patmos Letters," was a dentist and physician in Pergamos who was accused of disloyalty to Caesar and so he was given time to repent and he hid and when he was found he was put into a brazen bull that was heated red-hot. That's how he died for his faith. You can find that record in the book "Martyrs' Mirror."[1]

2:14

But I have a few things against thee, because thou hast there them that hold the doctrine of Balaam, who taught Balac to cast a stumblingblock before the children of Israel, to eat things sacrificed unto idols, and to commit fornication. What did Balaam do? Well, he tried to curse the children of Israel, he was unsuccessful and it says in this verse and we find out from Numbers 31 that he actually moved Balak, the king of Moab, "to cast a stumblingblock before the children of Israel." What was the stumblingblock? Numbers 22-24 are the story of Balaam, the prophet of Baal and it says that he was a Moabite. Moab is where Jordan is today. Of course, the boundaries are not exactly the same. It would be kind of foolish if I said, "Oh, by the way, they just changed the country's name, nothing else has changed." South of what used to be Moab is what used to be Midian and Midian can be pretty safely said that that is what is now Saudi Arabia. Apparently, Balaam was well-known as a necromancer or someone who could deal with curses and could talk with dead folks and could do sorcery and so, what happened is, the children of Israel have left Egypt, as you know, and they have traveled through the land of Sinai and then the land of Midian and now they're on their way up through the land of Moab. And Balak, the king of Moab, decided that he wanted to curse the Israelites because there were a ton of these Israelites traveling through their land. So, this King Balak says he's going to seek out a prophet by the name of Balaam to curse the Israelites. They go and find Balaam and say, "We need you to come and curse the Israelites. We're going to take you up to a high mountain and you're going to do what you do. You're going to curse them and we're going to pay you. You're going to be just amazingly rich and we're going to be on our way."

Well, Balaam wouldn't come the first time. He asked God if he could go; he couldn't go. Balak came again and said, "Well, we're going to send you another opportunity to come and be with our king and curse the Israelites." Well, he did that time and then he's riding his donkey. This is a funny story. Three times Balaam is riding his donkey and three times this donkey goes against where Balaam is trying to steer him and three times Balaam whips his donkey. The third time, the donkey turns his head and talks to him. You say, "Well, that can't happen." You have a talking serpent in Genesis 3. Okay? A talking donkey a few books later is not that hard to believe.

So, you've got a talking donkey. Now, as you look in chapter 23 and 24 of Num- bers, you're going to see that three times Balaam tried to curse the Israelites and three times, instead, he blesses them. He says, "I've got to say what God is telling me to say." So, he blesses them. You see in Numbers 24 at the end of the chapter, look there with me in verse 25, "And Balaam rose up, and went and returned to his place: and Balak also went his way," and so, it seems like, that's the end of the story. "Balaam, you're a horrible prophet. You can't curse anybody. You are a failure." Take a look at Numbers 25:1-5 and Numbers 31:1-15 for more of the story.

Near the beginning of Numbers 25, Balaam provided some form

of counsel: "Oh, by the way, everyone falls for pretty girls so what you need to do is send your women over there to cohabit with their men and you will cause them to anger their God because they'll serve other gods. They'll anger their Jehovah and then, probably, that's the best way to get them cursed because God has promised he will curse them if they choose cursing."

2:15

So hast thou also them that hold the doctrine of the Nicolaitans, which thing I hate. Acts 6 is not saying that the Apostles are super-duper and that they couldn't talk to the people, it's just that there were so many people to care for that the Apostles had to leave the very, very most important work they had which was spending time in prayer and preparing Bible teaching for their people. They had to leave that to go and take care of the menial issues of managing the funds that were collected to care for widows and so, they elected deacons.

> *And they chose Stephen, a man full of faith and of the Holy Ghost, and Philip, and Prochorus, and **Nicanor**, and Timon…*

We have two major guesses as to what Nicolaitan means. Remember, the etymol- ogy or the word meaning behind it means "the conqueror of the laity; the conqueror of the common people." However, it also means "a person who followed Nicolas; someone who followed Nicolas." Apparently this guy that's mentioned in Acts 6, later on became what is known as a Gnostic. A Gnostic teaches that the Christ is a spirit; it's not a particular person, it is a spirit that comes upon certain people in history. That's what a Gnostic teaches. Of course, there are several brands of Gnosticism, but a Gnostic teaches that Jesus was not the Christ until his baptism when the Holy Spirit came on him. When he died, he was no longer the Christ until his resurrection and then he was the Christ again. So, Gnostics taught that all things that were holy were not of this material world; they were spirit; they were part of a different kind of world.

You're probably thinking, "Well, I'm glad that stuff doesn't come up anymore." Oh, yes it does. The Christian Scientists teach that. The Buddhists teach that. So, you need to understand that this Gnostic idea didn't die in the early church. Plato says that all reality is found in the realm of the invisible.

2:16

Repent; It means to have a change of mind. It can mean turn away based on the context, but it means to have a change of mind; to think again. So, he says, "You have some people here in your church that are giving parlay to the people who love Balaam and his doctrine and to the Nicolaitans. You'd better change your mind about being hospitable to them. You'd better change your mind **or else I will come unto thee quickly, and will fight against them with the sword of my mouth.** See 2:12.

2:17

He that hath an ear, let him hear what the Spirit saith unto the churches; To him that overcometh will I give to eat of the hidden manna, and will give him a white stone, and in the stone a new name written, which no man knoweth saving he that receiveth it. Take a look at Revelation 12:7-11 and Revelation 15:1-2 for an understanding of what it means, contextually, to **overcome.**

I just wanted you to see the church at Pergamos was told "overcome." In John's context, we're dealing with overcoming the accuser of the brethren in chapter 12 and the beast in chapter 15.

To him that overcometh will I give to eat of the hidden manna, and will give him a white stone, and in the stone a new name written, which no man knoweth saving he that receiveth it. To the church at Ephesus, he says, "I'm going to give you a tree of life which is in the midst of the Paradise of God." To the church of Smyrna, you see in 2:11, "He that overcometh shall not be hurt of the second death." And now to the church of Pergamos: **hidden manna** and **a white stone** with **a new name**

written. What is the **hidden manna**? Let's do our very best to let Scripture inform our answer.

Take a look at Hebrews 9:1-4 and decide: Is this a literal promise that you get to, somehow, and every overcomer gets to share in this little golden jar in the ark of the covenant when we get to heaven? My answer is: no. Remember chapter 1:1 tells us what this is a book full of signs. The real problem with a lot of people who try and understand the book of Revelation is, that they are looking for literal, all the time literal fulfillment. "We are literal Bible believers. We believe the Bible literally." Let's talk about that hidden manna. What is it? Well, if the hidden manna was in the ark of the covenant and the ark of the covenant was in the earthly tabernacle and the earthly tabernacle was a picture of what is in heaven, then we have to ask ourselves a question: what does it mean when he promises hidden manna to the overcomer? It's in heaven. The real ark of the covenant, Hebrews 9, the Bible says that everything that was in Moses' tabernacle was made after a pattern that he saw in heaven.

There is another answer and the other answer comes to us from a guy by the name of Constable. He says that this white stone is *tesseron* in the Greek and it is an invitation to the inside of a temple in that day whereupon was written the secret name of the god in whose honor that temple was built. Let me say that again: in this day, a white stone was given to someone who was invited to worship at a temple and on that white stone was the secret name of the god in whose honor that temple was built.

Since the believer at Pergamos would have seen, "I'm going up here to the temple of Zeus, Satan's seat, and they give me a white stone and on this white stone, while I'm in the temple worshiping, there is a secret name of this Zeus-god or of the goddess, then if I'm an overcomer with Christ, I get invited to his Temple and a secret name written which no man can know." Therefore, when you're promised hidden manna and you know that that is an illustration of what is in heaven, that there is a real ark of the covenant in heaven and when you know that a white stone is an invitation to that same location, then you mark it down, these not only go together, but they're an invitation to the Temple of God which is in heaven. So, contextually, when I overcome the dragon and the beast and the false prophet, I don't get invited to some place to worship. I get invited far higher than that. I, as an overcomer, have a place reserved in the Temple of God which is in heaven where the hidden manna is.

Christ promises reward to all seven of these churches and that you see these promises realized at the end of the book because John is writing a story here with many themes. Remember, the theme is the Revelation of Jesus Christ but there are many supporting themes like overcomers. What do they get? Well, first they are not hurt of the second death says the church of Smyrna. Ephesus, what did they have to look forward to? The tree of life in the midst of the Paradise of God. You see, these are all promises of the afterlife for the believer and overcomer.

> *1 John 5:4 He that is born of God **overcometh the world**: and this is the victory that overcometh the world, even our faith.*
>
> *Revelation 19:11 And I saw heaven opened, and behold a white horse; and he that sat upon him was called Faithful and True, and in righteousness he doth judge and make war. His eyes were as a flame of fire, and on his head were many crowns; and he had **a name written, that no man knew, but he himself**."*

Revelation 2:17 and 19:11 talk about Jesus having a name which no man knows except he, himself. So, there is a name that Jesus has, it's going to be on this white stone which might be figurative. It might be figurative for an invitation to the Temple. Is the overcomer getting invited to heaven or to the New Jerusalem? You say, "Well, I thought they were the same thing." Well, look at chapter 21 of Revelation. We have all these invitations to temples or temple-type things. There is this Temple that Moses saw on the mountain. He made things on earth that resembled that. We're getting these invitations to a Temple.

> *Revelation 21:1, I saw a new heaven and a new earth: for the first heaven and the first earth were passed away; and there was no*

more sea. And I John saw the holy city, **new Jerusalem, coming down from God out of heaven**.

Revelation 21:22 And I saw **no temple therein***: for the Lord God Almighty and the Lamb* **are the temple** *of it.*

Therefore, there's no structure in the New Jerusalem that came down from God out of heaven called the "Temple;" God and the Lamb are the Temple. There is a temple in Heaven (Revelation 7:14-17).

See the heaven from which the New Jerusalem comes; heaven has a Temple. Moses made the tabernacle on earth based on the one he saw in the mountain, Mount Sinai. So, there is a Temple in heaven it says here right in chapter 7:15, but the New Jerusalem that comes from God out of heaven: No Temple.

The question we have to ask ourselves is: that church at Pergamos, are they get- ting a symbolic invitation to a symbolic Temple in the New Jerusalem? And who is the symbolic Temple in the New Jerusalem? God and the Lamb. Or, are they getting a symbolic invitation to a literal Temple in heaven? Remember, we have an example of a Temple, we have an allusion to a Temple, in the New Jerusalem: it's God and the Lamb. The New Jerusalem comes down from God out of heaven. We have a literal Temple in heaven out of which comes the New Jerusalem that does not have a Temple except for God and the Lamb.

Revelation 22:1, And he shewed me a pure river of water of life, clear as crystal, proceeding out of the throne of God and of the Lamb. In the midst of the street of it, and on either side of the river, was there **the tree of life**.

Where is the tree of life? Is it in heaven or is it in the New Jerusalem that comes down from God out of heaven? The New Jerusalem is still what is being described here. So, there is a tree of life in the New Jerusalem that comes down from God out of heaven but is not, itself, heaven. The New Jerusalem is not heaven, it comes from heaven. In the New Jerusalem that comes from heaven, there is a tree of life.

The figurative Temple in the New Jerusalem is: God and the Lamb, remember?

*Revelation 2:7 He that hath an ear, let him hear what the Spirit saith unto the churches; To him that overcometh will I give to eat of **the tree of life, which is in the midst of the paradise of God**.*

Where is the tree of life? It's in the New Jerusalem. In the midst of what? Paradise. So, we have the tree of life which is in the midst of the Paradise of God which is in, where? The New Jerusalem. It seems like that all seven of these churches are getting invitations to the New Jerusalem. So, to the overcomer at Pergamos he offers the hidden manna and the white stone which are figurative invitations to a figurative Temple in the New Jerusalem. What is the figurative Temple in the New Jerusalem? God and the Lamb. So, these seven churches are being promised fellowship with God and the Lamb in the New Jerusalem and we found it, with hardly ever leaving Revelation.

2:18

And unto the angel of the church in Thyatira write; This is a very small church, in fact, you might remember from another book of the Bible, Lydia was from Thyatira (Acts 16). Even as a small church in a small city, the church here is the recipient of the longest letter to the churches in Revelation. So, there is special emphasis on this church. Why would God put special emphasis on this church?

who hath his eyes like unto a flame of fire, "Alright, something's coming. I saw what you did."

and his feet are like fine brass; Feet that are strong yet fine and pure, they are strong enough to stamp out evil but they're pure enough, if you will, to discern good from evil.

*Daniel 10:6 His body also was like the beryl, and his face as the appear- ance of lightning, and **his eyes as lamps of fire**, and his arms and his **feet like in colour to polished brass**, and the voice of his words like the voice of a multitude.*

2:19

I know thy works, and charity, and service, and faith, and thy patience, and thy works; and the last to be more than the first. Not only does he repeat the word "works" but he uses the word "charity" which we normally translate to "love" and "ser- vice," so they do service to help other people. This is kind of contrasting the Ephesian church that was lacking that first love. This church has faith and they have this patience. Jesus is talking more than anything about "have patience until I come. You're going to go through a lot of different things. You're going to go through tribulations, you're going to go through hardships." He gives one verse of commendation and I think that's a good lesson to us. If we're ever trying to help somebody or correct somebody and we know they did wrong, we don't want to come at them and just say, "These are the things that you've done wrong." Jesus gives us a good example here, he gives them something they did right and then goes into something they did wrong.

2:20

Notwithstanding I have a few things against thee, because thou sufferest that woman Jezebel, Remember back in 1 and 2 Kings, there really was a person named Jezebel. She had a husband, King Ahab, who ran the country at that time. He had a problem because his wife told him everything that he needed to do. He wanted something so badly that she actually stepped in and killed the person that had it so that he could have it. She helped him fulfill selfish desires. "I want something so bad that you have that I'm willing to kill you for it so that I can have it."

The true story of Jezebel is that Jezebel usurps her husband's authority, fulfills the selfish desires there which is a reoccurring trend and leads the nation into a great trouble. One of the results of all the problems that she caused in the kingdom of Israel was that there was no rain. Elijah held back the rain per God's order that there would be no rain. When there's no rain, crops do not grow very well. I would say that would be a great trouble. That's the true story of Jezebel. Now, we would assume that the church of **Thyatira** either knows the story of Jezebel from the Old Testament or they could find it. They would have 1 and 2 Kings in some way, shape or form that they could go back and read about it so that could be why John is using Jezebel as an illustration here.

Then he says that there currently is a woman, **Jezebel**, in the church or Thyatira, a real person. Now, was her name Jezebel? Maybe not but I don't think that's what's important in this section here. He points out that this woman Jezebel claims to be a prophetess. If somebody says, "I'm a prophetess," she's taking authority that is not hers.

which calleth herself a prophetess, to teach and to seduce my servants to commit fornication, She caused God's people to sin or commit fornication. This is another story of another Jezebel usurping authority and causing the people of God to commit fornication.

and to eat things sacrificed unto idols. "Okay, what's the big deal with that?"

> *Revelation 2:14 But I have a few things against thee, because thou hast there them that hold the doctrine of Balaam, who **taught** Balac to cast a stumblingblock before the children of Israel,* **to eat things sacrificed unto idols, and to commit fornication.**

This is the same kind of problem: they believed in this doctrine of Balaam that they should eat things that are sacrificed to idols. Both were guilty of eating offerings to idols and teaching fornication to God's people. They are eating that food to idols because of who? This woman is causing them to commit fornication and to eat foods sacrificed to idols which causes a stumblingblock to the other Christians. So, her and hers are cast into a great tribulation.

Most striking about Jezebel is her idolatry. That is, she was a woman of many strange gods. A whole church was being held accountable for the actions of an idolater in their midst. Here's a more direct way to say it, perhaps: "a whole church was being held accountable for the flirtations of a woman after a different God."

2:21

And I gave her space to repent of her fornication; and she repented not. The church of Ephesus had a problem with apostasy. The church of Smyrna had a problem coming about them where they were very persecuted. Then Pergamos had both, apostasy and persecution. In **Thyatira**, it's more specifically focused on immorality but we can even see later that immorality can result in apostasy, can result in a false religion, can result in a belief against God.

2:22

Behold, I will cast her into a bed, She is cast into a bed. What's a bed? The Greek word for bed is used ten times in the New Testament, and those ten times it was either talking about a physical bed like one that you would sleep in as in Mark 9:2 and 6; or, in Mark 7:30, Luke 5:18 and Acts 5:15 it's a sickbed—somebody is dying. So, casting somebody into their bed brings great sickness unto, possibly, death.

and them that commit adultery with her into great tribulation, except they repent of their deeds. What is great tribulation? The only other time "great tribulation" is used is in 7:14. This Greek word is *megas*. This is "mega tribulation." God uses these great tortures, these mega tortures; some of them want to die and they can't die.

2:23

And I will kill her children with death… It's saying, "I will kill them unto death. It will be a deathly death. It will be a real death." "I will kill her children with **death and all the churches shall know that I am he which searcheth the reins and hearts: and I will give unto every one of you according to your works."** This is according to their bad works in context here. These are going to get the worst of it; they're going to get that great tribulation. **So that other people know that I search the hearts.** Jesus is trying to prove a point here that "I can search your heart and I know what you're thinking:" Christ gave this horrible person that led many astray space or time to repent of her fornications and then the saddest news of all: She repented not. Grace is still given to the Jezebel. She was given a place, a time to repent and she did not.

2:24

But unto you I say, and unto the rest in Thyatira, as in, the rest of these people that aren't committing fornication yet, these people that aren't wrapped up in the sin of Jezebel. **as many as have not this doctrine…** what doctrine? The doctrine of Balaam (verse 14). That doctrine where they cause others to be stumblingblocks and they commit fornication.

As many as not have this doctrine and which have not known the depths of Satan. You've heard them speak, you know the depths of Satan, you know the depths of the sin that they're in. They don't even want out at this point.

I will put upon you none other burden. None other burden is put upon you. You've been doing good works. What you started off doing, what you are doing really good, that's great because now you're even doing more than you were doing before. That's great. You had a little bit more love than you loved before. Keep that up. "I put unto you no other burden other than to keep doing what you're doing."

2:27

And he shall rule them with a rod of iron; as the vessels of a potter shall they be broken to shivers, little pieces, that's what shivers are. **Even as I received of my Father. 28 And I will give him the morning star.** There are lots of stars but there is a star, the star, but later in the book of Revelation (22:16), you'll see that there is a Morning Star. The Morning Star is Jesus. So, who does he give or what does he give to the overcomer? He gives them Jesus. He gives them salvation. He gives them a sonship. To overcome something means you had to have it first. Apparently, there are people in this sin of fornication following after Jezebel that are people of God, and they overcome that sin and they do receive salvation and they do persevere in the end and they do have that reward.

Is this reward to those in the millennium or to the New Heaven or to the New Earth, the New Jerusalem? Well, I don't think that's clear because it says that "I sent mine angel to testify unto these things in the churches. I am the root and the offspring of David, and the bright and morning star" (Revelation 22:16). This is all after the great tribulation so it has to take place either in the millennium or in the New Jerusalem.

And power over the nations. We will rule with him so Christ also promises a reward at the end of the book here. These overcomers come in 19:15, it says that they'll have "powers over the nation.

Chapter 3

3:1

And unto the angel of the church in Sardis write; These things saith he that hath the seven Spirits of God. What would the audience think if they just read this? Isaiah 11:1. How many Holy Spirit's are there? Just one but seven names.

And the seven stars

> *Revelation 1:20 The mystery of the seven stars which thou sawest in my right hand, and the seven golden candlesticks.* ***The seven stars are the angels of the seven churches.***

In other words, we have here in verse 1, we have the introduction as Jesus being the one who has possession of **the seven Spirits and the seven stars**.

> *Isaiah 11:1 And there shall come forth a rod out of the stem of Jesse, and <u>a Branch</u> shall grow out of his roots, and **the spirit of the LORD shall rest upon him, the spirit of wisdom and understanding, the spirit of counsel and might, the spirit of knowledge and of the fear of the LORD,***

So we have seven names there for the Holy Spirit in this Scripture and a comprehensive description in 11:3 while Zechariah 3:8-4:6 connect "seven eyes" with the Spirit of God. Those "seven eyes" will show up later in the next chapter.

In Isaiah 11:1 we have this spirit from God that has seven names and apparently the Branch that is to come is going to judge with the eyes of the spirit. Zechariah 3-4 says that there is a stone coming with seven eyes upon it and the eyes, according to 4:6, are the spirit of the Lord.

> *Acts 2:1 And when the day of Pentecost was fully come, they were*

*all with one accord in one place. And suddenly there came a sound from heaven as of a rushing mighty wind, and it filled all the house where they were sitting. And there appeared unto them cloven tongues like as of fire, and **it sat upon each of them**.*

On each of these 120 people in this upper room, the spirit of the Lord appeared. There is just one spirit of the Lord, but he appears individually upon these believers in this upper room as a cloven tongue of fire.

that thou hast a name that thou livest, and art dead (3:1). People know you by your name and they said "we live, we're alive."

> *Revelation 1:18 **I am he that liveth**, and was dead; and, behold, I am alive for evermore, Amen; and have the keys of hell and of death.*

Jesus says, "Hey, church full of Christians, you're supposed to be just like me. You're supposed to be people that were dead and are now alive and will live forever but, instead, you're dead. There is no life in you. You've got this fantastic title, people love your label. You're known for this and for that. You're even known for coming out of the paganism of the Acropolis in Sardis but you're dead." So, He says in verse 2, **Be watchful, and strengthen the things which remain.** You're not completely dead. It's like there's a case of death. You're dead, you're kind of dead, you're almost there. **that are ready to die: for I have not found thy works perfect before God.**

The biggest problem with the church at Thyatira was that they were messing around with this woman "Jezebel," a system of beliefs and probably an immoral woman. Their biggest enemy was compromise. The biggest enemy of Sardis is their self-deception. Look at 3:1, at the end of the verse, **you have a name that thou livest, and are dead.** "You think you're alive. You're not. The best thing going for you is your title. That's it. What you have over the door, that's the best thing going for you. You are deceived and you did it to yourself."

Sardis had this amazing huge fortress. It was amazing. 1,500 feet tall on a cliff was this acropolis and that was their fortress and that was their claim to fame. "**We have a name**. We're Sardis." And so the church still lived in that.

This is the first church where there are no good things to say. Jesus says, "I had some good things to say to Ephesus, Smyrna, Pergamos and Thyatira." And, by the way, Sardis read those letters because they read the whole book of Revelation. Sardis is next in travels of John, off the isle of Patmos and they're, "Oh good. Wow! God was hard on Ephesus. He thrashed them but at least he said something good about them." Got to Smyrna, "Man, he talked about what good workers they were. Of course, afterward he sort of let them have it. Pergamos." Then Sardis is thinking, "What is he going to say good about us?" Nothing. "I have nothing good to say about you."

We see that he introduces himself as the one who has the **seven Spirits and the one who has the seven stars**. Jesus has introduced himself to four different churches, we're on the fifth one and there are two left, and remember how John sees in Revelation 1 this vision of the Son of Man. What was he referring to then? Daniel 7. He's talking about this vision of the Son of Man in Revelation 1 and he got it from Daniel. With each of those seven churches he introduces himself in a way in which he describes himself in chapter 1.

I have not found your works perfect before God. Whatever they were doing, it wasn't mature at all, it wasn't complete. They were doing things half-heartedly. When it really mattered to do the right thing, they didn't do the right thing. They were very, very good at acting Christianese but when you sat down and looked them in the eyes and said, "What are you studying in the word of God these days?" Or, "What has God been talking to you about in the last week?" they had a name that they were alive but that that would be all. Jesus said, "Be watchful because you're about to be just completely dead."

3:3
If therefore thou shalt not watch, I will come on thee as a thief, and thou shalt not know what hour I will come upon thee. The question is whether the coming of Christ is unpredictable to all believers? Or is the coming of Christ like a thief in the night for all believers? Is it? Some propose that the rapture could happen at any moment because it happens like "a thief in the night," but wait a minute. Revelation 3:3 says that it is for the unprepared believer. If you're not looking for me, I will come upon thee as a thief.

> *Luke 12:36-37 Blessed are those servants whom the Lord when He cometh shall find watching, verily I say unto you that he shall gird himself up and make them to sit down to meat and will come forth and serve them and of he shall come in the second watch or the third watch and find them so blest are those servants. And this know, that if the man of the house had known what hour* **the thief** *come he would have watched and not have suffered his house be broken through. So be ye, therefore, ready also for the Son of man cometh at an hour when ye think not.*

Doesn't that sound like the language of Revelation 3:3? Now, if you have a pre-disposition to a secret catching away of believers that happens unpredictably, then you will not see this. The Lord comes as a thief on those who are not watching and that is why Revelation 3:3, one of the same apostles who was standing there in Luke 12 wrote Revelation 3 with the aid of the Lord, both are the words of Christ, interestingly enough. Christ is speaking the same through the pen of Luke as He is through the pen of John! Luke in the gospel of Luke and John in the book of Revelation and he says if you're not watching I'll come upon you as a thief. This same language is used in

> *1 Thessalonians 5:1 But of the times and seasons, brethren, ye have no need that I write unto you for yourselves know perfectly that the day of the Lord so comes as a thief in the night. 4. But you, brethren,* **are not in darkness that that day should overtake you as a thief.**

This being the fifth church of the book of Revelation, you might notice that this is also another promise of the coming, and to the church at Ephesus he says in

*Revelation 2:5 Remember, therefore, from whence thou art fallen and repent and do the first works **or I will come unto thee quickly.***

Now in the second church, the church of Smyrna, I don't see any promise or threatening of a coming. Interestingly enough, there are also no rebukes to this church at Smyrna. Interestingly enough, he doesn't have anything sharp to say to the church of Smyrna. Pergamos, he rebukes them and then warns them of His coming. Repent or I will come unto thee quickly and will fight against thee. And then, the church of Thyatira, the fourth church, he rebukes them because of Jezebel and then "says hold fast what you have till I come." So with all the churches with whom he has rebuked he has a warning of the coming. Isn't that something? We have a warning, and you have a threat of His coming. And so, at this fifth church we have a warning, **you have a name that you live but you're dead**, and a warning of His coming. So, notice first of all, that these comings are only unexpected to carnal believers. Not to believers who are watching for the signs that Christ gave them. Secondly, you might notice that the warning is only to the churches that have things that were rebukeable. Alright, so, still we're in verse 3 of chapter 3, **if you will not watch I will come upon thee as a thief and shalt not know what hour I shall come upon thee**. This had a particular, historical significance to the church at Sardis because the command to wake up is a reminder that twice in history Sardis had been sacked and with a 1500 foot tall fortress no one ever thought it would happen. Both Cyrus II and Antiochus III conquered or sacked Sardis when the watchmen on the walls failed to detect any enemies.

3:5

He that overcometh, the same shall be clothed in white raiment; and

I will not blot out his name out of the book of life, but I will confess his name before my Father, and before his angels. In each of these seven churches, we're seeing a pattern: he introduces himself, he says here's what I like about you, here's what I don't like about you and here's what you can expect. If you are an overcomer, you can expect white raiment, you can expect your name in the book of life and you can expect to have your name confessed before God and the angels.

"Well, if you have to overcome to stay in the book, what do you have to do to overcome?"

> *1 John 5:4, He who is born of God overcometh the world: and* ***this is the victory that overcometh the world, even our faith.***

What is the purpose of a book of life? It was customary to have registers of citizenship in which were entered the names of citizens both natural and adopted. Heaven is represented as a city and its inhabitants are registered. Some whom have not yet reached the heavenly city are regarded as citizens on their way home and in the case of Israel, they were citizens of a covenant community.

Philippians 3:14: Paul says, "I press toward the mark for the prize of the high calling of God in Christ Jesus." Verse 20, "For our conversation is in heaven." Do you see that? Our citizenship is in heaven. Who is the "our?" Believers in Philippi are the subject of this answer. Look at chapter 4:3, "And I intreat thee also, true yokefellow, help those women which laboured with me in the gospel, with Clement also, and with other my fellowlabourers, **whose names are in the book of life.**" If you went from 3:20 to 4:3, you would probably think it was the same thought, wouldn't you? We have citizenship in 3:20 in heaven and we have a book of life in 4:3.

What would you think about that book of life? It was a collection of citizens from where? Heaven. We're not talking about the same book that was spoken of in Exodus 32, Psalm 69 and Daniel 12. Different book. Why? How do I know? Context.

Then consider Hebrews 12:20-25 where we have a body of people "written" in Heaven.

Therein we have Moses, we have Mount Sinai, we have the blood of goats and calves, we have a book of life and it really just represents the book of the living community. Over here, we don't have that: we have Mount Zion; we have not Moses, but Jesus; we have not the blood of bulls and goats but the blood of Jesus, we don't have just the congregation of people living on earth known as covenant Israel but we have the church of the firstborn; we don't have a book of life that can be blotted out on planet earth but we have a church of the firstborn which is written in heaven—citizens, part of the general assembly and church of the firstborn written in heaven.

> *Revelation 13 who is like to the beast and who is able to make war with him and all that dwell upon the earth shall worship him whose names are not written in **the book of life of the Lamb** slain from the foundation of the world.*

"Can I be blotted out of the book of life?" The answer is "no." What is the distinguishing characteristic of those who do not bow to the antichrist in this verse? They are in the book of life. What would you have to do to get blotted out of the book of life if it were possible for you to be blotted out of the Lamb's book of life? What would you have to do? You'd have to do something worse than bowing to the antichrist because if you're in the book, you're not going to bow. If you're in the book, you're not going to bow so if you can be blotted out of the Lamb's book of life, you have to do something worse than worshiping the antichrist.

By the way, this is the first mention of the "Lamb's book of life." Revelation 17:8 looks a lot like it.

> *The beast that thou sawest was, and is not; and shall ascend out of the bottomless pit, and go into perdition: and they that dwell*

> *on the earth shall wonder, whose names were not written in **the book of life** from the foundation of the world.*

If your name is in the book of life, will you bow to the beast? No. Okay, it must mean that you overcame by the blood of the Lamb. You have to do something worse than bow to the antichrist to be removed from the book because you won't bow to the antichrist if you're in the book.

The Lamb's Book of Life is for residents of the New Jerusalem and not like the book that they could be blotted out of in Exodus 32. Those in that chapter were simply residents of an earthly community of Israelites. How were you blotted out then? You died. That's it. That's why David was praying for his enemies to be removed from it (Psalm 69); he wanted their death. Daniel 12, Michael the archangel stands up for those who are written in the book of life. Why are they in the book of life? Because they are living Jews, not because they're dead and not because they're citizens of heaven.

> *Revelation 20:11, And I saw a great white throne, and him that sat on it, from whose face the earth and the heaven fled away; and there was found no place for them. And I saw the dead, small and great, stand before God; and the books were opened: and another book was opened, which is **the book of life**: and the dead were judged out of those things which were written in the books, according to their works. And the sea gave up the dead which were in it; and death and hell delivered up the dead which were in them: and they were judged every man according to their works. And death and hell were cast into the lake of fire. This is the second death. And whosoever was not found **written in the book of life** was cast into the lake of fire.*

How did you get to go to the lake of fire? Your name is not in the book. What were we guaranteed that you would not do if your name was in the book? You would not bow down to the antichrist, the beast. So, we're told that you will go to the lake of fire and you will bow down to the beast if your name is not in the book of life. So, let's put it in some context.

21:2 says "And I John saw the holy city." Look at that. If that chapter division wasn't there, you would have the city and the registry (Book of Life) within two verses of each other. Context is awesome. 21:25, "And the gates of it shall not be shut at all by day: for there shall be no night there. And they shall bring the glory and honour of the nations into it." What are we talking about? Verse 23, the city. They will bring their glory and honor into the city, "And there shall in no wise enter into it any thing that defileth, neither whatsoever worketh abomination, or maketh a lie: but they which are written in the Lamb's book of life."

Mark it down: if you are born again, 1 John 5:4, you are born of God. You have put your faith in Christ. Revelation 12:10-11: you've overcome by the blood of the Lamb and your name is in the book of life because you belong in the holy city. Question: if you had to be born to be in this book of life of Exodus 32 and you're blotted out, when are you put in this Lamb's book of life? What kind of life do you have once you get saved? Eternal life. So, if you have eternal life and this is a Lamb's book of the living and you have eternal life, when can you expect to be blotted out? Never! Because you're in that Lamb's book of the living so long as you live. Whose life do you have in you? Christ's life. So, as long as Christ lives, you live. As long as you live, you're in the Lamb's book of life.

3:7

And to the angel of the church in Philadelphia write; These things saith he that is holy, We have this introduction of Jesus, "He that is holy, he that is true." Although one may find other things called "holy" in the book of Revelation, it is entirely because they are associated, in part, with a Holy God revealed in the Son.

Revelation 4:4 And round about the throne were four and twenty seats: and upon the seats I saw four and twenty elders sitting, clothed in white raiment; and they had on their heads crowns of gold....8. And the four beasts had each of them six wings about him; and they were full of eyes within: and they rest not day and night, saying, **Holy, holy, holy***, Lord God Almighty, which was, and is, and is to come.*

So, when we say **He that is holy,** we see in chapter 4 that Lord God Almighty is holy so are there two "He's" that are holy. The truth is, we believe that Jesus Christ is the same substance as God the Father. They are not the same people but they are the same God and so we have many who are made holy because of the holy one but there's only one "holy one." Someone might say it means "without sin." That is a result of what **holy** really means. **Holy** does not mean "without sin" but it is a result of what it does mean.

he that is true, he that hath the key of David, he that openeth, and no man shut- teth; and shutteth, and no man openeth.

> *Isaiah 22:7 And it shall come to pass in that day, that I will call my servant Eliakim the son of Hilkiah...And the key of the house of David will I lay upon his shoulder; so he shall open,* ***and none shall shut; and he shall shut, and none shall open***.

The key keeper had around his neck a particular a chain or whatever and he had the key. In this case, it was Eliakim and he was the son of Hilkiah. Hilkiah was the high priest back in the days of Hezekiah the king. So you have the high priest and then you have his successor, Eliakim. Eliakim, it was said that he had the key to the house of David. Apparently, he had access to where the king lived. If you had the key of the house of David, you could go anywhere you wanted to, but in particular, you could go before the king anytime you desired. You have the key and so Christ is saying, "I have the control of the access to God. I have the ability to open and shut."

In the context of one of our themes "kill the dragon; get the girl" we see that this is access to the King and that this is access only intimacy earns or gains.

3:8

I know thy works: behold, I have set before thee an open door, and no man can shut it: for thou hast a little strength, and hast kept my word, and hast not denied my name. Christ promises an open door to those who have kept the word of his patience. Jesus said, "I'm going to write you as the one who has the key." Now, please notice how he uses this key image all through this short letter to the church of Philadelphia. Look at verse 7, "I have this key and I open doors that **no one can shut and I shut doors that no one can open**." Verse 8, "I know thy works: behold, I have set before thee **an open door, and no man can shut it:** for thou hast a little strength, and hast kept my word." So, he talks about having this key, he **opens doors that no one can shut** in verse 7, he shuts **doors that no man can open** in verse 7. He says, "I am the one who controls things around here. I have the access before the Father." That does sound like John, though. Wasn't John the one who recorded Jesus saying "I am the way, the truth and the life. No man comes to the Father except through me (John 14:6).

3:10

Because thou hast kept the word of my patience, I also will keep thee from the hour of temptation, which shall come upon all the world, to try them that dwell upon the earth. So, we have this Christ who holds the key and he says, "I'll keep you; I'll give an open door. I'll give you a way of escape." This has the idea of "guarding outside of." The whole word behind "from" there is the Greek word *ek*. The word here, ek, means "out." It really looks like, based on verse 10, that those who keep the word of patience will be guarded outside of the hour of temptation that shall try them that come upon all of them that dwell upon the face of the earth.

In the statement "Revelation 3:10 guarantees that those who are saved will not be a part of the tribulation period." There are two major assumptions: 1. is that it is a promise to all believers. However, in verse 10 it says "because you've kept the word of my patience, I also will keep thee from the hour of temptation which shall come upon all the world to try them that dwell upon the earth." There appears to be a stipulation. If this is an escape before the tribulation period, it means that we are talking about only some people who are believers. They have kept the word of Christ's patience or have kept Christ's word in his patience.

It does definitely appear to be a promise to the entire church there in Philadelphia because in verse 8 he says, "you have kept the word of my patience." But what it doesn't appear to be is a promise to all believers. I'm saying that if the pre-tribulation rapture belief is in this verse, then we have to assume that it is for all believers who keep the **word of** his **patience**.

> *Revelation 2:22 Notwithstanding I have a few things against thee, because thou sufferest that woman Jezebel, which calleth herself a prophetess, to teach and to seduce **my servants** to commit fornication, and to eat things sacrificed unto idols. And I gave her space to repent of her fornication; and she repented not. Behold, I will cast her into a bed, and them that commit adultery with **her into great tribulation**.*

Who are the ones that were "seduced to commit fornication" with this "Jezebel?" The servants of Christ who are promised that if they don't repent of this, they will get what? The great tribulation John talks about in only one other place—within the chronology of Daniel's 70th week (Revelation 7:10-14):

> *Revelation 7:14. And I said unto him, Sir, thou knowest. And he said to me, These are they which came out of **great tribulation**, and have washed their robes, and made them white in the blood of the Lamb.*

Know this: John didn't have two great tribulations in the book of Revelation.

Those who are "coming out of Great Tribulation" can't come out if they didn't go into it. So either these are saved people that went in and came out; or they were saved (called "servants" in 2:20), got unsaved, went into "great tribulation," got saved and came out; but Revelation 2:22 promises that unrepentant servants of Christ will get great tribulation. If Revelation 3:10 is talking about a rapture of the church from the earth, it is only a proof text for a partial rapture. To assume that Revelation 3:10 requires a rapture is an assumption that being "kept from an hour of temptation" requires that you're being taken from the planet.

> *John 17:15.* ***I pray not that thou shouldest take them out of the world, but that thou shouldest keep them from the evil [one].***

Is it necessary from Jesus' perspective for his disciples to be removed from the world to be kept from the evil one? Apparently not. This is certainly parallel with Revelation 3:10.

We have an hour of temptation here in the very same book ten chapters later and it tells us what **the hour of temptation** is. These are kept from the evil one while being on the earth because their names are in the Lamb's book of life (Revelation 13:8). We can, therefore, assume that those who have **kept the word of [His] patience** are on the earth during the **hour of temptation** but that those who have not **kept the word** are flung into the full reality of Revelation 13:8 (like those in 2:22).

There is no need to believe that in order to be kept from the hour of temptation you have to be removed from the earth. Christ said that it was possible to be kept from the evil one without being removed from the earth. Also, remember that we are told that it is a conditional protection during that hour for those who have not committed adultery with whomever Jezebel is in chapter 2.

What ought to cause some level of pause among the reader is the first phrase of verse 11: **I come quickly**. This tells the reader that being excused from this **hour** is connected, at least with the coming of Christ.

Somehow, the "keeping" of some from **hour of temptation which shall try all earth dwellers** is accomplished through the coming of Christ. We must admit that if this is so, then all the promises of Christ to the believer to return only catch some away…a partial rapture (the closing verses of Luke 21 seem to leave this as a possibility) or we are left with the possibility that those in 2:22 are really not believers and are left behind to face **the hour,** or as intimated in 3:11, they are in danger of losing their salvation.[5] So, how about some summary questions?

1. Does one have to be removed from the earth to be kept from the Revelation 13:8 scenario? No, John 17's comparison bears that out.

2. Are there two classes of people (or three) in this passage (those who keep or those who do not keep but are saved) or is there but one? One: Overcomers are allowed in Heaven (3:12; 1 John 5:4), and those who do not fit this either were never saved or were, and are not (a can of worms for a different time).

3. Does the promise of His coming in 3:11 mean His 2nd coming or are there other options? His 2nd Coming: It is the one spoken of by John in the opening of the book (1:7), and described in the closing of the book (19:11-15).

4. Is there any chance that 13:8 occurs after 19:11-15? No, there is no reason to believe those who are here and tempted to bow (13:8) do so with Jesus Christ on the earth.

   Summary statement:
   The promised protection to those who are saved must be that they are not of those who will be tried, and that they are promised a quick return of Christ shortly after that hour. Those who are tempted, then, in the 13:8 **hour** must be those newly saved and out of the view of this promise.

---

[5] One is reminded that no "former believers" are ever promised salvation in the Bible.

Alternative:
There is a **coming** hinted throughout these letters to the churches well-spoken of (filled with true converts), and in the last passage of Revelation that is for only the believers as others wait for the distant, long awaited coming which "every eye shall see" (1:7). This would mean all those in the 13:8 scenario are those simply left behind.

3:14

And unto the angel of the church of the Laodiceans write; There are two churches in the book of Revelation that received letters from two different apostles. One of them is Ephesus. They got a letter from Paul and that letter is known as Ephesians and then they got this one from John in Revelation 2. Well, Laodicea is another church that got two letters. In Colossians 4:16, we find out there's a letter that Paul wrote to the church of Laodicea that didn't make the status of Scripture and was not included in our Bible. So, Laodicea did get a letter written to them by another apostle, we just don't have it.

They have a town about 10-12 miles north of them known as Hierapolis and they describe this as a place that has very, very warm and in most cases, hot mineral baths that were used for healing and for therapy. Hierapolis was known for its hot mineral baths. It might surprise you to know back in the Roman Empire days, they did have aqueducts. There there were ways to convey water long distances and there were some between Hierapolis and Laodicea. There were also aqueducts between Colossae and Laodicea. Colossae is about 15-20 southeast of Laodicea and it was known for its cold drinking water. So you've got one place that's known for its cold, refreshing drinking water. They lived at the foot of an 8,000 foot mountain and, of course, when snow melts off it makes for, in most cases, good drinking water, cold drinking water. Then when you went up to the mineral baths in Hierapolis they had hot mineral-based healing waters. That's going to mean something here in a short bit, isn't it?

These things saith the Amen, the faithful and true witness The Son of man is coming in clouds to the one sitting on the throne in Daniel 7 and in Revelation 1, John says he saw the Son of man and the reader would have certainly thought that John was saying that Jesus Christ was the fulfillment of Daniel 7 and every time Jesus introduces himself to the churches, he does so like right here: **the faithful witness.**

> *Revelation 1:5 And from Jesus Christ,* ***who is the faithful witness****.*

the beginning of the creation of God. Does that mean that he's the first created being or does it mean that he began creation? First, I want to look in the immediate context. Second, we need to look at all seven letters if there is nothing in the immediate context.

> *Revelation 2:8 And unto the angel of the church in Smyrna write; These things saith* ***the first and the last****, which was dead, and is alive;*

He's referred, in this verse, as "the amen." That means "That's it. I agree. Let it be done." As a matter of fact, the last word of the Bible is "Amen." So, right here in his introduction to the Laodiceans, he is saying, "I'm the end and I'm the beginning."

> *Revelation 1:11 I am* ***Alpha and Omega****, the* ***beginning and the ending****, saith the Lord, which is, and which was, and which is to come.*

So, if we can demonstrate that Jesus is talking in 1:8, we can demonstrate he's the uncaused cause. John 1:1-3, "In the beginning was the Word, and the Word was with God, and the Word was God. The same was in the beginning with God. All things were made by him; and without him was not any thing made that was made." Alright, so we have this God and Word who "was God" together creating everything to the point where John says twice that if he didn't make it, it wasn't made.

"And the Word was made flesh and dwelt among us." So, this very Christ is the one who is identified as the one who made everything that John went out of his way twice of saying, "If he didn't make it, it wasn't made." So, there are religions out there that teach that Elohim is not the uncaused cause. He is another god that was caused by another god. So, that's why we're being very articulate about this, the best that we can, the best that I can.

What difference does it make if God first created Jesus and then they created everything together or if Jesus actually did the creating? Why would matter to the church member at Laodicea? Everything that we believe about God affects our think- ing and then every way that we think affects our behavior.

There is creation occurring with each of Jesus' miracles (like the multiplication of fish, for example). If Jesus was the beginning of the creation of God in that he was the first created being, well, then so what? If this is so, He's great, but he's not THE creator. Whereas, if He's the one doing it, then we have quite a difference in potential. We have Jesus being the uncaused cause and all of a sudden, he is the God. Jesus is actually Jehovah.

And unto the angel of the church of the Laodiceans write. The person who is speaking in 1:10 and 4:1 is speaking. **These things saith the Amen**, that's the final word. **The faithful and true witness, the beginning of the creation of God.** He's the final word and he's the beginning. He's the first word and the last word. All of these introductions to these seven churches that take place in chapters 2 and 3 of Revelation begin with Jesus saying, "I am" and he fills in the blank. In this particular, he reaches back to chapter 1, the faithful witness. Revelation 1, then, reaches back to Daniel 7, and then Revelation 2 and 3 reach back to Revelation 1. This book comes unlocked when we see the Old Testament inside of Revelation.

Jesus gave compliments to five of the seven churches. Laodicea is not one of them. Of these five churches, there is also five that were told to repent.

3:15-16

I know thy works. I don't know if you've realized it or not yet, but he says that to all seven churches. Isn't that something? I suppose that the Lord said something once and that's pretty important but when he says it seven times, we should probably know he knows our works. That is one of the things that he says to all seven churches.

I know thy works, that thou art neither cold nor hot: I would thou wert cold or hot. Now, would this have meant something to the reader? Would they have thought about this and known exactly what he was talking about? Absolutely. "I wish that you were cold like the waters from Colossae, good for taste and refreshment or, I wish that you were hot and good for healing like those waters from Hierapolis." You are neither good for refreshing people or healing them. Out of the seven churches, only two of them are not complimented by the Lord. There are no compliments for the church of Laodicea. None.

I know thy works, that thou art neither cold nor hot: I would thou wert cold or hot. So then because thou art lukewarm, and neither cold nor hot, I will spue thee out of my mouth. If we were to live in that day, we would have known the author was referencing the hot waters that were brought in via aqueducts from Hierapolis and/or the cold waters being brought in via aqueduct from Colossae and we would have known, based on that this was not about a salvation ultimatum. If on Father's Day this coming June, I write a note to my three children. Here's the question: in about ten years, if you open up a letter from me to my oldest child and you read it, there are going to be some things there that you are going to need to know in order to understand what I am writing. I might reference the game on Friday. I might reference the car that she wishes she could drive. I might reference the license that she hopes to obtain. You would need to know whatever it is I'm talking about for the letter to make sense, wouldn't you? You might learn several things from the letter about the writer and you'll learn lots of things about the original reader by reading the letter. You can learn a lot from someone else's mail but that doesn't mean it's your mail. The Bible was written to particular people at a particular time and we glean learning from those letters but not a single person in here can say, "I was the first generation intended recipient of that letter." So we can learn things from the letter but it is not right for us to say, "Uh, I don't need to know the history behind that."

I looked across the table at someone I really care dearly for a couple of Thanks- givings ago and I said, "I think it's important that we know the historical context of the passages that we're reading." And that dear person to me said, "I think that's stupid." And I'm saying to you that the reason that we have so many cults and sects and groups that would all line up and say, "I believe the Bible," is because they don't understand or are not willing to acknowledge the historical context.

I will spue thee out of my mouth. Is this a proof text that a person who is lukewarm will go to hell? No. If we don't know that we're referencing healing waters from Hier- apolis or cold thirst-quenching waters from Colossae, then we might come away with thinking that John the Apostle is saying, "I wish you were all out for God or not for him at all. If you can't make up your mind, you make him want to puke." Rather, since we know that one town produced healing, warm, mineral waters and one town produced cold, thirst-quenching, satisfying waters, it sounds like Jesus is saying, "I wish that you were healing people or satisfying people but you're not doing either. You're not accomplishing anything. You're rancid, tepid and disgusting." We don't have the freedom to yank those two Scriptures and say it's to everyone. Well, hold on, no it's not. It's to believers in a local church, and Christ is saying the entire local church is like that. Can you imagine even supposing that Christ is threatening to send an entire local church who was saved to hell? That's what we're left with if we believe that that's what that Scripture is teaching.

3:17

Because thou sayest, I am rich, and increased with goods, and have need

of nothing. Did you know that for the most part, these seven churches endured lots of earthquake activity back around 60 AD and I'm pretty sure it was these four eastern cities (the last four of the seven) faced that earthquake and all four of them except for Laodicea, received help monetarily from the Roman government to rebuild. Laodicea did not. One of the reasons Laodicea was so well off was because they were right here at these crossroads going west and east to the mountains and then south into Colossae and north into Philadelphia. They are at a very intersection of the trade trails or spice trails. They were there collecting duties and they were there doing services amongst the traders.

They were very wealthy. They could say to the Roman government, "We don't really need your help. We're going to rebuild ourselves." That is a matter of history. Can you imagine being so well off that you're not taking government funds? To those who think that they don't need anything. He says, "You're miserable." That word there is the idea of pitiful or in need of mercy. "You don't know this but you are in need of supply and mercy." Grace is getting goodness you don't deserve, mercy is not getting the whipping that you do deserve. So, mercy and grace are both present at the cross. We're not getting the judgment we deserve. We are getting the righteousness we do not deserve. That's the difference between mercy and grace. Jesus said, "Not only are you so needy but you are actually in need of mercy because I should just spew you out of my mouth," is what he said in the preceding verse.

and knowest not that thou art wretched, and miserable, When the uncaused cause says to you, "You're miserable," that means something. When the uncaused cause says, "You need me," that means something because you've had the one who needs nothing telling you you need everything. If, on the other hand, Jesus is just the first created being, well, then, he needs someone too. He was caused. So, it matters to the listener which is true. It's an issue of authority.

and poor, and blind... Laodicea was known for their healing eye salve powders. So Jesus is picking on them in a big sort of way. He's taking their strengths and saying, "You don't have any strength here. You're blind. You're known for your eye salve and you can't see anything.

You're known for your riches and you're dirt poor."

3:18

I counsel thee. I know sometimes we get the idea that Jesus didn't like the Laodicean church. Well, if He didn't like them, then why would he counsel them? Sometimes you've got to like someone enough to give them some harsh counsel. **I counsel thee to buy of me gold tried in the fire.** You burn the precious metal, the impurities rise to the top because of their different weights and densities. The goldsmith or the person, the refiner, scrapes the top off and, hopefully, what you have left is a purer precious metal. As a matter of fact, they do it to silver.

> *Psalm 12:6 The word of the Lord is **pure as silver** tried in the furnace of earth seven times.*

He says here, "I want you to get gold tried in the fire. Well, you're rich but you've got the wrong kind of gold. You think you've got a lot but you really don't have anything. You're dirt poor."

So Jesus says, **I'm going to counsel you to buy of me gold tried in the fire that thou mayest be rich; and white raiment, that thou mayest be clothed, and that the shame of thy nakedness do not appear; and anoint thine eyes with eyesalve, that thou mayest see.** Now, I want you to notice, please: we're not dealing with a church full of unsaved people. How do I know this? Look at the next verse. Of course, the town of Laodicea was well-known for their ophthalmology. They had lots of eye aids and healing aids and so to look at them and say, "You're all blind," was no question taken, as an insult—at the very least, a rebuke.

3:19

As many as I love, I rebuke and chasten: be zealous therefore, and repent. He says, "I love you and I chasten you." Well, chasten has the idea of "spanking," not "flogging." I don't go around whipping other people's kids if I can help it. I spend time correct- ing my own children—hopefully a little less the older they get. **Be zealous therefore, and repent.** Just imagine what it would look like if we were zealous to repent. We're zealous towards a lot of things but getting sin and impurity and unholiness out of our lives is usually not one of them.

As many as I love, I rebuke and chasten: be zealous therefore, and repent. That is a quotation from Proverbs 3.

> *Proverbs 3:11-12. My son, despise not the chastening of the LORD; neither be weary of his correction. For **whom the LORD loveth he correcteth.***

Every one of these seven churches received a reference from the Old Testament.

3:20

Behold, I stand at the door, and knock: if any man hear my voice, and open the door, I will come in to him, and will sup with him, and he with me. Jesus is speaking to a church made up of believers. What kind of sense does it make to look at people who are sitting on a dock and saying, "You want to come out of the water?" So it makes no sense for Christ to offer salvation to the saved. It seems to me like Jesus is saying, "I want to have a relationship with you." Who is the "you" in the context? All the people in the church. Jesus says, "Right now, you make me want to vomit but if one of you will decide to let me into your church, I will come in and fellowship with you among that church." That means that you can be in the middle of a crowd where people are bored by the things of God and Jesus will sit right on your row and help you to enjoy the goodness of God in the land of the living.

3:21

To him that overcometh will I grant to sit with me in my throne, even as I also overcame, Notice how great it is that Christ is the first overcomer. We're not being commanded to do something here that Christ hasn't already done. He's overcome the wicked one. Remember? Context is king.

> *Revelation 12:11 And **they overcome** by the blood of the Lamb and by the word of the testimony, and love not our own lives even unto death.*

And the reason they/we are able to overcome is because of the Lamb who provided that same blood as He overcame.

and am set down with my Father in his throne. He that hath an ear, let him hear what the Spirit saith unto the churches. Promises to overcomers are given to all seven churches. All seven churches have an introduction from the Son of God; five have a commendation; all seven of them are given a quotation or a reference from the Old Testament. All seven of them are told "he that hath an ear let him hear." All seven of them are told that they have promises as overcomers.

Moreover, all seven of these churches have promises that appear in fulfillment at the end of the book (Revelation 22:1-3 and Matthew 19:27-29). It seems like that those who suffer with Christ will reign with him (2 Timothy 2:12). Revelation 20 talks about that as well. It seems like that they are separate thrones, same throne room so that you can actually say you're sharing the throne. It seems like overcomers will share his throne as he shares with the Father's throne. There are separate thrones but they are close enough together where they could be considered the same seat of authority.

Chapter 4

4:1

After this I looked, and, behold, a door was opened in heaven: and the first voice which I heard was as it were of a trumpet talking with me; which said, Come up hither, and I will shew thee things which must be hereafter. Many have said this is the rapture. Here are five reasons why I do not think this is the rapture of the church:

1. It doesn't say it is. That's pretty important. If a rapture were to be communicated here, why wouldn't John do at least what Paul did before him? Consider 1 Corinthians 15:51-54 and how it doesn't say it here. It's pretty explicit. We are not going to die; we are all going to be raised and changed, and those who are dead will be raised with us. But, isn't that strange? Paul says it plainly. He says here's how it's going to happen.

   *1 Thessalonians 4:16 For the Lord Himself shall descend from Heaven with a shout with a voice of the archangel the trump of God and the dead in Christ shall rise first. Then **we which are alive and remain shall be caught up together** in the clouds to meet the Lord in the air so shall we be with the Lord.*

   Let's not forget 1 Thessalonians 4:16-18. It is also quite explicit. And then we say with the very next moment, "the very next thing on God's calendar is a rapture," and John doesn't even care to tell us where it is? He doesn't even say "hey, the rapture is right here in chapter number 4! This is when all the saints go to Heaven and all the dead with them." That wasn't that important to him?

2. If John is the church in chapter 4:1, then why is it that the elders are often seen as the church 4 verses later? We

can't be changing symbology. I wouldn't do that to any other author in here. I'm going to take what you say and change the meaning half way through the paragraph?

3. Prophets who are caught up to Heaven use this very same language? For instance, the apostle Paul:

   2 Corinthians 12:1 ...I knew a man that was caught up to the third Heaven, in the body or in the spirit I cannot tell but God knows.

   Ok, so that's common language for a prophet to say "I was caught up to Heaven" when they were caught up to Heaven. Moses saw the pattern of the tabernacle in the mount, Ezekiel was caught up to Heaven, John was caught up to Heaven. Why can't this be "John was caught up into Heaven?" Everything he describes is from the Heaven's perspective. It simply need not be the "church being caught up to Heaven" as so popularly purported.

4. There is no resurrection in chapter 4:1. The two rapture verses out of 1 Corinthians 15 and 1 Thessalonians 4 have a resurrection of dead saints. There's no resurrection happening here! There's not even a supposed symbol representing the resurrection!

5. If John is the church when he's caught up to Heaven, how come he's not the church when he returns before the trumpets in chapter 8? We have a problem there! If he's the church when he goes up to Heaven how come he's not the church when he comes down? In chapter 19, how can the church be the armies of Heaven coming with Christ, but they were first John when he was caught up to Heaven? If chapter 4:1 is a rapture then it's not the rapture of 1 Thessalonians 4 or 1 Corinthians 15 or Matthew 24 because all of those involve angels and

resurrection. None of those take place here in chapter 4 of Revelation. Now, why did I say that? Because, if John is the church, then it's not John worshipping in chapter 5 and verse number 13. If John is the church of chapter 4 verse 1, then everywhere you see John in the book of Revelation you've got to say "well that's the church." And then when he returns in chapter 8 to say "I saw angels falling from Heaven..." he was the church back on earth? Of course not.

6. Then, how do we handle the next phrase where John says "He was in the spirit" and the church is supposedly "raptured" with glorified bodies? Come on now.

Immediately I was in the spirit. That would be as of a vision, John being in the spirit, and that takes place also in Revelation 1:10, 17:3 and 21:10. In all of those events it's "transported" or "in the spirit" and that is as opposed to physically being transported where if you look in Revelation 11:11-12 the two witnesses during the times of the trib- ulation or the pouring out of God's wrath, the witnesses are killed and then brought to life and it says that "after the three and a half days the breath of life from God came into them and they stood on their feet and great fear fell upon those who were watching them and they heard a loud voice from heaven saying to them, Come up here." Then they went up into heaven in the cloud and their enemies watched them and in that passage, there is no mention of "in the spirit." This is where the two wit- nesses were raised from the dead after they'd been killed and summoned into heaven but summoned up physically. So, that is a different sense than where John is speaking in several different instances where he was "in the spirit."

> *2 Corinthians 12:2 [Paul says] I knew a man in Christ above fourteen years ago, (whether in the body, I cannot tell; or whether out of the body, I cannot tell: God knoweth;) such an one caught up to the third heaven. And I knew such a man,* **(whether in the body, or out of the body, I cannot tell:** *God knoweth;) How that he was caught up into paradise.*

And we take that passage to mean Paul was talking about himself and where he had a special event in his life where God brought him up into the third heaven and even Paul was saying, "It was so real, I couldn't even tell whether I was in my body or whether it was a vision." John does relate to us that it was "in the spirit" and, therefore, a vision. John was still bodily in the isle of Patmos.

4:2

A throne was set in heaven, and one sat on the throne. Remember when even Moses saw the burning bush, was taken aback, he fell down. I believe it would be very diffi- cult to draw a correct representation of what some of these prophets and writers were seeing when they got a glimpse of God in his glory.

he that sat upon the throne was like a jasper and a sardine stone: and also there was a rainbow around the throne. One of the definitions of the word "the rainbow" is an iris, like the iris of your eye or a halo. So, when we see the word "rainbow" auto- matically we think of the multi-colored rainbow and, of course, God used the rainbow in the sky at the end of Noah's flood as a sign of a covenant. So, here we could look at this rainbow as being representative of the covenant but even more so, the fact that it said it had an emerald appearance which isn't multi-colored but if you think of it as the halo effect, then this facet of the halo or the rainbow which was mostly like and emerald or green.

"Jasper" was described as being mostly clear. So, we have the clear or the trans- parent or the crystal look around the one that is sitting on the throne and then the sardius was a red colored and in the Old Testament sometimes, the term translated sardius by some of the translators was translated "ruby." So, we have this image of a little bit of the ruby color around the crystal color and then, of course, the emerald hue from the rainbow. The first stone was the sardius stone and the last stone was the jasper stone. So, we have kind of symbology here from the Old Testament breastplate of righteousness, so to speak, from the priests attire. Then also in Revelation 21:19-20, the foundation of the New Jerusalem includes the jasper stone and the sardius stone.

4:3

And round about the throne were four and twenty seats: and upon the seats I saw four and twenty elders sitting, clothed in white raiment; and they had on their heads crowns of gold. There are no other passages in Scripture where we talk about the 24 elders that we see in this scene. If we were to look in Acts 20:17 and 1 Timothy 5:17 and Titus 1:5, **elders are** the leaders, the overseers of the church, individual churches, but also representative of the believers.

The term "crown" in this passage comes from the Greek word *stephanos* which is the wreath or garland which was given and awarded at public games. Those that were winners at public games as opposed to a crown that was worn by a monarch or somebody that was in a ruler authority. So, these crowns and the words used for these crowns are specifically not of those of the same crown that would be worn by a king or God on his throne. It seems, then, that these elders represent the believers before the throne of God. Furthermore, the Old Testament backdrop of Leviticus 4:14-15 (the command of the assembly to approach, yet only the elders do so) and Ezra 10:14 (which requires no explanation) show us that where you find elders, you find a myriad of others whom they would represent in their collective action.

Now, allow me to point out that their actions in 4:10 are not "casting their crowns at the feet of Jesus," for He does not arrive on the scene until chapter 5.[6]

4:8

See notes on 1:8.

---

[6] I noticed this first listening to this fine message: http://www.sermonaudio.com/sermoninfo.asp?SID=112116113142 [accessed January 26, 2017].

Chapter 5

5:1-3

And I saw in the right hand of him that sat on the throne a book written within and on the backside, sealed with seven seals. And I saw a strong angel proclaiming with a loud voice, Who is worthy to open the book, and to loose the seals thereof? And no man in heaven, nor in earth, neither under the earth, was able to open the book, neither to look thereon. Jeremiah 32:6 (and following) show us we're talking about a deed that this man signed proving that he had purchased a field.

> *Matthew 13:44, Again, the kingdom of heaven is like unto treasure hid **in a field**; the which when a man hath found, he hideth, and for joy thereof goeth and selleth all that he hath, and **buyeth that field**.*

> *Matthew 13:37 He answered and said unto them, He that soweth the good seed is the Son of man; **The field is the world**.*

In these Matthew 13 Kingdom parables, who is the one doing the action? The Son of man, Jesus. What is the field? The world. So, in verse 44, who is it that's buying the field? Jesus. And what is he buying? The world. He's buying the world to get some- thing precious (a kingdom?) hidden therein. When did that happen? On the cross.

Well, isn't Revelation 5 prophecy? Well, if Christ bought the world, doesn't He have possession of it yet? Legally, he does but in a very practical sense, he doesn't.

> *Psalm 24:1 **The earth is the Lord's** and the fullness thereof.*

But he hasn't taken true possession of it yet in a kingdom sort of sense. Is the king- dom of God existing? Yes. Is it in full power and manifestation here on the earth? No. That's why we pray, "Thy kingdom come, Thy will be done on earth as it is in heaven."

5:4

And I wept much. Think about this angel saying, "Who is worthy to open the book?" Nothing, and not just nothing but in this vision John saw "nobody in heaven or on earth or in hell." Nobody in heaven or earth or under the earth was worthy. Nobody was found that was worthy. Now, we want to know what makes someone worthy. Was this author of Revelation walking with Jesus when Jesus was on the earth? Why is he so forgetful? Because he's a man.

Here is John's reaction. Now, this is like a replay of Isaiah 6 except there is some more detail added. It's also a sort of a replay of Revelation chapter 1. Revelation 1 reminds us of Daniel 7 where you see an Ancient of Days sitting on his throne and the Son of man being brought to him by the clouds of heaven.

because no man was found worthy to open and to read the book, neither to look thereon. No one could even open the book. No one should even be looking at this scroll. The Greek word behind "scroll," behind "book" is *biblion*. It's where we get our word "Bible" and it means a scroll. We're talking about a scroll in the hand of the one sitting on the throne and it has seven seals on it. It's sealed seven times and every time a seal is broken in chapter 6, it opens slightly. Christ is being revealed in the book of Revelation chapter 19. Between chapter 5 and chapter 19, we have something happening. What is it? It is Christ slowly taking back possession of the earth during a period of seven years. He does it gradually. He does it a seal at a time in chapter 6 and unravels the judgment on the planet. Then in chapter 19, he comes back to the planet in the body and in chapter 20 we have a 1,000 year reign on this planet. Again, this is one story. You are seeing him lifted up here as the one who owns the world and in chapter 19 He comes back to take residence. Between here and there, he is slowly judging the earth and making it ready for his coming. It takes seven years.

5:5

And one of the elders saith unto me, Weep not: behold, the Lion of the tribe of Juda, the Root of David, hath prevailed to open the book, and to loose the seven seals thereof. We have this one sitting on the throne and then we have around him, and we have four beasts having six wings. They are always crying, "Holy, holy, holy." It seems like they're the same ones in Isaiah 6 called seraphim. It seems like they're the same ones in Ezekiel 1 called cherubim. In any case, you have them around the throne and then we found out last week in chapter 4, what else do you have around the throne? 24 elders. You say, "Who do they represent?" They represent a larger body. What would be the point of having elders if they didn't represent someone else? An elder is a leader, an overseer.

The reader knows the elders are not just a symbol. Why? Because one of them
steps out. So, if you're going to say 24 elders merely represent a group of people, then we have a problem because then what does just one represent? So they are real people even though they represent other people like a Republic sort of arrangement. We can look through Scripture: Job 1, 1 Kings 22, where you have councils taking place around the throne of God in heaven. So this is not far-out that you have elders—who are people—that are in heaven right now.

5:6

And I beheld, and, lo, in the midst of the throne. So, we're not talking about a particular chair called "the throne." We're talking about the throne area. We talked about this in Revelation 3 dealing with the church at Laodicea when we spoke about how Jesus said, "To him that overcomes, I will allow him to sit with me in my throne even as I am sitting with my Father in his throne."

and in the midst of the elders stood a Lamb as it had been slain. So you have people of the earth fearing "the wrath of the Lamb." That's hideous. When you think of a lamb, you probably don't get scared, do you? He's called the Lamb all through the book of Revelation.

1. <u>The Lamb is the only one found worthy to open the book with the seven seals.</u>

Look at chapter 5:5. Now, you might remember that the book of Revelation is the story of how Christ reclaims the earth. In chapter 5 we have this unveiling of this title deed and in chapter 19, he sets foot back on the earth. Between chapter 6 and chapter 19, we have a gradual reclamation of planet earth. Why? The earth is the Lord's.

Revelation 5:9 And they sung a new song, saying, Thou art worthy to take the book, and to open the seals thereof: for thou wast slain, and **hast redeemed us to God by thy blood** *out of every kindred, and tongue, and people, and nation.*

Colossians 1:20, it says he's reconciled the world to himself through the blood of his cross. Sometimes we think: well, he really just died for people. Hold on, let's just try to remember that the whole creation is cursed. Romans 8 links the sin of Adam with the curse of creation and when Christ comes at what Ephesians 4 calls "the day of redemption" it's not just the people he's redeeming to himself, it is the creation that's been groaning for this redemption. So, all of creation is linked somehow with the redemption of people.

The reason that He's found worthy to open the book is for the very reason that we assume he's a Lamb to being with, "**because you were slain and have redeemed us to God by thy blood out of every kindred, tribe, people and nation.**" That is the fulfillment of the promise to Abraham. Do you remember? What was the prom- ise that God gave Abraham? All nations would be blessed through Abraham. All the nations of the earth would be blessed and Paul said in Galatians 3:8 that that was the gospel that was preached to Abraham. So, we see in Revelation 5:9 the fulfillment of the promise that God made to Abraham, that the very seed of Abraham would bring redemption and bless all nations and now you have all nations being blessed because of the seed of Abraham, Jesus Christ (Galatians 3:16), who died to save all nations. That's a great thing.

*John 1:29 John seeth Jesus coming unto him, and saith, Behold **the Lamb of God**, which taketh away the sin of the world. This is he of whom I said, After me cometh a man which is preferred before me: for he was before me. And I knew him not: but that he should be made manifest to Israel, therefore am I come baptizing with water…35 Again the next day after John stood, and two of his disciples.*

Genesis 22: Do you remember that Abraham took Isaac and Isaac said, "Father, I see the wood and I see the fire but where is the lamb for the burnt offering?" And Abra- ham said, "My son, God will provide himself a lamb." Get that now: God will provide himself a lamb. The reason we know that that was not immediately fulfilled was because it was not a lamb caught in the thicket, it was a ram caught in the thicket. So, there was a very long view of that promise that Abraham made to Isaac. One day God will provide himself a lamb and so when John is recorded here as seeing this carpenter from Nazareth walking down the beaches of the Jordan River, he says, "Behold the Lamb of God which takes away the sin of the world." Maybe the audience in that day didn't catch the full significance of that but the reader did. The reader is a student of Genesis and all through the book of Genesis we see John connecting his gospel with the book of Genesis, the first thing of which being the first three words "in the begin- ning." So, it is no strange thing that this terminology is being used. John is clearly saying, "Jesus is the fulfillment of Abraham's prophecy to Isaac and Jesus is the Lamb of God." Therefore, a lamb signifies something: it signifies death, doesn't it?

2. <u>The Lamb is the one opening the seals.</u>

*Revelation 6:1 And I saw when **the Lamb** opened one of the seals.*

He opens all seven seals. It is indeed the Lamb who is opening this book and little by little he's opening each of the seals and he's revealing a little bit more of his plan at the grand old reclamation grand opening of the King and his Kingdom.

    3. <u>The Lamb is the One receiving the worship from the host heaven other than the one who sat on the throne</u> in chapters 4 and 5.

Here's John, going back to Exodus. In the gospel of John, John's always going back to Genesis. Well, if there's one thing that is going to be painfully obvious as you go through Revelation is that Revelation points back to Exodus. Here's one example of Revelation pointing back to Exodus.

> *Exodus 20:4 Thou shalt not make unto thee any graven image, or any likeness of any thing that is **in heaven** above, or that is **in the earth** beneath, or that is in the water **under the earth.***

Three realms: heaven, earth, water under the earth. We see John going back to Exodus. You're going to notice John continually goes back to Exodus in the book of Revelation. In the gospel of John, he goes back to Genesis which is the first book of the Bible. In Revelation, he goes back to Exodus which is the second book of the Bible.

    4. <u>The Lamb is full of wrath</u>. (Revelation 6:12-17)

There was a great earthquake. Then we have the sun becoming black or the sun becoming dark, whatever. Sun black. That's significant, that doesn't happen all the time. Moon blood or we could say, crimson or dark. And the stars falling from heaven. Now, we're going to talk about what that means, let Scripture tell us, but I just wanted you to be aware that this happens during the sixth seal. Heaven is parted as a scroll.

> *Acts 2:16, But this is that which was spoken by the prophet Joel...17 And it shall come to pass in the last days I will pour out of my Spirit upon all flesh: and your sons and your daughters shall prophesy, and your young men shall see visions, and your old men shall dream dreams: And on my servants and on my*

handmaidens I will pour out in those days of my Spirit; and they shall prophesy: And I will shew wonders in heaven above, and signs in the earth beneath; blood, and fire, and vapour of smoke. ***The sun shall be turned into darkness, and the moon into blood before that great and notable day of the Lord come.***

So we have the sixth seal of Revelation. Joel and Luke and Peter all say that it does not happen in the day of the Lord. When does it happen? <u>Before</u> the day of the Lord.

Matthew 24:15 When ye therefore shall see the abomination of desolation, spoken of by Daniel the prophet, stand in the holy place, Then let them which be in Judaea flee into the mountains.

Let's put this on a time marker here. Remember, Matthew 24:15 happens half way through the tribulation period. Everyone got that?

Matthew 24:21 For then shall be ***great tribulation,***

So we are supposed to ascertain from this that the Great tribulation begins half way through the 70th week of Daniel (tribulation period) and probably lasts how long 3½ years.

*Matthew 24:29 Immediately **after the tribulation** of those days shall the sun be darkened, and the moon shall not give her light, and the stars shall fall from heaven, and the powers of the heavens shall be shaken.*

When does it happen? After the tribulation. That means that the sixth seal of Revelation happens after the great tribulation and before The day of the Lord. So, one thing we know for sure, the day of the Lord does not happen until after the tribulation.

5:9-10

And they sung a new song, saying, Thou art worthy to take the book, and to open the seals thereof: for thou wast slain, and hast redeemed us to God by thy blood out of every kindred, and tongue, and people, and nation. And hast made us unto our God kings and priests: <u>and we shall reign on the earth</u>. So goes the climax of the Genesis 1 focal point. It looks like God is showing us in Genesis 1 where he created everything. Does Genesis 1 tell us how he created everything? No. Does he try to prove his existence? No. There are a lot of things that are given. What is given is: first of all, that the Hebrew audience assumed that there was a God, assumed that God created, assumed that God created everything and so he narrows the focus down to man. And so we get down to basics: God creates man in his own image and then you might remember Genesis chapter 5 begins a genealogy and it says that this guy lives so many hundreds of years, he had a son and then he died and his total number of years was this many years. Chapter 5, the genealogy begins, chapter 10 it continues. What happens in chapters 6, 7, 8, and 9? One story really, about Noah. And the reason that it's stuck right there in chapter 6, 7, 8 and 9 is because the last person spoken of in chapter 5 is Noah.

And what God is showing us through his writer, Moses, is that God is narrowing his focus. Think about creation week: he created day one like day two, the firmament or the heavens; day three the dry land and the herb yielding seed and their fruit bearing seed; day four he populated the firmament with heavenly bodies, cosmic bodies; day five he populated the water and the air; day six he populated the dry land with land animals and with man. And so, God gets all the way down to day six and he focuses <u>then on man</u>. He doesn't talk much anymore about the development of plant life or of animal life. We will come back to it, but that is not the goal of Genesis. God wants you to know the main thing happening in his economy is not what's happening on Neptune or what's happening on earth in the animal kingdom. God is not a green God; God's not going green. Mankind is the pinnacle of his creation and that is why after day six it says, "it was very good."

And he starts talking about mankind from there on and then what happens in chapter 12 as he narrows his focus even further? He pulls a man out of the Ur of the Chaldees named Abram and he is known as "the Hebrew" which means "wanderer." So, Abram becomes the first Hebrew. This is important because then you realize all a sudden that yes, other things happen in other countries but that wasn't God's focus. He did not want you to see everything that happened on Neptune, in the animal kingdom or even in the Moabites and the Hittites and the Gergasites and the Canaanites. No, that's not the focus. The focus is: what happens through Abraham. So, in Genesis 3 the focus gets very narrow: mankind and the redemption of mankind. We'll look at that in a minute. Then in Genesis 12 he says, "But who within mankind?" Ah, the line of Abraham, the one who I will call out of his luxurious retirement lifestyle at the age of 75.

So, I wanted you to see that God is narrowing our focus. He wants the reader to notice. We are not talking about creation in general, we're talking about the pinnacle of his creation, mankind (Genesis 1:26-2:1).

Now, you might notice that it says 2 or 3 times that man was created in the image of God. In the ancient world, the king would say, "Alright, I'm going to set up statues of myself in all the corners of my domain so that everyone knows it's mine." Well, God does the same thing with earth. Don't you remember Psalm 24:1, "The earth is the Lord's and the fullness thereof; the world, and all that dwell therein." And so, God says, "To prove that, I, the Sovereign, am going to put images of myself down there around my domain so that everyone knows every time they see someone, every time they see an image of God, they will know, Ah, God owns this place." That's good stuff.

> *Genesis 1:28 "And God blessed them, and God said unto them, Be fruitful, and multiply, and replenish the earth, and subdue it: and **have dominion**."*

Let's talk about 1:28: are we talking about males or are we talking about males and females? Who is to have dominion over the fish of the sea, the fowl of the air, the cattle, every creeping thing that creeps on the earth? Between 26 and 27 and 28 it says that "God blessed them" in verse 28 and "God said unto them, Be fruitful, and multiply, and replenish the earth, and subdue it; and have dominion." Now, how do we know we're not just talking to males? Verse 27 says, "God created man in his own image," so we know we're talking about mankind and not males. Why? Because he defines man at the end of the verse, "male and female created he them."

Christianity raises women to the level of men. Men are the nurturing leaders and they are restored to the pre-fall condition of men and women with the man gently leading, men and women together conquering God's creation. Men and women together conquering God's creation within the institution of marriage is God's idea. It is furthermore God's ideal for man to gently lead his wife as they both dominate the earth to the point where they are both conquering what God has given them to do through the vision of the husband. It's the idea that the man is to be the king of his home and the wife is to be the queen and there is no trampling underfoot. There is a gentle leadership taking place with one vision in the home.

Here's how it used to be: Psalm 8, "you created mankind a little lower than the angels" and they are both under the Creator/God. Both of them are under the Creator/God. And then we see a reality that we'll look at here in a few minutes, 2 Corinthians 4:4, where Satan is the god of this world. Somewhere Satan took the dominion of man. Take one trip through Ezekiel and Daniel and you'll find the Prince of Persia, the Prince of Damascus, the Prince of Moab, the Prince of Babylon, all spirit entities that are in charge of certain sections of this world.

> *Ephesians 6:12, "We wrestle not against flesh and blood but against principalities, powers, rulers of the darkness of this world, spiritual wickedness in high places."*

Since the fall, the spirit world has been under the watchful eye and the sovereign hand of God. So, we see how we were intended to be in Genesis 1 and I wonder if we'll ever get back there? Christ subdues Satan and restores all things and subjugation of Satan will fully occur at the Second Coming.

We're reminded of Genesis 3:15, the seed of the woman will crush the serpent's head. So, eventually, Satan will be a defeated foe. Now, he is and he is not yet. Those are realities that you're going to have to get used to as a student of the Word of God: There are things that are effective and there are things that are not yet taking place.

In Psalms 8:1-6 he goes back to creation week there. I intended you on ruling things with glory and honor. Verse 6, "Thou madest him to have dominion over the works of thy hands." That's how he was made. Man was created in God's image. What does that mean? Well, God is a Sovereign, man was intended to be a sovereign. Do you see how we are marred images of God? **Mankind is intended to rule**, not be afraid. Fear is something that came with the fall. So, I'm looking forward to restoration, aren't you?

In Isaiah 11, we're looking forward to a day when everything will be as it was before the curse. And it's not the first Adam that's going to make it happen. 1 Corinthians 15 and Romans 5 speak of the last Adam. Remember, the first Adam brought a curse to us by sinning with a tree in the Garden? And the last Adam took away our curse by becoming the curse for us on a tree in a garden. The Bible is not a collection of disjointed tales, it is one story of redemption.

Look at Luke 4. This is a pretty key Scripture and something I said earlier. We are in the middle of the temptation of Jesus in the wilderness. This is also, by the way, found in Matthew 4. Matthew 4:4 and Luke 4:4 are almost identical. It's easy to remember it that way. Look at the second of three temptations in Luke 4's account.

> *Verse 5, "And the devil, taking him up into an high mountain, shewed unto him all the kingdoms of the world in a moment of time. And the devil said unto him, All this power will I give thee, and the glory of them: for that is delivered unto me; and to*

whomsoever I will I give it. If thou therefore wilt worship me, all shall be thine. And Jesus answered and said unto him, Get thee behind me, Satan: for it is written, Thou shalt worship the Lord thy God, and him only shalt thou serve."

Do you see what Jesus did not do? He did not say, "You Bozo, no it's not. Are you kidding? I'm the Creator. Do you think I'm going to let you have this thing?" He didn't do that, though, did he? But here's what Satan is offering Jesus, we got this in Matthew 4 like three years ago. Here is what Satan was offering Jesus, "You can have what you came to get without dying for it if you'll just worship me. You can have what you came to get without dying for it." He's trying to trick Jesus.

By the way, you might be interested to know that Satan offers him here all the power of the kingdoms, in verse 6. Well, after the crucifixion and resurrection in Matthew 28:18, Jesus says, "All power is given unto me in heaven and earth." So, Jesus says, "It is accomplished. The wicked one is cast out." Paul says to the saints in Rome (Romans 16), "It won't be long. Satan will be crushed under your feet shortly." So, we're just waiting for the Second Coming for all this to take affect. The curse has been removed, it's just a matter of it being removed. The earth has been re-won, it's just a matter of it being taken back. It's already owned. It's already taken back. It's already been paid for.

Ephesians 1 it says that the Holy Spirit is put within our hearts as the earnest of redemption. I paid $500 nonrefundable dollars on my house called "earnest money" and I went back and closed. I didn't want to lose $500. The earnest of this entire cre- ation will take place very soon and to guarantee that, God has invested earnest money down here and he says the earnest money, Ephesians 1, is the Holy Ghost in the heart of the believer. So, do you want a guarantee that soon this thing is going to come to pass and Jesus is going to take over the planet again? Do you want a guarantee? Okay, the Holy Spirit in your heart is the earnest money from the Lord. Very soon, he's going to close and move on in.

Think about 2 Timothy 2:12, "If we suffer with him, we will also reign with him." We will be able to do with the second Adam what the first Adam could not secure for us. We will reign over the earth with the second Adam, with the last Adam, with Jesus Christ we will rule the earth. Review: God created man to rule over his creation, man gave that rulership in an accursed state to the wicked one, Christ crushed the head of the wicked one and took back ownership, not from a sovereign God standpoint but from a resident standpoint. That's even inadequate, I don't even know how to say it. I'm not saying God was on vacation during the Old Testament before Christ died. At the death and resurrection of Christ, Satan's head was crushed, dominion was given back to the last Adam and now Revelation 5:9 we find a scene in the future, **And they sung a new song, saying, Thou art worthy to take the book, and to open the seals thereof: for thou wast slain, and hast redeemed us to God by thy blood out of every kindred, and tongue, and people, and nation. 10 And hast made us unto our God kings and priests: and we shall reign on the earth.** We'll have dominion again with our last Adam. We lost it with Adam, we get it back in Jesus. When? 2 Timothy 4:1. Here's what Paul said to Timothy, "I charge thee therefore before God, and the Lord Jesus Christ, who shall judge the quick and the dead at his appearing and **his kingdom**." The prayer of the disciples in Matthew 6 was "**Thy kingdom come**, Thy will be done in earth as it is in heaven." When Jesus comes visibly, literally, physically, he is coming to bring the Kingdom of God to earth so that things that are done in heaven are done on earth and those of us who have been redeemed, Revelation 5, we will share in that rulership.

What are they doing near the end of the book in chapter 20? They are reigning on the earth. Whatever, then, takes place in chapter 5 is significant to what ends up happening in chapter 20. We are dealing with a title deed to the planet that Christ is taking over (Revelation 1:7, 3:10, 6:10, 9:1-4).

Chapter 6

6:1-2

Before anybody thinks we are getting into something that is only for end times, per- haps they should read Jeremiah 32:23-24 for a good example of God judging a city in these analogous terms by a previous empire. This is clearly on the minds of those who hold to a preterist perspective and an early dating of Revelation.

And I saw when the Lamb opened one of the seals. Remember, in chapter 5, the Lamb was the one worthy opening the seals. **and I heard, as it were the noise of thunder, one of the four beasts saying, Come and see. 2 And I saw, and behold a white horse: and he that sat on him had a bow; and a crown was given unto him: and he went forth conquering , and to conquer.**

> *Zechariah 6 And I turned, and lifted up mine eyes, and looked, and, behold, there came four chariots out from between two mountains; and the mountains were mountains of brass. In the first chariot were red horses; and in the second chariot black horses; And* **in the third chariot white horses;** *and in the fourth chariot grisled and bay horses. 5.And the angel answered and said unto me,* **These are the four spirits of the heavens**

We understand that Zechariah has already used the imagery that John is using. John is using old imagery. He's using old information. It is up to us to be willing to open the Bible and say, "What has God already said about this?"

Here's what we know about from Zechariah: there are historical particulars about what Zechariah is saying but what is also very true is that the white horse is "winds or spirits that go throughout the whole earth." Now, if I say, "Well, there's a good spirit in here. I like the way that we're all ready to learn and read truth," the reader would know what I was saying. The army calls it *esprit de corps* and it's supposed to be sort of this idea that you're part of an organization that just loves being a part of the organization. Same idea here in Zechariah, we have these white horses and the white horses are a spirit or a wind that go throughout the whole earth. Well, that's not much help but it's some help. It's some help because the last time we see a white horse and a vision, it's representing a spirit and it was by a prophet.

> *Matthew 24:1 And as he sat upon the mount of Olives, the disciples came unto him privately, saying, Tell us, when shall these things be? and what shall be the sign of thy coming, and of the end of the world? Jesus answered and said unto them,* ***Take heed that no man deceive you. For many shall come in my name, saying, I am Christ; and shall deceive many.***

So far with the first seal we have that it is a spirit (or wind) and that it is a false Christ. How many horseman are there?

> *Revelation 7:1 After these things I saw four angels standing on the four corners of the earth holding,* ***the four winds.***

I would suggest that these angels are holding the reins to these four horses we saw in the first four seals. Why? Because Zechariah says that these different color horses represent different spirits or winds. I don't think it's far fetched to say that John was a student of Zechariah.

6:3-4

And when he had opened the second seal, I heard the second beast say, Come and see. 4 And there went out another horse that was red: and power was given to him that sat thereon to take peace from the earth, and that they should kill one another: and there was given unto him a great sword. Is Zechariah talking about something different? Maybe, but when he used red horses it was describing a spirit that travels throughout all the earth.

> *Zechariah 6 And I turned, and lifted up mine eyes, and looked, and, behold, there came four chariots out from between two*

> *mountains; and the mountains were mountains of brass. In **the first chariot were red horses;** and in the second chariot black horses; And in the third chariot white horses; and in the fourth chariot grisled and bay horses. 5.And the angel answered and said unto me,* **These are the four spirits of the heavens.**

Then we're taken to the Olivet Discourse. Jesus says after the white horse, the false Christs…

> *Matthew 24 You'll hear of **wars, rumors of wars,** see that you be not troubled for all these things must come to pass but the end is not yet for nation shall rise against nation, kingdom against kingdom.*

Was John, Revelation's author, on the Mount of Olives with Jesus when he gave this discourse? He sure was. So, it's not far-fetched to see that Jesus is putting the first five seals right in order here in that Olivet Discourse and they show up again when John is 60 years older on the isle of Patmos. We know that we have the second horse, it's a spirit and it is wars and bloodshed that begin prior to the middle of the tribulation period based on what Jesus tells us.

6:5

And when he had opened the third seal, I heard the third beast say, Come and see. And I beheld, and lo a black horse; and he that sat on him had a pair of balances in his hand. Wheat apparently was for the richer folks and barley was pretty well for the peasants and all others who wanted it.

> *Zechariah 6 And I turned, and lifted up mine eyes, and looked, and, behold, there came four chariots out from between two mountains; and the mountains were mountains of brass. In the first chariot were red horses; and in **the second chariot black horses;** And in the third chariot white horses; and in the fourth chariot grisled and bay horses. 5.And the angel answered and said unto*

me, ***These are the four spirits of the heavens.***

*Revelation 7:1 After these things I saw **four angels** standing on the four corners of the earth holding,* ***the four winds.***

Now, the antichrist will be of particular interest to the Jewish people which is why Daniel 9 says that this seven year tribulation period begins with a covenant between the Prince that shall come, the antichrist, and the Jews. Then, halfway through, he does what Daniel calls the abomination that makes desolate where he probably, from what we can tell from Scripture—2nd Thessalonians 2 and Daniel 9—he sits in the temple of God claiming to be God. So, what appears to occur some time in the future is that a temple is erected somewhere on the Temple Mount in Jerusalem. It seems like that somewhere around the 3.5 year mark, he takes over and actually sits on the mercy seat, the ark of the covenant. So, it seems like he actually takes up residence sitting on the ark of the covenant in that temple that will be built.

Jews will be expecting a Christ figure that does signs and wonders and miracles. By the way, if it seems far-fetched that the Lord would be sending deceitful spirits into the world, I want to remind you of 1 Kings 22 where there is a crowd of angels around the throne of God and Ahab needs to be deceived to go up to Ramoth-Gilead to be killed in battle and the Lord looks around and says, "So what should we do?" And one of the spirits steps forward and says, "I'll go be a lying spirit in the mouth of his prophets." And God said, "Okay." And he went and Ahab went to battle and was killed. So, that was revealed to us, that's something that actually did take place.

The fact that we're not getting new material in the book of Revelation is mind-bog- gling because some folks have never even thought about the Old Testament shedding light on the book of Revelation. It seems fitting, then, that one of the key miracles of the anti-Christ figure will be to somewhat cure this famine.

And I heard a voice in the midst of the four beasts say, A measure of wheat for a penny. The Greek word there is denarius and that was usually a day's wage.

and three measures of barley for a day's wage; and see thou hurt not the oil and the wine. For some reason, the famine was not bad enough at that point to affect the oil and the wine or orchards and vineyards.

6:7-8

8 And I looked, and behold a pale horse. "Pale" is, we're going to learn, a light green or verdant.

> *Zechariah 6 And I turned, and lifted up mine eyes, and looked, and, behold, there came four chariots out from between two mountains; and the mountains were mountains of brass. In the first chariot were red horses; and in the second chariot black horses; And in the third chariot white horses; and in **the fourth chariot grisled and bay horses**. 5.And the angel answered and said unto me, **These are the four spirits of the heavens.***

> *Revelation 7:1 After these things I saw **four angels** standing on the four corners of the earth holding, **the four winds**.*

and his name that sat on him was Death, and Hell followed with him. Hell followed with him. And power was given unto them over the fourth part of the earth, to kill with sword, and with hunger, and with death, and with the beasts of the earth. You might notice, by the way, that under the fourth horse you have hunger, just like the black horse, and you have the sword just like the red horse. So, it seems like whenever the pale rider or the spirit of the pale horse is sent into all the earth some time in the first half of the tribulation period, it seems like it's going to be an increase in famine, an increase in bloodshed and then we have some things added here: We have this thing known as death, it's just labeled as death. And with death and with the beasts of the earth.

> *Ezekiel 14:8 Though Noah, Daniel, and Job, were in it, as I live, saith the Lord GOD, they shall deliver neither son nor daughter; they shall but deliver their own souls by their righteousness, For thus saith the Lord GOD; How much more when I send my four sore judgments upon Jerusalem, the* **sword, and the famine, and the noisome beast, and the pestilence,** *to cut off from it man and beast?*

You see four things discussed there, don't you? Hunger, death, beast, sword. Instead of "death" in Revelation, you have "pestilence." By the way, pestilence means plague and in some versions, in Revelation 6:8, it reads "plague." It looks like John is preaching old material. You have the same four things in both verses and look who it's against: Jerusalem. It seems like, then, the fourth horse is effective primarily in Jerusalem. If the Bible is going to teach us, then my best guess tells me that the fourth horse or the pale horse, takes a fourth of the population of the land of Jerusalem in Israel and he does it through four judgments of which it has happened before (in Ezekiel 14). So, it looks like the fourth horse is an increase in famine, an increase in bloodshed and plague and evil beasts. If that means it is a climax of the three plagues, it also means that those three probably only happen around Jerusalem. Of course, when everyone is starving that includes the animals so they're going to be a real problem and then when there's corpses everywhere from all the death, then of course beasts are going to be a problem. Again, my best guess says this happens in and around Jerusalem. Then, of course, there's Jeremiah 29:17 where Jews--the Jewish King in particular--is promised (essentially) seals 2-4.

6:9

And when they had opened the fifth seal, I saw under the alter This is just another example of temple talk in the book of Revelation. Towards the end of the book of Revelation we find that the new Jerusalem does not contain a temple, but we are told all through Revelation that Heaven itself does contain a temple, and that the new Jerusalem that does not contain a temple merely comes down from God out of Heaven. Revelation 2:17 speaks of hidden manna, and hidden manna as we know from the book of Hebrews chapter 9, in the book of exodus, the manna was placed in a jar in the Ark of the Covenant. The Ark of the Covenant was placed in the Holy of Holies, and the Holy of Holies was the innermost sanctum, if you will, of the temple in the Old Testament. So this is temple talk. God promises the hidden manna or that which is in the Ark of the Covenant or that which is in the Ark of the Covenant in the temple in Heaven is promised to the overcomer. The second of the mentioned so far temple talk comes in 3:12. So here again we have talk of temple in heaven, and then thirdly this passage discusses souls of them that were slain for the word of God being under the altar.

the souls of them that were slain for the word of God, and for the testimony which they held: Are we to assume this is a small piece of furniture wherein are crammed a numerable company of those who have been slain for the word of God? I think not. I think from the perspective of John, he is looking at an enormous altar and a gathering, a multitude if you will, of people waiting below an altar that is, perhaps, elevated and they are, from his perspective, below them-standing below them. Let me also point out to you that the end of verse 9 they were slain for the word of God and for the testimony they held. The word of God and the testimony they held. This is reminiscent of the opening of the book.

> *Revelation 1:9 I John, who also am your brother, and companion in tribu lation, and in the kingdom and patience of Jesus Christ, was in the isle of Patmos,* **for the word of God, and for the testimony of Jesus Christ.**

Before he comes back to the earth, he is showing us that there is a great company of predetermined number that should be killed. Why do I say predetermined?

6:10-11

11 And white robes where given unto every one of them; and it was

said unto them, that they should rest yet for a little season, until their fellowservants also and their brethren, that should be killed as they were, should be fulfilled. There's a number of martyrs that fits this episode and God knows that number. This, also, was forecasted by Jesus (Matthew 24:9).[7] We see it answered in 7:9. Two different groups.

When you see that this crowd of souls that were slain on earth are under the altar, does that mean they're all crammed underneath a mourner's bench somewhere in heaven? No, it's the idea of the perspective of John as he's looking into the temple in heaven, he sees an altar and then a mass of martyrs.

The 2nd time these prayers are mentioned are in chapter 8 and the reference to these prayers being incense before the Lord. These prayers of the saints are a sweet aroma to the Lord. They are to wait until the number is complete. What happens in chapter 7:12-17? The numbers are becoming complete. You have saints coming out of great tribulation.

It would fall into the contextual flow well if we saw that the seven trumpets are an answer to prayer (see chapters 8-11). The people in the fifth seal are clothed in white robes after a certain time and some people are joining them with white robes in answer to the promise that was given them in chapter 6:11, "Hey, you have more people joining you. Here are some white robes." All of a sudden in chapter 7, we see people with white robes joining them. And where are they joining them from?

*Revelation 7:14 I said unto him, Sir, thou knowest. And he said to me, These are they which come **out of Great tribulation.***

So they came out of here. This is well-reflected in the ESV and in the NASB as "they are coming out of great tribulation." It's a present continual tense. They are coming out great tribulation so this crowd is dying for their faith and they have white robes and they are currently

---

[7] One should be able to ascertain that Jesus names the first five seals of Revelation in the same succession in the Olivet Discourse. John is not using new material.

coming out of great tribulation by the time John sees the vision. So, it makes sense that the fifth seal is somewhere around the middle of the week and, therefore, pushes the trumpets into the Great Tribulation toward the last 3.5 years.

6:12

And I beheld when he had opened the sixth seal, and, lo, there was a great earthquake; Are we talking about the same great earthquake as discussed in Revelation 11:12-19? Because we have earthquakes on earth today. Are they "the great earthquake?" No, I believe there is definitely going to be a great earthquake some day. Just as 1 John speaks of "many antichrists" today, *the* antichrist has not come yet. It seems they are the same "great earthquake."

> *Revelation 16:17 And the seventh angel poured out his vial into the air; and there came a great voice out of the temple of heaven, from the throne, saying, It is done. 18 And there were voices, and thunders, and lightnings; and there was **a great earthquake** such as was not since men were upon the earth, so mighty an earthquake, and so great.*

It's one that's never happened before. It's not just a great earthquake that's never happened before but it's a mighty earthquake and so great, putting emphasis on this is the worst one ever.

> *Hebrews 12:26 Whose voice then shook the earth but now he hath promised, saying, Yet **once more I shake not the earth only, but also heaven.** 27 And this word, Yet once more, signifieth the removing of those things that are shaken, as of things that are made, that those things which cannot be shaken may remain.*

and the sun became black as sackcloth of hair, and the moon became as blood.

> *Matthew 24:29 Immediately after the tribulation of those days*

> *shall the sun be darkened and the moon shall not give her light and the stars shall fall from heaven and the powers of the heavens shall be shaken.*

What about Old Testament passages like Jeremiah 15:9? Does anybody really think the audience had any reason to believe this was a far-away time, 1000's of years into the future? Or, rather, that it was a poetic way of describing national judgment from God?

6:13

And the stars of heaven fell unto the earth, even as a fig tree casteth her untimely figs, when she is shaken of a mighty wind. Picturing a tree, it's autumn, the trees' untimely figs are shaken and fall. If there is a great shake on the earth so much that it shakes heavens, that things fall from heaven, that's going to have a relation to what we're talking about here.

6:14

And the heaven departed as a scroll when it is rolled together; and every mountain and island were moved out of their places. The great flood caused the mountains to be formed. Now, were there mountains back before then? Think about Japan and the plates. Japan is on a mountain of sorts, it's on an earthquake plate and when the plate goes under Japan, it lifts Japan up. We get mountains like Mount Fuji which is a huge mountain also caused by a volcano related to earthquakes and that earthquake that's been happening for a long time has caused the mountain to raise, or caused the land to rise and the land below it to go under and cause things like tsunamis that we've had before.

That's what's happening here: the heavens departed as a scroll and rolled together
as we read back in Isaiah. Just like it said, and the host of heaven shall be dissolved and they shall be rolled together as a scroll. That's the same exact language we're using here and "every mountain and island were

moved out of their places." This can be found elsewhere in Scripture (Isaiah 54:10; Jeremiah 4:23-24; Ezekiel 38:20; Nahum 1:5-7).

Chapter 7

7:1

after this is the same way that 4:1 begins. If you believe that this is written in chrono- logical order, then you have the sixth seal occurring after the great tribulation and the 144,000 being sealed after the sixth seal which happens after the great tribulation. I don't know of a person on the planet that believes that the 144,000 Jews are sealed in the millennium somewhere. There is no point in that. But look, it happens again in verse 9

7:5-8

And I heard the number of them which were sealed: and there were sealed an hundred and forty and four thousand of all the tribes of the children of Israel. Of the tribe of Juda were sealed twelve thousand. Of the tribe of Reuben were sealed twelve thousand. Of the tribe of Gad," and so forth, Aser, Nepthalim, Manasses, Simeon, Levi, Issachar, Zabulon, Joseph and Benjamin.

> *Genesis 49:1, "And Jacob called unto his sons, and said, Gather yourselves together, that I may tell you that which shall befall you in **the last days**."*

Did you notice what was of interest to Jacob there? He wanted you to know what was going to happen to his 12 sons, when? The last days. Now, please look at verse 16,

> *"Dan shall judge his people, as one of the tribes of Israel. Dan shall be a serpent by the way, an adder in the path, that biteth the horse heels, so that his rider shall fall backward."*

When is that supposed to happen according to verse 1? Last days. So, we have Dan being difficult in the last days. Many Old Testament scholars think that the antichrist will actually come from the tribe of

Dan; the beast of Revelation will actually come from the tribe of Dan. Dan in the last days is to rule his people and that is found in Genesis 49. Remember, the main function of prophesy is not to tell you what will happen but most of the time it's to tell you what's happening. Let me say that again: the function of prophesy is often not to tell you what will happen but to tell you what is happening.

> *Ezekiel 6:11, Thus saith the Lord GOD; Smite with thine hand, and stamp with thy foot, and say, Alas for all the evil abominations of **the house of Israel**! for they shall fall by the sword, by the famine, and by the pestilence. Alas for all the evil abominations of **the house of Israel** for they,*

Who is "they?" The House of Israel. Let's remind ourselves here: the white horse is antichrist; the black horse is famine. The red horse is death by sword & wars. Then you have the pale horse which is plague or death or pestilence, wild beasts. That's Revelation 6 and we'll get back to that. Isn't it interesting that you have seals 2, 3 and 4 mentioned here and who is the recipient of seals 2, 3, and 4? The House of Israel.

> *12 He that is far off shall die of the pestilence; and he that is near shall fall by the sword; and he that remaineth and is besieged shall die by the famine: thus will I accomplish my fury upon them. Then shall ye know that I am the LORD, when their slain men shall be among their idols round about their altars, upon every high hill, in all the tops of the mountains, and under every green tree, and under every thick oak, the place where they did offer sweet savour to all their idols.*

Who is he talking to again? The House of Israel. And where did they live? Israel.

> *14, "So will I stretch out my hand upon them, and make the land desolate," the land, the land of what? Israel. "More desolate than the wilderness toward Diblath in all their habitations: and they shall know that I am the LORD. Moreover, the word of the*

> LORD came unto me, saying, Also, thou son of man, thus saith the Lord GOD unto the land of Israel; An end, the end is come **upon the four corners of the land."**

In Ezekiel 6 we find that at least seals 2-4 occur in the land of Israel. See also Ezekiel 9:1-7, and see those marked in Jerusalem are spared and we see that from Ezekiel 9:1. They are marked for their righteousness. Where do you see that again? They are sickened by the abominations taking place in the city. Now look at chapter 47 of Ezekiel, verse 13.

> *Thus saith the Lord GOD; This shall be the border, whereby ye shall inherit the land according to the twelve tribes of Israel:* **Joseph shall have two portions.** *And ye shall inherit it, one as well as another: concerning the which I lifted up mine hand to give it unto your fathers: and this land shall fall unto you for inheritance.*

So we're looking forward to a day when the Israelites by tribe will have an inher- itance. Did that happen after Ezekiel 47 and up until this point yet? Has that hap- pened? Joseph will have two shares in the inheritance and that is inheritance in the land of Israel. You're going to see that all of this neat stuff makes studying Revelation just a little bit easier. Now, let's move to the New Testament.

> *Matthew 19:27, "Then answered Peter and said unto him, Behold, we have forsaken all, and followed thee; what shall we have therefore? And Jesus said unto them, Verily I say unto you, That ye which have followed me, in the regeneration when the Son of man shall sit in the throne of his glory, ye also shall sit upon twelve thrones, judging* **the twelve tribes of Israel."**

Do you see that? There's coming a day when the Apostles, at least, were promised that they would judge the twelve tribes of Israel. Now, read James 1:1 and see that it is addressed to the "twelve tribes." I'm trying to get you to see that it is not an accurate statement to say that the twelve tribes were extinguished in the first century. It's not accurate to say that ten of them were lost completely in the Assyria siege of 722 BC.

In Revelation 5-6 we've been discussing the seven sealed book. This is a deed to planet earth and the Lamb, the only one who is worthy to open the book because he died and purchased creation with his own blood, is willing to open the seals. The fourth seal was found probably in Jerusalem. So, notice, please, 2-4, I'm going to put a question mark here. It seems like seals 2-4 happen in the land of Israel.

Revelation 3:10 promises an hour of temptation that shall come upon the whole earth. So, there is a specific end time scenario where the whole planet will be rocked and I think Revelation speaks to that, but I also don't want to close the door on the fact that it might have some things that are localized to Israel. I think it's a safe thing for me to say that John goes back to Ezekiel and writes about it. He goes back to Ezekiel and writes about it.

So, the fourth seal we see takes place probably in Jerusalem. We saw the four horseman in Zechariah. Remember that? It's not a sin for you to write Zechariah 6 in your Bible next to Revelation. There is nothing sacrilegious about that. You might notice, please, that they're identified as four spirits or four winds that are sent into all the earth. Do you see that? Do you remember that? The four horseman are seen as four winds. Let me remind you what we see in chapter 7:1 in Revelation, "And after these things I saw four angels standing on the four corners." Four corners. Interest- ing. Everyone see that? "Standing on the four corners of the earth, holding the four," what's that? "Four winds," four spirits "of the earth."

You can look for a new interpretation but this guy is not doing that. I'm going to look at Zechariah and Ezekiel and I'm going to say, "Nope, probably John was already referring to an existing prophecy." And he's probably talking here that you have an angel, you have four angels holding the first four horses, the first spirits, the ones that are mentioned in Zechariah 6. Let me say that again: if the four horses are four spirits or four winds, contextually my best guess, my translucent guess is that you have four angels in chapter 7:1 holding the four winds that are already spoken of in the previous chapter which are the four horses.

My point was Zechariah does a good job of identifying what these four horses are. They are spirits. We shouldn't sensationalize them. They are spirits going out into all the earth. We're going to have a spirit of an antichrist. John told us it was already happening in his time. We have the spirit of famine, the spirit of sword, the spirit of pestilence and wild beasts.

You might notice the sixth seal. Well, look at Luke 23. "Jesus turning to them said, Daughters of Jerusalem," remember he's on his way to the cross, "weep not for me but weep for yourselves and for your children then shall they," who is "they?" The children of the daughters of Jerusalem. There we are localizing it again. I hope you're at least learning that, that the six seals are probably taking place in a localized area—or that they are at least focused there.

Twelve is a number frequently seen in the book of Revelation. Remember the 24 elders? It's two times twelve, right? So, 12 x 1,000 which is a way of completing a number often in Scripture. So, twelve is both squared and then multiplied by a thou- sand which is two ways of saying emphasis.

Please notice Judah is first instead of Reuben like in all the other genealogies mentioned in the Bible. Also notice that Joseph is given two shares. In Ezekiel 47 Joseph is mentioned in verse 8 and his son Manassah is mentioned in verse 6. Other than that, you have brothers of Joseph, right? So, Joseph gets two shares. Dan is not mentioned. The first time in a genealogy that Dan is not mentioned. Why is he not mentioned? Because he is playing another role, probably, in the book of Revelation. Interestingly enough though, he is mentioned as having a share in the life to come. So, Dan does get restored but he is not mentioned in this genealogy where 12,000 are seen as converted.

7:9

After these things I looked, We need to first of all point out that this is not necessarily the order in which these things occur, but rather that these things are seen by John in particular order. **and behold, a great multitude which no one could number, of all nations, tribes, peoples, and tongues,** I am really surprised, honestly, that these distinctive groups are preserved in Heaven. I guess I had never considered, until a point in my life, that God is going to actually have people of different colors in Heaven. Believe it or not, I was told in my earlier years of studying the Bible that we would all look like Jesus in Heaven: you know "33 year-old, Jewish males".

standing before the throne[8] and before the Lamb, clothed with white robes, with palm branches in their hands, This appears to be the

---

[8] It sounds so nice to say "you can worship God anywhere." It's true. The only issue is that it is usually said by somebody who is excusing their conscience for rarely being with other believers on the Lord's Day. Here you'll find saints...together (in the same location)...around God and Christ. Two thoughts follow:

1. There is no question where worship was happening. Most will agree that "where two or three are gathered, Christ is in the midst." Did you know that is found in Matthew 18? Did you also know that it is on the heels of a passage about church discipline? Now, before you say "well, wherever there's believers, there's the church." Again, very cute cliche, but not at all what this passage is talking about. What sense would there be in "sending people away" from the church if we were not talking about a real, local, established, organized group of believers known as the church? So....since this passage is talking about a real, local church, then the real, local church experiences Christ "in their midst"..........when they assemble. **The earthly reality of the heavenly throne scene is when the church assembles.**

2. The scene recorded in Revelation 7 is a scene that is heavenly reality. It pleases God. We don't find anybody upset that they have to be with the church around the throne. Nobody is saying "can we cancel the meeting?" Nobody is "praying about attending." Nobody is saying "Again? We have to worship around the One on the Throne again?!" In other words, nobody is looking for a reason not to meet.

Today, in our churches, we are not seeking to meet less if we seek for "His kingdom to come and His will to be done on earth as it is in Heaven." **Heavenly reality is when the church can be described as "always together worshiping."** Read the passage for yourself. How can you get anything different? Is worship expressed in singing? Yes. Is worship expressed in prayers? Yes. But the chief way we worship is by exalting God's written Word to a place of prominence in our meeting times. It crowd represented by 24 elders of Revelation 5:9-10. In other words, those 24 elders said "you did redeem us to God by thy blood out of "every kindred, tribe, people, and nation" and we know that elders represent those whom they oversee. For example, if you are an elder of the city and perform the elder of the city in the gates of the city, you speak for the city. These, then, are the people for whom those 24 elders speak. I think I can back this up when we consider verse 11. The "elders" are, in fact, present.

Furthermore, if the halls of heaven are populated with people of all colors, we find out that we will probably not all have the same skin color in Heaven. This has been God's plan for a long time. Do you remember God's Word in Genesis 12: "In thee shall all the nations of the earth be blessed?" Galatians 3:8 calls this the "Gospel to Abraham."

After this I beheld, and, lo, a great multitude, which no man could number, of all nations, and kindreds, and people, and tongues, stood before the throne, and before the Lamb, It's not talking about having palms of hands in their hands. This speaks of "palm branches." He describes a multi-ethnic multitude. He says he sees a multitude, a multi-ethnic multitude. We have a different group the 144,000. We have every tribe here, every nation. No one could number them. You have these 144,000 Jews which are set aside and protected from the judgment of God and now we're getting on to another group of people that is multi-ethnic.

You can find the gospel all the way from Genesis 3:15 to really Revelation 5:9, 7:9. Remember what God told Abraham, "In thee shall all the nations of the earth be blessed." Do you remember that? All the nations of the earth being blessed. Jesus is born of the tribe of Judah, one

---

was/is good enough for God (Psalm 138:2), and it should be more than sufficient for us.
    Heavenly reality, then, is seeking to worship more, centered around Bible preaching with your fellow church members. "...even more so...as the last day approaches." (Hebrews 10:25) If believers are doing anything as to the frequency of their worship and worship-centered fellowship, it is....increasing it.

of the tribes of Jacob, one of the sons of Isaac, one of the sons of Abraham.

clothed with white robes, and palms in their hands. Looking back, you should see this crowd described in 6:11 as those who have been martyred. Look under those notes for more.

Matthew 24:9 says "You'll be killed and hated of all nations and then you shall see the abomination of desolation spoken of by Daniel the prophet." We find out that happens half way through the tribulation period so we know the five seals at least begin in the first part of the tribulation period. We also know from Matthew 24:16 and 29 that the last half of the tribulation is known as the "Great Tribulation."

Revelation 7:14 And I said unto him, Sir, thou knowest. And he said to me, These are they which **came out of great tribulation**, *and have washed their robes, and made them white in the blood of the Lamb.*

So this crowd came out of that second half of the tribulation period so that they are the fulfillment to what the folks under the fifth seal were expecting. They begin to be killed under the fifth seal and they are seen *en mass*.

7:10

and crying out with a loud voice, saying, Please take note that as it describes these men and women, boys and girls of all ethnicities, they cry out that all **"Salvation *belongs* to our God who sits on the throne, and to the Lamb!"** They are doing so to the point where it is called **crying** and to where we are told they are waving **branches.** Perhaps it is at this point where we should consider why it is we raise our hands when we worship? Perhaps it is because we are signifying what it will be like when we do so around the throne.

to our God who sits on the throne, and to the Lamb!" This is the reality of chapters 4 and 5 and Daniel 7. There are two in the scene.[9] Furthermore, we find them both promised in Revelation chapters 21 and 22.

Lamb!" Here again we find a reference to Genesis: Genesis 22:8, that is where God promised Abraham that He would provide a Lamb. So, the 2nd time in Genesis, and the 2nd time a promise to Abraham.

And they cried with a loud voice, saying, Salvation to our God which sitteth upon the throne, and unto the Lamb. They cried with a loud voice and you might notice that the folks under the altar also cried with a loud voice. Both groups are martyred; both groups are wearing white robes. One is crying out for judgment, one is praising for salvation. One is under the altar, one is before the throne. One is waiting, the other is serving.

> *Revelation 7:15 Therefore are they before the throne of God, and **serve him** day and night in his temple.*

These are the gradual fulfillment of what the people under the altar in the fifth seal were being told.

> *Revelation 4:2 And immediately I was in the spirit: and, behold, a throne was set in heaven, and one sat on the throne.*
>
> *Revelation 5:1 I saw on the right hand of him **that sat on the throne a book**…6 I beheld and lo in the midst of the throne and of the four beasts and in the midst of the elders **stood a lamb** as it had been slain…7 And he came and took the book out of the right hand of him that sat upon the throne.*

7:11-12

---

[9]This will keep us from modalism: believing there is only one person in the "trinity" manifesting himself in three different ways at different times.

These saints in white and angels and elders are not looking around for something to do. Rather, instead of somehow dreading they have nothing else to do but worship the One on the Throne, they fall to their faces—demonstrating to us that there is need for both joyful praise, and for somber adoration.

And all the angels stood round about the throne, and about the elders and the four beasts, and <u>fell</u> before the throne on their faces. Now we have the angels falling down.

Saying, Amen: Blessing, The word behind "blessing" is the word *eulogia*. What does that sound like? Eulogy: a statement of grace upon somebody.

and glory, *doxa* What does that sound like? Doxology, right? We all love that song.

and wisdom, Behind "wisdom" is the word *sophia*. That is how we get "philosophy" or "love of wisdom."

and thanksgiving, and honour, and power, and might, be unto our God forever and ever. Amen. How many things do you hear ascribed by the angels concerning the Lamb? Seven. Look back at 5:12 and you will find they are saying seven things but they're not saying this to the person on the throne, they're saying it to the lamb. Seven blessings to the lamb in chapter 5:12 and seven blessings to the one who is sitting on the throne in chapter 7:12. Remember, we have the one on the throne and then we have the lamb who is in the midst of the throne.

7:13-14

Then one of the elders answered, Is this the same "elder" that offered clarity to John's consternation in 5:5? And what is he "answering?" Who asked anything? Is he answering the inquisitive thoughts of John?[10] It

---

[10]Robert Jamieson, A. R. Fausset, and David Brown, *Commentary Critical*

must be that He is answering the loud worship of the angels, elders, and four living creatures. Versions that ignore this terminology of "answer" (or exchange it for "ask" as the HCSB does) do so without manuscript support.[11]

14 And I said to him, "Sir, you know." So he said to me, "These are the ones who come present tense…translated so by the NKJV. As they die, they show up in Heaven. **out of the great tribulation, and washed their robes and made them white in the blood of the Lamb.** The read must at least admit that there are, in fact, saints…who are "coming out of great tribulation." They are talking about "salvation" (7:10) and that this "salvation" is through **the blood of the Lamb.** Are you having a hard time with this? Do you think God is any less worthy of Worship than He will be on this future day? Do you think that those in Heaven today are there because of some action other than God's salvation through the blood of Jesus? Do you think that we should do less today in His presence than we will do that day when we stand before the throne? If your response is "No," then you will have no problem with what we're about to read.

These are they which came out of great tribulation, It should be "and they are coming out of great tribulation." This is the continual collection of those who are dying for Christ assembling before the throne. These are they which are coming out of great tribulation. As they're dying, they're appearing before the throne of God with white robes and palm branches in their hands. As they're dying, the chapter 6:11 promise is being fulfilled to those who were in the fifth seal and heaven is being populated. As they're dying, they are appearing before the throne.

> *2 Corinthians 5:8 To be absent from the body is to be present with the Lord.*

---

and Explanatory on the Whole Bible, vol. 2 (Oak Harbor, WA: Logos Research Systems, Inc., 1997), 570.
[11] https://www.blueletterbible.org/lang/lexicon/lexicon.cfm?Strongs=G611&t=KJV [accessed June 14, 2016]

Philippians 1:22 I have to choose between dying and being with Christ or staying with you in the flesh.

*Revelation 2:22 I will cast her into a bed, and them that commit adultery with her **into great tribulation**, except they repent of their deeds.*

Here we spoke that not all believers are guaranteed deliverance from the great tribulation. We've been dogmatic about that so far. We have church members here who are seen as servants of God, who are promised great tribulation and here we see a snapshot of people who are brought out of great tribulation as they die. Incidentally, the English translation you are using may not utilize the article found in the Greek. This is "the Great Tribulation"[2] probably referenced in Revelation 2:22 as a pronounced punishment against the fornicators of that local church, and in Matthew 24:21 as a pronouncement against the land of Israel.

7:15

Therefore they are before the throne of God, and serve Him day and night in His temple. As John relays the elder's explanation of the condition of those multitudes, he starts off by giving their location. Then, he completes the description by giving their function. And he starts off this three verse function with an immediate description: **they serve Him.** Isn't this wonderful? Actually, some folks think that "work is a curse," but then we see that it is the relative fruitlessness of man's work, not work itself, that is the result of the curse in Genesis 2 and Genesis 3. It is not the will of God for you to hate your work. Now, I am not interested in confusing this place **around the throne** with our forever home in the New Jerusalem found at the end of the book, in which we're told "there is no temple there" (Revelation 21:22). Consider, though, that Heaven is the beginning of our eternal state and people are…what?…they're working!

Furthermore, Revelation 22:3 says that those in the New Jerusalem are doing the very same thing. "And there shall be no curse: but the throne of God and of the Lamb shall be in it; and His servants shall serve Him. This is exceptionally good news for those among us who thought Heaven would be boring with nothing but choir practice and harp recitals. Imagine being "useful" forever.

And He who sits on the throne will dwell among them. This translation is a little weak. For while the English here can put someone in mind of John 1:14 and the "tabernacling" of Christ "among us",[12] The Greek in this same John's writing here is more "on us."[13] Therefore, while we are there, there is no sun crushing our souls with its relentless heat (referenced in the next verse). So in this passage we have reference to both the tabernacle and the temple. At any rate, the Lexham English Bible references this as "the one seated on the throne will shelter them." This, as one might expect, reminds the reader of another Old Testament Scripture: Psalm 91:1 and the sheltering of children of God under the Almighty.

Therefore are they before the throne of God, and serve him day and night in his temple. This is how we know they are not yet in the New Jerusalem. They are in heaven and the New Jerusalem comes down from God out of heaven. Revelation 21:22 says there is no temple in the New Jerusalem, but there is one in heaven.

> *Revelation 3:12 Him that overcometh will I make a pillar in **the temple of my God** and he shall go no more out and I'll write upon him the name of my God and the name of the city of my God which is New Jerusalem.*

> *Revelation 4:5 Out of the throne proceeds lightnings and*

---

[12] https://www.blueletterbible.org/kjv/jhn/1/14/t_conc_998014 [accessed June 14, 2016]

[13] https://www.blueletterbible.org/lang/lexicon/lexicon.cfm?Strongs=G1909&t=KJV [accessed June 14, 2016]

> *thunderings and voices and there were **seven lamps of fire** burning before the throne.*

A menorah, right? Where do we find the menorah? In the temple. Right, so this is more temple talk. We have the Ark of the Covenant being spoken of when we see the hidden manna.

> *Revelation 2:17 He that hath an ear let him heart what the spirit says to the churches, to him that overcometh will I give to eat of the **hidden manna**.*

Where is the manna stored in Hebrews 9 and in the Old Testament where was the jar of manna? In the Ark of the Covenant.

serve him day and night These are people that are no longer subject to the curse. Work continues after death. In heaven we are working for God in his temple. Let's back up to before the curse. What was Adam doing before the fall? He was working and he found joy in it. It is not the perfect will of God that you hate your job. You need to find a line of work that you enjoy or consciously take joy in your labor. It is not a curse. It is a curse to be inefficient, says Genesis 3. Part of being cursed was that we work hard and receive less fruit, but work itself is not part of the curse.

7:16-17

17 For the Lamb which is in the midst of the throne shall feed them, and shall lead them unto living fountains of waters: and God shall wipe away all tears from their eyes. This most certainly refers to Isaiah 40:10 and 49:8-11.

Since when does a lamb feed anyone? A lamb is going **to feed them**? And then a lamb is going to **lead** them? Anyone ever seen a lamb lead anything? It's usually a goat, right? Or a sheep dog or a shepherd. But we have a lamb leading and feeding. What do those two things go with? Who does the leading and the feeding of a flock? A shepherd! However, in

Isaiah 53 we have the shepherd becoming a sheep and now in Revelation 7 we have the lamb becoming a shepherd. It's a complete switch-around. The suffering lamb is a shepherd.

In Isaiah 53:7, The shepherd of verse 6 becomes a sheep. There is the Incarnation right there in Isaiah 53. Now, who are these sheep that went astray? It's us, right? So we're the sheep that have gone astray and the shepherd of Isaiah 40 becomes a sheep and suffers as a sheep for sheep who have gone astray.

Everything that's been spoken of has been spoken of before in the Scripture. In Isaiah the shepherd becomes a sheep and in Revelation the lamb, or the sheep, becomes a shepherd.

> *Revelation 6:11 White robes were given unto every one of them and it was said unto them that they should rest yet for a little season until their fellowservants also and their brethren should be killed as they were and that it should be fulfilled.*

There are a fixed number of people who are going to die for Christ for this period and the crowd that we see in chapter 7:12-17 is the fulfillment of the promise given to the martyrs in the fifth seal in chapter 6:11.

You might notice in chapter 6:12 and here in 7:12, both crowds are wearing white robes. One is already in heaven assembled and the other is joining them.

Jesus calls the last 3.5 years of the 7 years "great tribulation." Seals 1-5 begin somewhere around the beginning part of the tribulation period and continue, it seems like, most of the way through the tribulation period. The sixth seal, according to Matthew 24, happens after the "Great Tribulation." This is how the great multitude that no man can number arrives in heaven, through great tribulation.

17 for the Lamb who is in the midst of the throne will shepherd them and lead them Not only do we find that this **Lamb** is a lion (5:5), but we also see that this **Lamb** is a **Shepherd**. This is the opposite of Isaiah 40:10 & 53:6-7 where the shepherd becomes a lamb. At any rate, nobody is expecting a "lamb" to do anything mighty. This is captured in songs like

> *Wonderful, merciful Savior, precious Redeemer and Friend;*
> *Who would have thought that a Lamb could rescue the souls of men?*
> *Oh, You rescue the souls of men.*[14]

More could be said about the shepherding character of Jesus? Is this not what He does? Does He not minister to your hearts that He is both guiding you from behind and leading from before? Does He not whisper to your soul that while the shadows lengthen, they do not even faintly touch the extents of His piercing watch? Consider the contemplations of John Newton, author of *Amazing Grace*.

> *"...the wise and good providence of God watches over his people from the earliest moment of their life, overrules and guards them through all their wanderings in a state of ignorance, leads them in a way that they know not, till at length his providence and grace concur in those events and impressions which bring them to the knowledge of him and themselves."*[15]

to living fountains of waters. And God will wipe away every tear from their eyes."

To the believer: May I share with you a verse from Charles Wesley

> *Come, Almighty to deliver, Let us all Thy grace receive;*
> *Suddenly return, and never, Nevermore thy temples leave.*
> *Thee we would be always blessing, Serve Thee as Thy hosts above,*
> *Pray, and praise Thee without ceasing, Glory in Thy perfect love.*

---

[14] Philip Webb, ed. *Hymns of Grace* (Los Angeles: Master's Seminary Press, 2015), 162.

[15] John Newton *The Works of John Newton, vol 1* (Carlisle PA: Banner of Truth Trust, 2015), 7.

To the lost: As a final warning, I am compelled to say that those who are, in this passage, "day and night serving in the temple" are placed in juxtaposition to those who suffer "day and night forever and ever" (14:11).

Chapter 8

8:1

And when he had opened the seventh seal, so we have the seven sealed scroll, the deed to earth. Revelation chapters 4-19 is a study of Christ retaking the earth.

And when he had opened the seventh seal, there was silence in heaven about the space of half an hour, but the question is: what is silent in heaven according to that verse? What has been going on? We found out in chapters 4 & 5 that there is much praise and worship taking place. Imagine how long that's been going on. Isaiah 6 it was happening. Job 38:7 says that it was happening when God laid the foundations to the globe. So, it has been happening for at least 6,000 years, possibly more. Here in chapter 8:1, there is nothing going on.

So, somewhere between the number being fulfilled in chapter 7 in answer to their cry for justice in chapter 6 we have prayers being brought up before the trumpets are blown. Chapter 6, they are told justice will come after your brothers join you. Chapter 7, brothers and sisters are joining them. Chapter 8, we have prayers mentioned and before we have the prayers mentioned, what do we have happening in heaven? Silence. Apparently, what was about to happen was so grievous that it made heaven shut up and apparently, it was in answer to the prayers of the martyrs in the fifth seal.

space of half an hour That's interesting in itself because I don't know, did he have a wristwatch? How did he know that it was a half hour? We do know that in that time there were 12 hour increments, there were 12 one hour increments in daylight and so for him to say, "Well, probably half an hour," means that it wasn't exactly an hour, it was less than an hour, **about** the space of half an hour. Now, what I want to know is: what is causing this silence? What silences the worship?

8:2

And I saw the seven angels which stood before God; and to them were given seven trumpets. They were given seven trumpets. This word "trumpet" is the same Greek word that could be equated with the Hebrew *shofar*. So, this is a ram's horn probably.

We have seven angels in heaven, each of them is assigned a *shofar*, a trumpet. We have already identified in the book of Revelation some people who are a part of the crowd around the throne since chapter 4: 24 elders; 4 beasts; The Lamb in the midst of the throne; souls under the altar in the 5th seal; the multitude which no man could number in Revelation 7; the seven-fold Holy Spirit of God is there. So the Trinity is there; John is there; 100 million angels finish up the group according to Revelation 5:11. I think that might be everyone and now we have an additional group: seven angels with seven trumpets that are before the throne of God.

And another angel came and stood at the altar. How many altars were in the Old Testament temple? Two. one inside and one outside. Here outside the temple we have this brazen altar, then you have this thing known as a laver. There are six pieces of furniture. We have the altar where the sacrifices were offered, the laver where the priests would wash their hands. Inside we have the menorah, we have the table of showbread, we have the altar of incense and inside the Holiest of Holies we have The Ark of the Covenant.

It says there in Exodus 25:40 and in Hebrews 9 that Moses made the taberna- cle based on the pattern that he saw when he looked into heaven. Isaiah looked into heaven and saw a temple. John is now in heaven, sees a temple.

Another angel came and stood at the altar, having a golden censer. This is a fire box or some sort of holy way to transport coals from the altar to the altar of incense. Aaron had four sons: Ithamar, Eleazar, Nadab and Abihu and two of them were killed in the book of Leviticus for offering strange fire. We don't know where they got the fire, we don't know if they brought it from a different altar, but apparently they did not do what they were supposed to do and God killed them right in the holy place. This is the eighth angel and it says that he's offering incense which are the prayers of the saints.

8:3

Having a golden censer; and there was given unto him much incense, that he should offer it with the prayers of all saints upon the golden altar which was before the throne. I'm guessing that the throne is probably in the Holiest of Holies in heaven and that God himself is sitting on this mercy seat. Instead of the glory abiding on a mercy seat in heaven, it's God himself abiding on the mercy seat. I don't know. See more in my notes on 6:9-11 regarding the **prayers of the saints.**

8:7

The first angel sounded, and there followed hail and fire mingled with blood, and they were cast upon the earth: and the third part of trees was burnt up, and all green grass was burnt up. The first angel sounded, and there followed hail and fire mingled with blood, and they were cast upon the earth: and the third part of trees was burnt up, and all green grass was burnt up. And the second angel sounded, and as it were a great mountain burning with fire was cast into the sea: and the third part of the sea became blood. Remember we're told in chapter 7 that the earth, the sea and the trees cannot be hurt until the 144,000 of the first half of chapter seven were sealed. Then we see in the first two trumpets that the sea, the earth and the trees are hurt. So, it seems like the trumpets have to happen after the 144,000 are sealed. That we can find in chronology. The angels who bring the trumpets are not allowed to hurt the trees or the earth or the sea until after the 144,000 are sealed.

Why do I believe this occurs in the great tribulation period?

We have these souls that were killed for their testimony in Jesus Christ, we have them being killed and we have them all now given these white robes and they're told this, "You guys just be patient with these white robes until your fellowservants are killed" (6:9-11) So, when does this happen? Revelation 7:9. See notes in 6:9-11.

8:12

And the fourth angel sounded, and the third part of the sun was smitten, and the third part of the moon, and the third part of the stars; so as the third part of them was darkened, and the day shone not for a third part of it, and the night likewise. It's possible, based on the last phrase, that either a third of the magnitude of the light that shines in the day or a third in the night, one of the possibilities here is that it's less visible at night, less visible at day. That's one of the possibilities but based on the last phrase of the verse, it seems like it throws the world into such chaos that they're not even sure how long a day is anymore. So, that is how it's possible for us to have a determined time of seven years and for Jesus to still be correct when he says you won't know the day of my coming because the days are almost where you can't tell when one starts and the other ends because of the calamity that happens here with the sun, the moon and the stars. The fact that there are still stars and a moon and a sun to shine, it seems like we can place trumpets 1-4 between seals five and six.

8:13

And I beheld, and heard an angel flying through the midst of heaven, saying with a loud voice, Woe, woe, woe. "Anguish, anguish, anguish to the inhabiters of the earth." He's giving a forecast here of the fifth, sixth and seventh trumpet which are to be hideous for those who dwell either on the earth or in the land.

There are some variant readings between the translations on whether it should read "angel" or "eagle." We don't find an eagle speaking from the heavens before this or after this in the book of Revelation but we do have one more case of an angel speaking from the heavens in chapter 14 where he preaches what's called the Everlasting Gospel. So, based on that evidence alone, I am going to go with the reading of "angel."

Chapter 9

9:1

I saw a star fall from heaven unto the earth: and to him was given the key of the bottomless pit. We're going to find it in Luke 8, is where we get our word "abyss" from. What does "abyss" mean? It means "a place of deepness"; it refers in the Old Testament almost exclusively to the floor of the ocean and sometimes it is used interchangeably with the ocean itself.

See Luke 8:26-28. Now, please notice the demon is asking for what in verse 28? He's asking for the Son of God not to torture him. Do you get that? That's a strange thing for a demon to ask.

Noticing verses 29-31 of Luke 8 see two things: they did not want to be tormented and they did not want to be sent into the deep. The word behind "deep" there is that word "abyss." It is translated differently in the book of Revelation; it is translated "bottomless pit." So, if you want to you can use the same language all through the five usages to follow; you could say that the demons asked not to be tormented in the bottomless pit. It's the same word, that word "abyss" is used here.

8:32-33, "And there was there an herd of many swine feeding on the mountain," so right away you know they're probably not in Israel, right? They're actually on the eastern side of the Sea of Galilee. "There were swine feeding on the mountain and they besought him that he would suffer them," or allow them, "to enter into them. Then went the devils [demons] out of the man, and entered into the swine: and the herd ran violently down a steep place into the lake, and were choked."

So, as you're coming to this passage, you would probably say, "Well, you already said that the abyss was indicative of the deepest part of the ocean or of the ocean itself at times in the Old Testament," and that's true. So, if you had just that, you could say that the demons were asking not to be dumped into the lake. But the fact that they asked not to be tormented tells me that's not what they were getting at. There was a particular place that they were afraid of going to be tormented and they called it the "abyss." So, I don't believe they were talking about the lake (contextually).

That's the first time we see it is that the demons were afraid to go there. Now, I would like to just suggest that the reason they were afraid to be tormented in the abyss is because they knew some beings that had gone there. 2 Peter 2:4 uses the word "*tar- tarus*" behind that word "hell" and it's the only place it's used and it's used to describe a particular class of angels that sinned prior to the flood of Noah.

Look at Romans 10 next and let's confirm this. Remember the Bible doesn't tell us everything, but I'm going to suggest first of all that abyss = *tartarus*. In other words, they are at the same location or at least there is some overlap—maybe part of the abyss is *tartarus* or part of *tartarus* is the abyss. But, in any case, we've spent an entire lesson teaching that a particular class of demons were put in Tartarus [See commentary on Genesis (6:1-4) one for more information], and yet these demons are asking not to be tormented in the deep. So, I would suggest that the abyss of Luke 8 and the Tartarus of 2 Peter 2 are probably the same.

Paul actually says that Christ went where when he was dead? The deep, the abyss (Romans 10:5-8). That's what Paul says. Now, a lot of people say, "Why doesn't Paul talk about *hades* too much?" Well, he just uses a different word, a different word in the language and I don't know how to explain it.

But what we have described here is that the abyss of Romans 10:7 appears to be equal with the Hades of Acts 2. Now, remember we already talked about how Christ definitely went to Hades (Psalm 16; Acts 2). So, the rich man and Lazarus is an occur- rence that took place and we have a man who is simply known as Lazarus, not the one who is raised from the dead in John 11, but a different one, who was seen in or near Abraham in Hades. So, the issue is: did Abraham go to a place of torment? No. He was a saint; Hebrews 11 says he was a saint; Romans 4 says he was a saint; James 2 says he was a saint; Genesis 15 says he was a saint. There is no need to think that any person who's ever been saved in any age went to a place of torment. But if Hades means, and it does, "the place of departed dead," well, then, it's okay for us to say that Christ went to the place of departed dead but was not tormented in the flames.

So, when I say that **the abyss** of Romans 10, where Jesus went when he was dead according to Paul, and the Hades of Acts 2, which is where Jesus went when he was dead according to Peter and David, there is no need to say that Christ was tormented there simply because a portion of abyss/*tartarus* or the portion of *hades* of the portion of *sheol* is torment. We will grant you that a portion of it is but apparently not all of it.

Ephesians 4 says that Christ went to the lower parts of the earth when he was dead to lead the captivity captive, the lead the captive ones away, to take something out of the center of the earth, the lower parts of the earth, to rescue them. They were captive, they were imprisoned and he led them out. So, the major function, it seems, of him going to h*ades* was to let the righteous ones out. And Revelation 1:18 says that Jesus said, "I am he that liveth, and was dead; and, behold, I…have the keys of Hades and death." So, he has keys and then Colossians 2 says that when he was there he spoiled the demons, he whipped them, "made a show of them openly." There is a lot of understanding, a lot of activity, a lot of information in the Bible about what happened when Jesus was dead. Rest assured, though, it is a fallacy to say that Jesus had to go to hell and burn for our sins. That's ridiculous. When he said, "It is paid for. It is finished," it's a banking term meaning the accounts are settled. And then he died, that's what it says in John 19.

> *Revelation 9:1-11 And the fifth angel sounded, and I saw a star fall from heaven," remember a star is otherwise identified as an angel in the book of Revelation, "I saw an angel fall from heaven unto the earth:* ***and to him was given the key of the bottomless pit.*** *And he opened the bottomless pit; and there arose a smoke out of*

> *the pit, as the smoke of a great furnace; and the sun and the air were darkened by reason of the smoke of the pit. And there came out of the smoke locusts upon the earth,*

We discussed in that these appear to be demonic locusts coming out of the bottomless pit. Now, if that is the case and if we're dealing with the same group of demons here that we have coming out of the pit in Revelation 9, they are going to be anxious to inflict problem. They are going to be anxious to inflict catastrophe and chaos. If they have been chained since Genesis 6, they are not happy and they are being let loose, it says, "to torment for five months," in verse 10. Verse 11, "And they had a king over them, which is the angel of the bottomless pit, whose name in the Hebrew tongue is Abaddon, but in the Greek tongue hath his name Apollyon," or destroyer.

So, it might look bottomless, but that's not the point of the translation. So, you could say, "I saw a star fall from heaven," verse 1, "and to him was given the key of the abyss." Or, "the key to *tartarus*." And, again, the only demons I know that are in a place of confinement right now are the ones of 2 Peter 2:4, the ones that sinned with human beings in Genesis 6. So, I don't know why these wouldn't be them coming out of that place. You see them going in, in Genesis 6, and coming out in Revelation 9.

> *Revelation 11. And I will give power unto my two witnesses. 7 And when they shall have finished their testimony, the beast that ascendeth out of **the bottomless pit** shall make war against them, and shall overcome them, and kill them."*

Right away, this antichrist figure, this beast, we're told where he comes from. That's not said about anyone else in Scripture as far as I know. There is something particular about this antichrist figure known as "the beast." He is known as the one who came from the bottomless pit. That means he was put there at one time. I don't know of anyone that started out there.

Revelation 17:8, The beast that thou sawest was, and is not; and shall ascend out of **the bottomless pit**, and go into perdition: and they that dwell on the earth shall wonder, whose names were not written in the book of life from the foundation of the world.

Again, we see that this beast, this antichrist figure in the book of Revelation. Why do I keep saying it like that? Because the word "antichrist" is not in the book of Revelation. He's not called "the antichrist" in the book of Revelation, he's called "the beast." And, apparently, it says twice, he comes out of the bottomless pit.

Let's review: we have demons who have been chained there, we have demons that are coming out of there in the future; we have a particular figure of some kind coming out of there and he is going to deceive the whole world, generally speaking, and then he's going to go back into destruction.

*Revelation 20:1, "And I saw an angel come down from heaven having the key of **the bottomless pit** and a great chain in his hand."*

Remember, 9:1 that angel that fell from heaven was given the key, so apparently it was repoed because now we have an angel coming down from heaven after the seven year tribulation period and he has the key to the bottomless pit and a great chain in his hand (Revelation 20:1-9).

Notice the devil will be in the bottomless pit or the abyss or the great deep or the place Jesus was when he was dead, or the place the demons were chained before the flood, Satan will be bound there for a thousand years—the thousand year reign of Christ on the earth that will take place upon his return and he will return after the tribulation period.

9:13

And the sixth angel sounded, and I heard a voice from the four horns of the golden altar which is before God. I want to remind us that John is sharing his vision of things that have already been exposed or revealed to us in the Old Testament. When we go back to Exodus 30 and Exodus 27, we see that in the law, when Moses was given the law and the preparation for the worship and for the various events of the tabernacle, there were two altars described that should be created. One altar is the brazen altar, and that altar was to be for the blood sacrifices. The size of that altar is not significant for what we're talking about but it was was approximately 7 ½ feet square and about 4 ½ feet tall. It was made of acacia wood and covered with bronze. This was where they made the blood sacrifices, burnt offerings for the atoning of the sins of the people in the tabernacle.

The second altar was about 1 ½ feet square (18 inches square) and 3 feet tall. It also was made of acacia wood, but covered with gold. This one was for the burning of incense prior to going into the Holy of Holies, before the Mercy Seat.

Part of the blood from some of the sacrifices was then used to mark the golden altar on the horns. The golden altar was just outside of the Holy of Holies where the Ark of the Covenant and the Mercy Seat were, which represented God's presence in the temple. And so we see that this altar, the golden altar, was before the Lord as its placement in the tabernacle. Now, the golden was symbolic of Christ. As the incense being the sweet-smelling savor that goes up before the Lord after the sacrifices, the incense had to be a particular type (there were those incenses that were forbidden) and the savor going up before the Lord or before God's presence. It also could be spoke of as a symbol of the worship of the saints in the New Testament. After those of us that have trusted Christ as personal Savior and are worshiping our God, worshiping our Savior, this altar before God could be representative our future worship. (future to the Tabernacle time)

and I heard a voice from the four horns of the golden altar which is before God. Is the altar that we're looking at in this passage in Revelation 9:13 the same as in the fifth seal which is back in Revelation 6:9.

Notice that in chapter 9, when it talks about the altar, it talks about the golden altar. And when we look at the passage in Revelation 6, there is no adjective; it just says the altar that is before the Lord. I may be taking a little bit of liberty here, but if you look at the passage in chapter 6, it says that there were those that were slain for the word of God that were under the altar and they cried with a loud voice saying, how long O Lord, holy and true. What I'm drawing your attention to here at this point is that they cried with a loud voice. In chapter 9 it says **I heard a voice from the horns of the golden altar which is before the Lord crying out saying to the sixth angel.** So, could it be that those who were crying out in the sixth chapter and asking for God to avenge their death, the martyred saints, are the voices that are coming out from the horns. Now the angel is being told to go release the angels which are bound. We see continuing on in chapter 9, that there is going to be massive death. Maybe this is the vengeance and so it could be the same altar. I'm not going to specifically say. When you look at some of the cross references in various Scriptures, the word "altar" used with the golden altar and the term "altar" used without the adjective golden is the same word. But when the chain references reference back, they don't always reference the same group of passages that have the word "altar." So, we really can't find a direct connection between the altar in chapter 6 and the altar in chapter 9 other than the voices.

9:14

Saying to the sixth angel which had the trumpet, Loose the four angels which are bound, and in the King James it says **bound in the great Euphrates.** That word "bound in" or "at"; in some translations it's expressed as "bound at the river Euphrates." First consider the angels that were bound. Obviously these are demonic angels because angels that are godly angels or of God's army are never referenced anywhere to have been bound. But we do know that God did bind a part of the angels that fell with Satan. And so this definitely, in my mind, is referring to angels that were bound which would be demonic angels and they are now going to be loose from being restrained at the river Euphrates. The Euphrates River is going to show up again in the book of Revelation

16:12.

> *And the sixth angel poured out his bowl upon the great **river Euphrates** and its water was dried up that the way may be prepared for the kings from the east.*

The sixth trumpet, then, seems related in some way with the sixth vial.

9:15

were loosed which were prepared for an hour and a day and a month and a year for to slay the third part of men. And, again, the word "men" comes from a Greek word which means "mankind" or "all mankind." Not just particularly a male person but all of humanity. And so, a third of the humanity is going to be slain by the events that happen as these angels are loosed.

9:16

And the number of the army of the horsemen were two hundred thousand thou- sand and I heard the number of them. Well, two hundred thousand thousand is 200 million and when you think about that, that's a pretty sizable army. There were 70 million people involved in WWII and there is going to be 200 million people involved with this movement of whatever troops, armies, horsemen, John was seeing. Just remember that what John was writing, based on what he was seeing, would have no words to describe in that timeframe things that were of modern warfare that we know of today. So, it's possible that he was seeing some of the things use in warfare today. But, there is no way to definatively claim such.

There is some good evidence that considering how much we depend upon the computerized world, with our power system controlled by computers, our grocery distributions controlled by computers, our banking system controlled by computers; all it would take is some massive magnetic or nuclear disturbance, that we end up with is the inability of any of this equipment to work. Then it's back to horses again. So, I'm not saying it couldn't be literal horses, but whatever it is, it's pretty massive and this force is moving in such a way that a third of mankind is slain or murdered.

It's very possible that we have demonic forces possessing the armies. Take a look at the North Korean leader right now. How many of us would call him level-headed or logical? I think some of the world's insanity is spawned by demonic or Satanic influence, but the Scripture is pretty clear: "the heart of man is deceitful above all things and desperately wicked. Who can know it?" Mankind left to his own devices can be quite evil.

You notice that it says that they are **bound at the river Euphrates.** The Euphrates was the eastern boundary of the Roman Empire. It's also symbolic of the separation of the east from the west and so it is very possible that the armies from the east, which has been the focus of a lot of speculation over the years that it is the Chinese army marching against Israel or against the forces of God at this point. Or, in this case, it appears that it's against anybody. We don't know who might be in the way? There are over 2 billion Chinese right now so a tenth of the Chinese population wouldn't be far-fetched to be the size their army. I don't have any specific tie-in Scriptures that are specifically saying this is one or the other, but I'm just throwing this out here. We must be careful about putting into the Scripture something that's not there.

9:21

Neither repented they of their murders, nor of their sorceries, nor of their fornication, nor of their thefts. The term "sorceries" comes from a word which is *pharmakeia* in the Greek which is drugs or the use of drugs and the term "fornication" of course from the word *porneia* which is elicit sex. Coming from a Christian perspective I have a predisposed, and I believe a properly predisposed view of the world and the events of the world. I'm glad I have it, but it's easy to forget that the Scriptures didn't affect everybody from the beginning of time as I have been affected. We know that God already destroyed the world once by a flood because of probably sexual immo- rality, things that were just blatantly pungent in the nose of God and putrid. And then it was several hundred years later that Moses presented the law. Prior to the time of Abraham, sex seemed to be just something that you did with anybody that you could do it with or anything you could do it with. That was just the culture of many people and it was Judaism and God's command to have one man and one woman that took away the pagan worship that so involved promiscuity. I realize it was Moses that wrote Genesis 1 and said God created male and female, but the cultures of the world up to the flood and then after the flood, deviated to the point that God established a unique people to demonstrate his unique practice amongst humans, where marriage became sanctified and a particular place in God's mind to represent the relationship that would later come between God, Christ and the church.

Chapter 10

10:2

And he had in his hand a little book open: and he set his right foot upon the sea, and his left foot on the earth, And cried with a loud voice, as when a lion roareth: and when he had cried, seven thunders uttered their voices. Do you see Psalm 29 there? Go count the "voice of the Lord" references. Notice here, there are a partic- ular set of seven thunders that John knew. John knew his reader would think about the seven thunders. Well, that's not mentioned anywhere in the book of Revelation before this place.

10:4

And when the seven thunders had uttered their voices, I was about to write: and I heard a voice from heaven saying unto me, Seal up those things which the seven thunders uttered, and write them not. Almost like Daniel 12:3-6.

10:5

And the angel which I saw stand upon the sea and upon the earth lifted up his hand to heaven, And sware by him that liveth for ever and ever, who created heaven, and the things that therein are, and the earth, and the things that therein are, and the sea, and the things which are therein, that there should be time no longer. Now, what that means is time remaining no longer or "there should be no more delay." This takes us back to the middle part of Daniel 12.

10:7

But in the days of the voice of the seventh angel, when he shall begin to sound, the mystery of God should be finished. As good Bible students, the first question we should ask if we're wondering what John means by "the mystery of God" is "Where else does he use that in the book of Revelation?" He doesn't use it elsewhere in this book. So, then I would be thinking, "Well John, did you write any other books?" No, he didn't use "the mystery of God" in those. We look in the immediate context to find out, "Is there anything mysterious that God did or said that leads me to believe that we're dealing with something in particular." Yes, seven thunders uttered and John had his little book. What is he writing in his little book? Revelation.

We, then, have two books in the context here: the one that the angel is holding and the one that John is writing. He hears seven thunders and he's told not to record it. Now, whatever those seven thunders are, they are the mystery of God. They are God's mystery. He's not telling you but there is not much time left until they're ful- filled. Remember, we have seven seals, seven trumpets, seven thunders and seven vials which apparently are judgments but we're not told what the thunders are. God tells us what we need to know in his word.

He's declared this to **the servants, the prophets**. Well, we know of one prophet in particular that he declared this mystery to. We read it in Psalm 29: David. David told us about these seven voices. Whatever these thunders are, they have at least been mentioned to a prophet. Well, the only place that I've found it so far is Psalm 29.

10:8

And the voice which I heard from heaven spake unto me again, and said, Go and take the little book which is open in the hand of the angel which standeth upon the sea and upon the earth. So what distinguishes this from the seven-sealed book in chapter 5 and the Lamb's book of life in chapter 3 and the book that he's writing (Revelation) from this "little book?" This is a book that hasn't showed up yet in the book of Revelation.

10:9-10

And I went unto the angel, and said unto him, Give me the little book. And he said unto me, Take it, and eat it up; and it shall make thy belly bitter, but it shall be in thy mouth sweet as honey. 10 And I took the little book out of the angel's hand, and ate it up; and it was in my mouth sweet as honey: and as soon as I had eaten it, my belly was bitter. If you would like some backdrop on this you may consider Ezekiel 2:3-3:3.

10:11

And he said unto me, Thou must prophesy again before many peoples, and nations, and tongues, and kings. Probably, this harkens back to a promise of the same type to Daniel (Daniel 10:5-12).

What did the Son of man say to the trembling John in Revelation 1? "Fear not." We're seeing that John is using old material in Revelation 1 when he shows us Jesus for the first time. When you see that he's identified as Jesus in Revelation, who should you assume that he is in Daniel? Jesus. Yeah, the one in linen, the one whose eyes are a flame of fire, the one who has this ability to put his hand on a trembling prophet. You should assume that it's Jesus before He was "Jesus."

> *Daniel 12:1 And at that time shall Michael stand up, the great prince which standeth for the children of thy people: and there shall be **a time of trouble, such as never was since there was a nation even to that same time.***

We're talking about a time of Jacob's trouble "such as never was since there was a nation even to that same time: and at that time thy people shall be delivered, every one that shall be found written in the book." That sounds familiar, doesn't it? Except we're reading the prequel, not the sequel.

> *Daniel 12:13 But go thou thy way till the end be: for thou shalt rest, and stand **in thy lot** at the end of the days.*

What was Daniel's lot? He was a prophet. So at the end of days Daniel will reappear. You know, in Daniel 12 we see a mighty angel present with a book, a prophet for- bidden to reveal truth, something to be finished, the end is discussed, hands raised, swearing by an eternal one, a period before the end is 3 ½ years and a promise of another time of ministry to that prophet. Interestingly enough, **every one of those** is found in Revelation 10. We have a perfect match and so if I'm a simple student of the word, which I think I am, then I'm probably going to believe that what was being taught in Daniel 12 is being re-taught in Revelation 10 and that we're near to the end.

What do Daniel and John have in common? They are both promised—last verse of Revelation 10, last verse of Daniel 12—another time of prophecy at the time of the end.[3] Who are the two witnesses in Revelation 11? Are they Moses and Enoch? Are they Elijah and Enoch? Are they Daniel and John? Well, I'm just saying: you have a clear cut promise to both of these men that they will appear to prophesy again at the time of the end and the time of the end is identified in both passages as 3 ½ years.

> *Revelation 11:2 The court which is without the temple leave out, and measure it not; for it is given unto the Gentiles: and the holy city shall they tread under foot **forty and two months**. And I will give power unto my two witnesses, and they shall prophesy a **thousand two hundred and threescore days**.*

These witnesses have a ministry of 3 ½ years. Both Daniel and John are promised that they will appear at the time of this 3 ½ years to prophesy. While I'm at it, what was the rumor about the apostle in John 21 but that he would be around at the time of his Christ's coming?

Chapter 11

11:1

And there was given me a reed like unto a rod: and the angel stood, saying, Rise, and measure the temple of God, and the altar, and them that worship therein. Because they didn't have inches and feet and yards and centimeters and all the things we use today, they used rods that were passed around and measured from an original rod. One person would have a rod in a marketplace that was measured from some other person that had a rod in a marketplace that was measured from some other person that had a rod somewhere else and they tried to keep them all the same.

11:2

But the court which is without the temple leave out, and measure it not; for it is given unto the Gentiles: and the holy city shall they tread under foot forty and two months. Find the backdrop for this in Zechariah 2.

This is Zechariah talking about the rebuilding of Jerusalem and I think it parallels a lot of what's going to happen in Jerusalem. Hebrew and Greek are not the same words but I think they're kind of similar here: measuring line/measuring rod. I don't know if I can take it as far as to say "multitude of men" would be Gentiles but we do know Jerusalem is packed full of people, a multitude of men.

	Daniel	Revel
A Mighty Angel is present with a	12:1	10:1
Prophet Forbidden to reveal certain	12:4; 9	10:4
Something is to be finished.	12:7	10:7
The end is discussed	12:4, 6	10:6
Hands raised	12:7	10:5

Swearing by Eternal One	12:7	10:6
Period before "end" is 3.5 years	12:7, 11	11:3
Promise of another time of ministry	12:13	10:11

11:4

These are the two olive trees and the two candlesticks standing before the God of the earth. And if any man will hurt them, fire proceedeth out of their mouth, and devoureth their enemies: and if any man will hurt them, he must in this manner be killed. Well, in trying to figure out who these two witnesses are, we're not given a description of them, we're given a description of what they can do. In the backdrop of this you will find Zechariah 4.

There are only two people that God would set apart to speak or to be for the whole earth, but we know if it's happening to Jerusalem, a lot of it's happening to the entire earth. One of the things that we know is happening to the entire earth, is the two witnesses are preaching to the entire earth. I was listening to an old commentator about this passage and he said, "Obviously there will be some way that these two wit- nesses will be on television and everybody will be able to see it or maybe there will be a new way that we haven't even thought of yet that will we'll all be able to see it right away." That commentator didn't know what a cellphone was but I guarantee you that in that day, there would be a very easy way for us all in the entire world to just look down at our hand-held you name whatever it is.

So who are the two? Who in the past has had the power to "devour their enemies with fire?"

> *2 Kings 1:9 And they answered [Elijah], He was an hairy man, and girt with a girdle of leather about his loins. And he said, It is Elijah the Tishbite. Then the king sent unto him a captain of fifty with his fifty. And he went up to him: and, behold, he sat on the top of an hill. And he spake unto him, Thou man of God, the*

> *king hath said, Come down. And Elijah answered and said to the captain of fifty,* **If I be a man of God, then let fire come down from heaven, and consume thee** *and thy fifty. And there came down fire from heaven, and consumed him and his fifty. Again also he sent unto him another captain of fifty with his fifty. And he answered and said unto him, O man of God, thus hath the king said, Come down quickly. And Elijah answered and said unto them, If I be a man of God, let* **fire come down from heaven, and consume thee** *and thy fifty. And the fire of God came down from heaven, and consumed him and his fifty.*

Then another person that may have possibly had ability to control fire: John proposes, possibly, that two have this power. Let me talk about Moses here for a second.

> *Numbers 16:29 These men die the common death of all men, or if they be visited after the visitation of all men; then the LORD hath not sent me. But if the LORD make a new thing, and the earth open her mouth, and swallow them up, with all that appertain unto them, and they go down quick into the pit; then ye shall understand that these men have provoked the LORD.*

If you remember the story of Korah, he was the one that was going against Moses. He was trying to take over and he said, "I'm just as good as Moses so I'm not sure why he's in charge." Well, he's in charge because God put him in charge.

> *And it came to pass, as he had made an end of speaking all these words, that the ground clave asunder that was under them: And the earth opened her mouth, and swallowed them up, and their houses, and all the men that appertained unto Korah, and all their goods. They, and all that appertained to them, went down alive into the pit, and the earth closed upon them: and they perished from among the congregation. And all Israel that were round about them fled at the cry of them: for they said, Lest the earth swallow us up also. And* **there came out a fire from the**

> **LORD**, *and consumed the two hundred and fifty men that offered incense.*

We're talking about people that were with Korah but they weren't Korah's family. They saw what happened to Korah and they said, "At least I'm not with Korah." And as they ran away, God sent fire down from heaven and consumed them.

11:6

These have power to shut heaven, that it rain not in the days of their prophecy so they're going to say that it's not going to rain at all, during their 42 months of prophecy the rain will stop, **and have power over waters to turn them to blood, and to smite the earth with all plagues, as often as they will.** The next power that they are supposed to have is they're supposed to be able to have the power over rain, power over weather, and we need to look back in the Bible and see if that's ever happened before. And particularly they'll have the power of plagues, particularly a power of water to blood.

> *1 Kings 17:1 And Elijah the Tishbite, who was of the inhabitants of Gilead, said unto Ahab, As the LORD God of Israel liveth, before whom I stand,* **there shall not be dew nor rain these years,** *but according to my word.*

> *James 5:17 Elias was a man subject to like passions as we are, and he prayed earnestly that it might not rain: and* **it rained not on the earth by the space of three years and six months.**

Of course, Exodus 7-10 shows Moses as the ultimate agent of controlling waters— making them blood. This appears to make Moses and Elijah some real, possible fulfillments to this Scripture.

11:7-9

And when they shall have finished their testimony, the beast that

ascendeth out of the bottomless pit shall make war against them, and shall overcome them, and kill them. And their dead bodies shall lie in the street of the great city, which spiritually is called Sodom and Egypt, and killed them where also our Lord was crucified. The Lord wasn't crucified in Egypt, he was crucified in Jerusalem so not only are the inhabitants of Jerusalem identified with Sodom and Gomorrah with all their fornications, they're Egypt with all their idolatry. All three in one spiritually, it says.

11:14

The second woe is past; and, behold, the third woe cometh quickly.

> *Revelation 8:13 And I beheld, and heard an angel flying through the midst of heaven, saying with a loud voice,* **Woe, woe, woe,** *to the inhabiters of the earth by reason of the other voices of the trumpet of the three angels, which are yet to sound!*

So the fifth, sixth and seventh trumpts are known as the Woes. It is from this verse, dear friends, that I would probably have to say that the two witnesses' ministry was in the last half of the tribulation period, not the first half. The word "quickly" occurs six times in the book of Revelation. Five of the six times that word "quickly" is used in the book of Revelation it deals with Jesus coming. If five of the six times we see this word being used by John he is trying to make something make sense to us. If he uses a word six times and five of the times it is an overt reference to the coming of Jesus, what do you think the sixth time is? Probably a reference to the coming of Jesus. So, I want you to know that regarding the timing of the rapture which is a big interest because it keeps coming up every week in here, this is the first time I've seen any kind of time sensitive reference towards when the rapture occurs.

11:15

And the seventh angel sounded;

*Revelation 10:7 But in the days of the **voice of the seventh angel, when he shall begin to sound**, the mystery of God should be finished, as he hath declared to his servants the prophets.*

Now we're going to see the evidence that the seven thunders that we heard about in chapter 10 are completed during the days of the sounding of the seventh trumpet. Remember we have four little sets of judgments: first of all beginning in chapter 6, we have the seven seals. In chapter 8 we have another set of seven judgments known as the seven trumpets. Then in chapter 10 we have another set of seven judgments known as the seven thunders. Remember that's the set of judgments we're not told anything about. They're a mystery; it's a mystery of God, apparently, from Revelation 10:7, that will be completed during the seven trumpets. And, of course, the fourth set of seven judgments comes later on in chapter 15 and 16 known as the seven bowls or vials.

and there were great voices in heaven, saying, The kingdoms of this world are become the kingdoms of our Lord, and of his Christ; and he shall reign for ever and ever. This is not the first time where we see Christ and the kingdoms of this world. You might remember the temptation of Jesus in the wilderness. You have the devil tempting Jesus. You might remember the first temptation was to "turn these stones into bread." He'd been fasting for 40 days, it seems like he'd be hungry. Then, Satan takes him to the pinnacle of the temple and he says "throw yourself off and let the angels catch you." The pinnacle of the temple, that's the southeast corner of the temple complex of Herod's Temple. There is this third temptation. Again, the devil takes him up into an exceedingly high mountain and shows him all the kingdoms of the world and the glory of them and he says to Jesus, "All these things I will give you if you'll bow down and worship me." Satan offers Jesus the kingdoms of this world and probably the kingdoms of this world he would have if he would just bow down to Satan. You don't see Jesus arguing with Satan, "No, you don't have the authority to give me the kingdoms of this world. You don't have the right to give me that." But Jesus did not bow before Satan. Here's what Jesus would have had had he bowed down to Satan in my opinion: he would have had the kingdoms of this world and no cross and no honoring of the Father and no salvation for you and I.

> *Revelation 5:9 And [the four beasts and twenty four elders] sung a new song, saying, Thou art worthy to take the book, and to open the seals thereof: for thou wast slain, and hast redeemed us to God by thy blood out of every kindred, and tongue, and people, and nation; And hast made us unto our God kings and priests: and we shall reign on the earth.*

What did we say that this book with seven seals was? A deed to the earth. So this is looking forward. "You are worthy to take control of the earth, you have the deed and we're going to reign with you on the earth because of your bl ood."

> *Revelation 5:11 And I beheld, and I heard the voice of many angels round about the throne and the beasts and the elders: and the number of them was ten thousand times ten thousand, and thousands of thousands; Saying with a loud voice, Worthy is the Lamb that was slain to receive power, and riches, and wisdom, and strength, and honour, and glory, and blessing.*

That's looking ahead to chapter 11, it's the very next time we see the 24 elders assembled.

11:16

And the four and twenty elders, which sat before God on their seats, fell upon their faces, and worshipped God, Saying, We give thee thanks, O Lord God Almighty, which art, and wast, and art to come; because thou hast taken to thee thy great power, and hast reigned. Remember what they said in chapter 5? "You are worthy to take power and we will reign." Here they said, "We thank you because you did take your power and are now reigning." So, you have looking forward in chapter 5, and you have looking back in chapter 11. Again, some are going to choke on this a little bit because, "Wait a minute, if we're already at the end of the seven years of tribulation, how in the world do we still have 8 chapters until He comes?"

11:18

And the nations were angry, and thy wrath is come, You have loud voices coming out from before the throne, 24 elders bowing. In chapter 4, they are saying "you're worthy to take power." Here, they are saying "we thank you because you did take power." Chapter 5 says "We are going to reign on the earth." Chapter 11 says "The kingdoms of this world are the kingdoms of our Lord and of his Christ."

> *Revelation 6:12 And I beheld when he had opened the sixth seal, and, lo, there was a great earthquake...17 For the great day of **his wrath** is come; and who shall be able to stand?*

So you should see from this Scripture that the sixth seal happens around the same time as the seventh trumpet because the wrath of God does not show up in the book of Revelation until the sixth seal.

Matthew 24, Mark 13, Jesus said, "There will come a time of great tribulation and immediately after this tribulation, the sun shall be darkened, the moon shall be turned into blood, the stars shall fall from heaven." He uses the same language and tells us it comes "after" the great tribulation. And yet, this is the first mention of the wrath of God in the book of Revelation, it's the sixth seal that comes after the great tribulation. And we're told that this seventh trumpet takes place somewhere after the sixth trumpet.

and the time of the dead, that they should be judged, and that thou shouldest give reward unto thy servants the prophets, and to the saints, and them that fear thy name, small and great; and shouldest destroy them which destroy the earth. I want to show you three things about this verse:

1. It is the first time where we see mention of the resurrection of anybody other than the two witnesses. The

Seventh trumpet comes sometime near the end, if not after the end of the great tribulation and it is the first time there is any mention of a resurrection other than the two witnesses. If we had something as profound and worldwide as a resurrection of believers, why isn't it mentioned before this?

2. This is the first time we see any mention of judging of anybody other than those who dwell on the earth in the book of Revelation and yet we see that it takes place here under the seventh trumpet. The first time judgment of anybody is indicated other than unsaved earth dwellers who are alive. But these are the dead being judged. That's the first time that's mentioned in this book of Revelation. Now, if we have a worldwide snatching away of hundreds of millions of believers and the tearing open of graves of hundreds of thousands of dead saints of generations past, why isn't it mentioned yet in this book? Let's just say there are 100 million believers. You say, "That's just too many." I don't think so. They're being saved by the thousands in the East every day. I don't think it's less than 100 million but we're not even talking about the snatching away of them that live, how about the generations of 2,000 years of church history of graves being ripped open and a resurrection and it not being mentioned yet before chapter 11 of Revelation! That is profound!

3. This is the first time we see anything about rewarding anybody in the book of Revelation. Now, some would say, "Well, we see the rewarding of the 24 elders." Yeah, that's true. We do. In chapter 5 it says, "Unto them was given crowns," but we're not told when they're given the crowns and we're not told how long the elders have sat there but I ask you: if multitudes of millions of believers are getting rewarded, somehow both living and dead, in this book, before chapter 11, why isn't it mentioned yet?

So this is the first time we see these three things in the book and yet we have an entire segment of Christianity that is emotionally involved in having a pet doctrine that's nowhere to be found in the book of Revelation: The Pretribulation Rapture.

The elements of that event do not happen until chapter 11 and the seventh trumpet. So I'm asking you: if you're going to disagree with this, at least, at least do yourself the service of finding some Bible before you say it belongs in the book of Revelation.

> *2 Timothy 4:1 He's going to **judge** the living and the **dead at his appearing and his kingdom**."*

So, when he appears he's bringing his kingdom and he's judging the living and the dead, right? So I need to assume that somewhere around the seventh trumpet which happens somewhere after the sixth seal, he's coming and we find out that he is, from 2 Timothy 4, bringing his "kingdom" and "judging the quick and the dead."

> *Matthew 24:15 When ye therefore shall see the abomination of desolation, spoken of by Daniel the prophet...21 For then shall be great tribulation, such as was not since the beginning of the world to this time, no, nor ever shall be...29 Immediately after the tribulation of those days shall the sun be darkened, and the moon shall not give her light, and the stars shall fall from heaven, and the powers of the heavens shall be shaken.*

Which seal does that sound like? Sixth seal. It happens after the great tribulation, yes? Is everyone with me?

> *Matthew 24:30 And then shall appear the sign of the Son of man in heaven: and then shall all the tribes of the earth mourn, and they shall see the Son of man coming in the clouds of heaven with power and great glory.*

So, Christ comes and he comes after the sixth seal. Revelation 11 has the seventh trumpet happening after the sixth seal. We have 2 Timothy 4:1 saying that when he appears, like Matthew 24:30, he'll bring his kingdom and he'll judge the dead. Matthew 25 follows with more "kingdom parables." Why is Jesus talking about the Kingdom on the heels of talk about His coming? Because that is when He sets up His Kingdom.

> *Isaiah 40:5 And the glory of the LORD shall be revealed, and all flesh shall see it together: for the mouth of the LORD hath spoken it....9 O Zion, that bringest good tidings, get thee up into the high mountain; O Jerusalem, that bringest good tidings, lift up thy voice with strength; lift it up, be not afraid; say unto the cities of Judah, Behold your God! Behold, the Lord GOD will **come** with strong hand, and his arm shall rule for him. Behold, his **reward** is with him, and his work before him.*

11:19

And the temple of God was opened in heaven, and the ark of the covenant was opened. There is a temple in heaven. Look, we have this hidden manna in chapter 3. Where was the manna held? In the ark of the covenant. We have a temple of God, altar with souls under it (6:9-11). We have an altar with a golden censer (8:1-4), a golden altar. All of this is found in the Old Testament temple.

Chapter 12

12:1-5

And there appeared a great wonder in heaven; a woman clothed with the sun, and the moon under her feet, and upon her head a crown of twelve stars: 2. And she being with child cried, travailing in birth, and pained to be delivered. Rick Larsen, in his documentary *The Bethlehem Star*,[16] identifies 9 clues about the "star" of Matthew 2 while pointing out shooting stars (which, among other things, doesn't stop) and comets (which would have been an omen of doom) are ruled out.

He then uses "starry night" software to talk about Jupiter ("the King planet") "Planets" use to be called "wandering stars" to distinguish them from "fixed star."[17] He sets the viewer's perspective for Babylon until the point of the narrative where the wisemen arrive in Jerusalem and then changes the viewer's perspective to what the wise men would have seen on the approach from Jerusalem to Bethlehem. He charts the "king planet" (Jupiter) and the "king star" (*regulus*) in the night sky and found a "triple conjunction"—or Jupiter making three passes to "king star." Genesis 49:9, of course, draws conversation of a scepter and the "Lion of the Tribe of Judah" (Revelation 5:5).

These "three passes" have been happening in the constellation of *leo* (Lion) (Here in this Scripture we have a continuation of the "scepter"). Now, at this point *virgo* (Virgin) follows the Jupiter ("king star") into the sky and in the midst of this constellation is the son **(woman clothed with the sun),** and at her feet was a small crescent moon **(and the moon was at her feet).** He sees this in his software in September of 3B.C.

---

[16] http://www.bethlehemstar.com/ [accessed 12/21/17].
[17] "planet" actually comes from a Greek word that means "wanderer", **https://tinyurl.com/yad3nyc9** [accessed 12/21/17].

Larsen further states, with the aid of his software that Venus ("mother star") and Jupiter stacked atop each other (not blocking each other) some 9 months later (in June of 2B.C.) thus becoming the brightest "star" to the naked eye in the east.

Then, astoundingly, he shows that the star stopped ("stood" is the language in Matthew 2) above Bethlehem (now from Jerusalem's perspective) on December 25th of 2B.C.—6 months after the brightest star anybody had ever seen. In other words, December 25th of 2B.C. is the first time anybody had celebrated the young boy's coming.

3. And there appeared another wonder in heaven; and behold a great red dragon, There have been those who think this makes good reference to constellations and stellar activity. It seems that since we have much in common here with Genesis [identifying this as Israel (Genesis 37:9-11)] that we should seek meaning primarily in the stars. It is tempting, but since I cannot ascertain a "dragon with 7 heads" in any constellation, it seems like that would not be my first choice.[18]

12:14 says "And to the woman were given two wings of a great eagle, that she might fly into the wilderness," so if I'm talking about a literal human being, then she should probably have literal wings. She's going to go and hide in the wilderness in verse 14 and we're going to find out that she is there for 3 ½ years? Now, I've got to find a place somewhere in the life of Mary where after she had Jesus, went and hid in the desert somewhere for 3 ½ years. I don't think that's a good guess. Rather it seems that there are times in Scripture where "eagles' wings" and "flood" are quite figurative (Exodus 19:2-4; Jeremiah 46:7), and that this trip to the wilderness is rather end-times in its reference to Israeli believers fleeing to nearby desert (Hosea 1:10-11; 2:12; Matthew 24:15)—specifically, half way through Daniel's "70th week" (Daniel 9:24-27). I have no reason to believe that John is giving us brand new material. So, number one about the woman: she is identified with Jacob, Rachel and their sons and not just their sons but all of the sons of Jacob.

---

[18]https://www.space.com/16755-draco-constellation.html [accessed 12/20/17].

And there appeared another wonder in heaven; and behold a great red dragon, Meanwhile, this dragon and its demise are old material (Psalm 74:14; Isaiah 26:19-27:1), and found in concert with the wrath of God at His coming and the resurrection of the saints.

having seven heads and ten horns. More old material (Daniel 7:7-8), and we later see n decrease from 10 kingdoms to seven at some point from Daniel's (and it seems John's) future, and that they will have solidarity for 3.5 years (Daniel 7:23-25).

And his tail drew the third part of the stars of heaven, and did cast them to the earth: and the dragon stood before the woman which was ready to be delivered, for to devour her child as soon as it was born. Who is the dragon? Satan (12:9). So, Satan pursues Israel into the wilderness and it happens for 3 ½ years she's finding refuge in the wilderness. Maybe he kills 1/3 of them while they're yet in Jerusalem (Daniel 8:9-10), I don't know. Remember, prophecy is translucent not transparent until it's fulfilled.[19]

---

[19] If the stars are literally in heaven are they bodies of gas that this human being by the name of Antiochus Epiphanes (seemingly the Greek general referenced in Daniel 8), one of the "four winds," lassoed somehow? Okay, that can't be. Everything else that we see in this prophecy is symbolic, we should not be surprised that the stars of heaven are symbolic as well. If they are then, symbolic in Daniel, why not in Revelation? I have heard that this is a proof text for his taking 1/3 of the angels of God with him when he fell as Lucifer (Isaiah 14:12–14), but it seems improbable that this is what the passage is saying in light of Daniel's usage (If you take that verse out, we don't really know how many angels Satan took with him in the fall). It is possible that these are the angels: 1/3 of the angels are cast out of heaven with him, but I don't think so because in Daniel 8, the stars could not possibly be angels. Why? Who is pulling the stars out of the heavens then? A man by the name of Antiochus Epiphanes is doing this. A man is yanking angels out of heaven?

I am fully aware that in the book of Revelation so far, stars have pictured angels, but I think Genesis provides some of the material for Revelation (Genesis 15). So, the first time we see stars in the heavens other than creation week. Is God comparing the offspring of Abraham, otherwise known as the children of Israel, the Jews, as stars of the heaven? So I have to believe this is a reference to him killing 1/3 of the Jews. Antiochus Epiphanes hated Jews. He threw a pig on their altar in an act of

How is it possible that the dragon was waiting on the Jews to bring forth a Messiah? Herod. He was Satanic. I speak more about this regarding the application of this passage behind Matthew's birth narrative in my commentary on Matthew (chapter 2), but as it applies to Luke, consider all the application if one only had the narrative of Luke to go with the book of Revelation. What do we see in Luke that shows this reality? By the way, even though Herod is the most obvious personification of Satan, biblical scholars are so busy speaking of the wise men's arrival as perhaps two years after Christ's birth. This provides a problem to then see Herod as **the dragon before the woman for to devour her child as soon as it was born.**

As a matter of fact, it seems quite a bit more probable that **a dragon** ready **to devour [Jesus] as soon as [He] was born** reaches back to nine months before His birth more than it reaches beyond the birth two years! What if this is true, then? What dangers would the reader of Luke be aware of if we were to consider the potentially Satanic attacks on Jesus if we were to reach back nine months—to Jesus' conception?

1. How about a culture that would stone a young woman who was pregnant before marriage? [We discuss this more in Matthew's commentary, but since the dilemma is at least suggested in Luke (1:34) it seems at least conceivable (pardon the pun) here as well.] This would be a hazard on the unborn Jesus.

2. How much should her prenatal travels both to the hill country of Judea and that of hers and Joseph's back to these same areas some eight months later be considered (1:36-39; 2:4)? How many marauders or hazards or weather patterns were

---

desecration. He stomped down Jerusalem. If anyone could say, "Hey, give me an historic figure after the Babylonian captivity that just decimated Jerusalem. What would you say?" Most everyone who studies this says Antiochus Epiphanes. So it's not far fetched here that since the dragon is pursuing Israel into the wilderness, that he flung 1/3 of them to the earth picturing that he killed them.

potential wrecks—with protection from Satan keeping them shrouded?

3. How much should normal birthing hazards and the ensuing risk of infection after birthing in a stable-like environment be considered as potentially Satanic attacks—if we knew the whole of it (2:7)?

4. Having considered the war that takes place in Revelation 12:7, shouldn't we at least consider what type of onslaught was taking place—necessitating the "host of angels" (2:13) to be this close anyways?[20] Shouldn't we consider that Luke 2:14 is Luke's version of Revelation 12:10? In other words, what demonic warfare was taking place in and around those Bethlehem fields?

And she brought forth a man child, who was to rule all nations with a rod of iron: This is Jesus (Revelation 2:26-27).

12:6

And the woman fled into the wilderness, where she hath a place prepared of God, that they should feed her, that they should feed her there a thousand two hundred and threescore days. There is going to be somebody, a third party, who is going to feed this nation of Israel when she flees into the wilderness and she'll be there a thousand two hundred and threescore days or 3 ½ years. Look how easy this synchronizes, folks. Matthew 24, middle of the tribulation period, middle of the week, those who are in Judea flee to the mountains. Hosea 2, towards the coming of Christ when Judah and Israel have one king, Israel will be drawn into the wilderness.

If you look at verse 14, "And to the woman were given two wings of a great eagle."

---

[20] It seems strange that a "host" from "Heaven" is usually identified as a "heavenly army" (Joshua 5:14; Revelation 19:11-16).

We should assume that it has something to do with the first time it's found when she fled into the wilderness. Remember the two witnesses (Revelation 11)? What city did they die in? Jerusalem, yes, but look at verse 8, "And their dead bodies shall lie in the street of the great city, which spiritually is called Sodom **and Egypt**, where also our Lord was crucified." So Israel half the way through the tribulation period is going to flee Jerusalem which is known as Egypt. So at the end of time, Israel is going to <u>leave</u> <u>Egypt again for the wilderness</u>.

Contextually, it seems like but you'd have to get them from Jerusalem to the wilderness somehow. The "they" could be the two witnesses that are feeding them. It could also be the 144,000 that could be feeding the nation of Israel in the wilderness. Certainly, if they are alive in Jerusalem, spiritual Egypt and they're preaching truth and if they're doing Mosaic things like turning water into blood, then they could also do Mosaic things like drop manna on them in the wilderness.

She flies into the wilderness, probably eastward, and probably into an area known for little settlements etched in the cliffs.

12:10-11

I heard a loud voice saying in heaven, Now is come salvation, and strength, and the kingdom of our God, and the power of his Christ: for the accuser of our breth- ren is cast down, which accused them before our God day and night. And they, overcame him by the blood of the Lamb, and by the word of their testimony; and they loved not their lives unto the death.

> *Revelation 12:7 And there was war in heaven: Michael and his angels fought against the dragon; and the dragon fought and his angels, And prevailed not; neither was their place found any more in heaven. And the great dragon was cast out, that old serpent, called the Devil, and Satan, which deceiveth the whole world: he was cast out into the earth, and his angels were cast out with him.*

About the time that the woman flees into the wilderness, the devil is cast out of heaven and so he's free to do something…

Satan's thrown out of heaven. What's he doing in heaven? He has some level of access to God. It looks like it because up until that point he's doing something; he's accusing the brethren. He's accusing them and so what interest would he have in accusing the brethren? The devil is known in Ephesians 2 as the "Prince of the Power of the Air." Somehow he has some access in some way to some part of heaven until this point right here.

Jesus never told Satan he didn't have the authority to give him the kingdoms of the world in Matthew 4 or Luke 4. He sees that he has a short time and right now as we speak, he has some level of access to the throne. Now when I say that, I'm not saying he has the same access he once did; I'm not saying he has the same access you do; I'm saying he has some level of access of right now.

*Zechariah 3:1 And he shewed me Joshua the high priest standing before the angel of the LORD, and Satan standing at his right hand **to accuse** him.*

At any rate, He's overcome by the brethren (10-11). In Matthew 12, Jesus said "Whoever does the will of my Father, they are my brothers." So, we're talking about followers of Christ here who have overcome Satan "by the blood of the Lamb and by the word of their testimony."

I read where a man said "Jesus would never whip his bride and leave her behind during the tribulation period." At first, that sounds like good bumper sticker mate- rial—if there were no saved people here at all during the tribulation. Oh, "there are saved people here and they're not a part of the bride?" They're dying, they're giving their life blood and all this, they're being beheaded but they're not a part of the bride?

You're saying the bride left the beginning of the seven years?

That's pretty unfair. Jesus said, "I'm not going to whip my whole bride, just a part of them. The ones that are born-again during the seven year period. They're going to pay with their blood." That doesn't make any sense. That is saying either that there is a partial bride rapture and part of the bride gets saved, becomes part of the bride and then dies or we're saying that they are not a part of the bride of Christ. If you don't know what I'm talking about, don't worry about it. The bride is something that Paul calls the church. He calls the church the bride of Christ, Ephesians 5. So, we're always trying to correct our theology.

12:12-14

14. And to the woman were given two wings of a great eagle Well-foreshadowed in Jeremiah 48:9. Once again, literalness should be soberly weighed in light of all the poetic nuance here. **that she might fly into the wilderness, into her place, where she is nourished for a time, and times, and half a time…** "3½ years" in two ways: "1,260 days," and "time, times and half a time."

And the serpent was cast out. Clearly, then, there is a difference between the "breth- ren" of 12:11 and the "woman" of 12:13.

12:15

And the serpent cast out of his mouth water as a flood after the woman, that he might cause her to be carried away of the flood. Jerusalem is "Egypt." And the dragon is apparently in some way, chasing the people of Israel out of Egypt. There is apparently a remnant of Jews that flee Egypt for the wilderness again and they do it halfway through the tribulation period and it's because the dragon is chasing them. The dragon is doing something. What's happening in Jerusalem where they feel like they have to leave? Matthew 24, the abomination of desolation spoken of by Daniel the prophet.

We have this dragon persecuting the woman and he does so with a flood. He's on the earth but something is happening in Israel or Judea that's causing the woman to flee to the wilderness. The dragon is involved in a place known as Jerusalem also known as spiritual Egypt and he casts out of his mouth a flood. Okay, so we have a flood coming from Egypt. Well, look there, we have old material. Jeremiah 46, the floods of Egypt or the armies of Egypt. Are they really the armies of Egypt? Are they coming from the real Egypt or are they coming from spiritual Egypt? Spiritual. So, we have the armies of the dragon or the armies of a personality that we still have to meet known as the beast, chasing the woman out into the wilderness from Egypt and apparently there are armies involved because coming out of Egypt are armies or a flood. Jeremiah 46 says that it's the armies of Egypt. I don't think Jeremiah knew he was going to be talking or prophesying about a far term occurrence that takes place from a spiritual Egypt but, after all, prophecy is not transparent in its fulfillment until it's happening. Most of the time it's translucent and we're left with best guesses.

12:16

And the earth helped the woman, and the earth opened her mouth, and swallowed up the flood which the dragon cast out of his mouth. Let's go through the history together. Here we are, the year is 1446 BC. You have Moses and the children of Israel leaving Egypt, they come to The Red Sea. They go through the Red Sea on dry ground and the armies of Egypt follow them. Jeremiah calls the "armies of Egypt" a "flood." So, a flood follows the children of Israel through the Red Sea. What was it that killed the armies of Egypt known as a flood? The Red Sea did, correct? Alright, I want you to see what God calls the Red Sea in the book of Exodus.

> *Exodus 15:12 Thou stretched out thy right hand and **the earth swallowed them**.*

God said through Moses that the earth, the Red Sea, swallowed up the armies of Egypt. "Why does he call the Red Sea the earth?" The sea is a part of the earth, isn't it? So, Exodus says that the earth swallowed up the armies of Egypt. Another proof that Revelation is the "Ultimate Exodus." I am not saying is going to geographically relocate and swallow up whoever it is the dragon is sending after the Israelites. I'm just saying they use similar language and whatever it is the dragon is sending after the Jewish people into the wilderness at this 3 ½ year time period, apparently it is armies if Old Testament prophecy means anything. Furthermore, John chose by aid of the Holy Spirit to use Exodus language to say that the earth swallows up those armies.

12:17

And the dragon was wroth with the woman, and went to make war with the rem- nant of her seed. Who is the seed of the woman? The seed of the woman is not the Jews in the beginning of the chapter. The woman is the Jews. Who is the seed of the woman? We have the seed of the woman promised in Genesis 3:15 and it's Christ, isn't it? And here we're told that the dragon is so angry that he can't just pummel the nation of Israel, the people of Israel, that he goes after the remnant of Christ. He goes after those who follow Christ. How do I know they follow Christ? The last phrase of the verse, **which keep the commandments of God, and have the testimony of Jesus Christ.** The seed of the woman is Christ; the remnant of the seed are folks that remain of Christ. At that point, that's whoever is alive who is a follower of Christ. See how they are referenced in 12:10-11 as "brethren."

Chapter 13

13:1-4

And I stood upon the sand of the sea, and saw a beast rise up out of the sea, below in verse 11, we have another beast coming out of the earth. In Daniel 7:3, four great beasts come out of the sea. In Daniel 7:17, these four beasts come out of the earth. Apparently, there is a way that these four beasts that Daniel is talking about are pic- tured in both the beast that comes out of the sea here in Revelation 13:1 and the false prophet, the beast that comes out of the earth, in 13:11. All through Revelation you see the earth and the sea, the earth and the sea. Remember chapter 10? You had a mighty angel come down from heaven and he put one foot on the sea and the other on the land and said time should be no longer. That is a theme. How about Revelation 20:12-13? The earth gave up the dead which were in it and the sea gave up the dead which were in it so earth and sea happened in combination all through the book of Revelation. Daniel 7 says that the beasts came from the sea or are coming from **the sea** and one saying they will come out of the earth.

We have John following up the vision of the dragon with a vision of the beast. This is not an accident. The placement of one vision after the other is not an acci- dent. As you look at the first 10 or 11 verses you will find the beast hurting the saints. Remember, in chapter 12 there is a distinction made between the Jewish people and the saints. The Jews flee into the wilderness, the dragon pursues them and then the dragon can't get to them and the last verse in chapter 12 of Revelation says that he turns and goes after "the remnant of the seed of the woman." Who is the seed of the woman? Christ. Who is his remnant? Christians. So, the dragon is angry with Christians, "the remnant of the seed." So, if the dragon is mad at the Christian, then Revelation 13, John immediately turns and finds a vision of a beast who is picking on who? Believers. Now, how do we know they're Christians? Because of the last verse of chapter 12: what do they have? "The testimony of Christ." These are not unbelieving Jews. The dragon was unsuccessful at targeting the Jews, it says it in chapter 12, the earth swallowed up his efforts to kill the woman, the nation of Israel and so he turns and he uses what according to chapter 13:4, he uses what to go after the saints? What does he use? Chapter 13:4? He uses the beast. So, whatever the beast is, it doesn't exist until what about halfway through the tribulation period. We know this because the woman is cared for, according to chapter 12, 1260 days and the beast in chapter 13 is given 42 months (13:5).

having seven heads and ten horns, and upon his horns ten crowns, and upon his heads the name of blasphemy. You might notice if you compare chapter 12:3 with chapter 13:1, the beast and the dragon both have seven heads. We already talked about the seven heads having crowns on them which means they're probably kings. Then we might notice that they both have ten horns. Now we let Scripture interpret Scripture: what are these ten horns? Kingdoms. Here, we see the dragon has crowns on his seven heads while the beast has names of blasphemy on his seven heads.

> *Revelation 17:9 Here is the mind which hath wisdom. The seven heads are seven mountains, on which the woman sitteth. 10 And there are seven kings.*

"7 kings" are the empires of the world that find their consummation or their fulfillment in this great beast, Daniel 7, Revelation 13: This would be Egypt, Assyria, Babylon, Medo-Persia, Greece, Rome. "Five are fallen, and one is." What empire was going around when John was alive? Rome. Apparently, this kingdom of Revelation 13 and 17 is like the preceding six, it's even a little bit like Rome, and it hasn't happened yet. I would suggest that this "7th kingdom" which "is to come" (17:10) is the one world government that will take place around the first part of the tribulation period. That's my suggestion.

> *Revelation 17:11 And the beast that was, and is not, even he is the eighth.*

So, this beast is "the eighth" and shows up in power in the last half of the 3 ½ year period. He's empowered by who? The dragon who is kicked out of heaven halfway through the 7 year period. So he looks like the first 7 kingdoms. He's the eighth but he's one of the seven. How is that possible?

> *Revelation 13:11 And I saw one of his heads as it were wounded to death; and **his deadly wound was healed**...12 He exerciseth all the power of the first beast before him, and causeth the earth and them which dwell therein to worship the first beast, **whose deadly wound was healed**. 14 And deceiveth them that dwell on the earth by the means of those miracles which he had power to do in the sight of the beast; saying to them that dwell on the earth, that they should make an image to the beast, which had the wound by a sword, **and did live**.*

So, he's probably involved with this kingdom number seven. He's probably the seventh emperor; he's probably the one world leader at the beginning of the tribulation period and he is the seventh king. Then it looks like, based on the fact three times in Revelation 13 it says "he died and was raised, a deadly wound was healed," he's going to have a sort of death and resurrection and come back but it's not him. He's a separate king altogether. What makes him different? Satan is empowering him.

And the beast which I saw was like unto a leopard, and his feet were as the feet of a bear, and his mouth as the mouth of a lion: and the dragon gave him his power, and his seat, and great authority Who is the dragon? Satan. And we know that because of 12:9.

And I saw one of his heads as it were wounded to death; and his deadly wound was healed: and all the world wondered after the beast. 4 And they worshipped the dragon which gave power unto the beast: So they worship Satan who gave power to the beast. **and they worshipped the beast, saying, Who is like unto the beast? who is able to make war with him?** If the dragon is a person and the beast is referred to as a "him" we should probably assume that this beast, just like the dragon is symbolic of Satan, the beast is symbolic of a person at least. We're just going to use parallelism.

the people of the earth worshiped the dragon because of the authority that he gave to the beast. The beast comes back to life or revives or becomes an imitator of Jesus Christ in a sense, being revived, and they recognize that it was the beast or the dragon that did it. So the kingdom and the throne gets its authority and its power from the dragon. They worshiped the dragon and they were not only worshiping the beast. Satan has been desiring worship ever since he lifted himself up with pride and tried to be like God, and Satan now seemingly has obtained his goal. I really believe that he will have deceived himself by this time when we see this event happening whether we are personally seeing it from this vantage point or from heaven's vantage point. He will have deceived himself into believing that just because the masses of people of the whole world are worshiping him, he will have wrested the authority away from God.

> *Revelation 4:11 Worthy art thou, O Lord, and our God to receive glory and honor and power for thou didst create all things and because of thy will they existed and were created."*

They worshiped the dragon because he gave his authority to the beast.

13:5

And there was given unto him a mouth speaking great things. The question is: who is giving it to him? It should be probably the end of verse 2, right? Satan gave power to him, gave him authority, gave him his seat and so there was given unto, verse 5, the beast **a mouth speaking things and blasphemies; and power was given unto him to continue forty and two months**. We know it's these 3 ½ years because from chapter 12 we have something happening halfway through. What is it? If the dragon is giving power to this man on earth to subdue the whole earth, that means the dragon has to be where? On earth. When is he cast down to earth according to chapter 12? Halfway through. How do we know? Because he pursues the Jewish nation into the wilderness in chapter 12:14 for one thousand two hundred and threescore days or 3 ½ years. So, if the dragon is cast down here and he empowers the beast for 42 months, then it must be that this is the half of the week that we are talking about—the last half.

And there was given unto him a mouth speaking great things, and you'll notice the worshiping is taking place of the beast and of the dragon but now notice the contrast between the entity that the people of the earth are worshiping here and those that are in heaven that were worshiping in chapter 4.

13:6

And he opened his mouth in blasphemy against God, to blaspheme his name, and his tabernacle, and them that dwell in heaven. And it was given unto him to make war with the saints, and to overcome them. and blasphemies and power was given unto him to continue forty and two months What a dark contrast to the real God in heaven, the real eternal Jehovah sitting on the throne and the fake god sitting on his throne on earth desiring and calling for the worship of people. There's nothing about him being the Creator and the sustainer and worthy, all he can do is blaspheme God and blaspheme those that are followers of God. So the beast was given power to overcome the saints. "And power was given him over all kindreds, and tongues, and nations." and I think if you have an ESV in your lap, it probably says "and peoples." You should have four things there, right?

13:7

And it was given unto him to make war with the saints, and to overcome them: and power was given him over all kindreds, and tongues, and nations. Notice that 7:9-11 provides a scene where God is surrounded by those that he's redeemed. Jesus Christ has redeemed from every tribe, every kindred, every nation and the parallel to the antichrist, the anti-God now has persons that are around him and worshiping him who were from every kindred, every tongue and every nation. So we have the antithesis of the real God, the real Christ, and the real heaven. The subjects must be conquered, it seems, to bow down.

13:8-10

And all that dwell upon the earth shall worship him. In verse 4, they're worshiping Satan when they worship the beast because the beast gets his power from Satan.

> *Revelation 17:8 The beast that you saw was, and is not and is about to rise from the bottomless pit and go to destruction, and the dwellers on earth whose names have not been written in the book of life from the foundation of the world will marvel to see the beast, because it was and is not and is to come.*

This is a real conundrum, so-to-speak, because it says that all that dwell upon the earth at this time shall worship him, and it's those names that are not written in the Lamb's book of life. If we were not already instructed in the last verse of chapter 12 that the beast was persecuting the "seed of Christ," we might conclude that there were no saints upon the earth at all. On the other hand, verse 7 seems to say that there will be significant war against the saints and they will apparently "lose."

13:9

If any man have an ear, let him hear. He that leadeth into captivity shall go into captivity So here's the demise of the beast. **He that killeth with the sword must be killed with the sword. Here is the patience and the faith of the saints.** Saints, you can be comforted knowing that the dragon and the beast have to be killed and they have to be chained up. What happens in chapter 19 when Jesus returns? The beast and the false prophet are thrown into the lake of fire and are killed, that's the second death, and who is thrown into captivity? The dragon, chapter 20:1, he's bound for a thousand years in the bottomless pit so this covers both of them.

13:11

And I beheld another beast coming up out of the earth. See notes under 13:1.

> *Daniel 7:3 And four great beasts came up from the sea, diverse one from another. The first was like a lion...a bear,...a leopard,...one with ten horns....24 And the ten horns out of this kingdom are ten kings that **shall arise**: and another **shall rise** after them; and he shall be diverse from the first, and he shall subdue three kings.*

Alright, so you have these kings that are coming up and they have not occurred yet from Daniel's perspective so these represent kingdoms. After the Babylonians empire we have Medo-Persian, Greece and then Rome and so it looks like we're dealing with those three successive empires. I just wanted you to see that it looks like Revelation 13 is telling us that this beast, the one with the ten horns, the fourth beast of Daniel 7, also has some of the characteristics that the first three beasts had. The first beast of Revelation 13 is a conglomeration of all the great kingdoms of history. It's going to look like Babylon, it's going to look like Medo-Persia, it's going to look like Greece, it's going to look like Rome, all wrapped up into one.

You need to know that the ten horns that are coming out of this beast in chapter 13:1 of Revelation are ten kingdoms with their kings according to Daniel 7:24. This beast in Revelation 13 has ten kings associated with it.

Remember that pretty much everything we read in Revelation 13 is found in Daniel 7. For example, you might look in verse 5 of Revelation 13: It continues 42 months. In Daniel 7:25: "a time, times and dividing of time.: I'm trying to say, "I have a guess as to what this beast is but it's informed, it's an informed guess based on Daniel 7." It looks like it's a conglomeration of previous kingdoms and yet this beast is going to have particular power for 3 ½ years.

You might notice in Revelation 13:12, it says, "And he," the other beast, "exer- ciseth all the power of the first beast before him." They have almost the same power, the same ability. It's almost like you have beast number one, beast number two and they both look like the beast of Daniel 7 who comes both "out of the sea" and "out of the earth."

And I beheld another beast coming up out of the earth; and he had two horns like a lamb, We notice this beast has two horns. He's coming up out of the earth as opposed to the first beast that came up out of the seas. This beast is going to have authority over the earth but he also has two horns like a lamb or what I would call a ram. Most of us today recognize, even Dodge uses that as a symbol of power, the Dodge Ram, the two horns. Not a meek lamb which Christ calls us—not to mention this is how Christ is presented when He is introduced into the vision in Revelation 4.

13:13-14

14 And deceiveth them that dwell on the earth by the means of those miracles which he had power to do in the sight of the beast; saying to them that dwell on the earth, that they should make an image to the beast. Elijah was this type of prophet. 1 Kings 18 bears this out to be sure. So this is, again, an anti-prophet—just as Satan is the anti-God and the first beast is the anti-Christ. Furthermore, anybody that has a Jewish perspective, considering Malachi 4, is looking for Elijah. It is inter- esting that the Jews are looking for a miracle-working Messiah figure like the beast and an Elijah-like prophet like this "other beast," the "false prophet" (as he is called in Revelation 20:10).

Chapter 14

14:1

And I looked, and, lo, a Lamb stood on the mount Sion, and with him an hundred forty and four thousand. What is the setting? Mount Sion; The heavenly Jerusalem, the city of the living God or as we generically refer to it in one word: Heaven.

> *Hebrews 12:18 For ye are not come unto the **mount** that might be touched, and that burned with fire, nor unto blackness, and darkness, and tem- pest.19. And the sound of a trumpet, and the voice of words; which voice they that heard intreated that the word should not be spoken to them any more…22 But ye are come unto **mount Sion**, and unto the city of the living God, the heavenly Jerusalem…*

Just in case you think that Mount Sion in the Bible always speaks of the earthly Jerusalem, this writer says, "No. We're talking about the heavenly Jerusalem. Mount Sion is the heavenly Jerusalem, the city of the living God."

> *…an innumerable company of angels, To the general assembly and church of the firstborn, which are written in heaven, and to God the Judge of all, and to the spirits of just men made perfect, And to Jesus the mediator of the new covenant, and to the blood of sprinkling, that speaketh better things than that of Abel.*

All these things can be found in heaven on Mount Sion. An innumerable company of angels? Haven't we seen that in Revelation before? "Thousand and thousands and ten thousand times ten thousand gathered around the throne?" Okay, so the writer of Hebrews, who I think is Luke, and John in the book of Revelation agree.

In Hebrews 11, Abraham was called out of Ur of the Chaldees to seek for "a city whose builder and maker is God." So, even Abraham knew that when he was looking for the Promised Land, he was really looking for a land that was just a foreshadow of a heavenly land where he would go and live with his Maker.

Is this the same group of the 144,000 (7:4; 14:1) that we saw in chapter 7? I think you're going to see that there are five or six comparisons so that you can see that we are dealing with, probably, the same group: Both groups have the seal of God on their foreheads (7:3; 14:1); a multi-ethnic groups is seen in both contexts (7:9; 14:6); both are before the throne (7:11, 15; 14:3, 5); they follow the Lamb (7:17; 14:4) beside "fountains of waters" (7:17; 14:7).

This is translucent, folks. Remember translucent says we have a good guess. And based on the information I'm given, is it possible we have two different groups of 144,000? Yes. But I don't think so. I think because of the comparison between the two groups.

having his Father's name written in their foreheads. What do you see as a characteristic of those who follow the dragon of (chapter 12) [or the beast (chapter 13)] and a characteristic of those who are described in the first five verses of Revelation 14? They both have a mark. Chapter 13 closes with those who follow the beast having a particular mark. Then the author comes back in the next chapter and says, "Now, let me tell you about a different group that has a different mark."

14:2

And I heard a voice from heaven, as the voice of many waters, and as the voice of a great thunder: and I heard the voice of harpers harping with their harps: We have mention again of a voice from heaven. This happens like 20 times in the book of Revelation where John hears things from heaven. Let's try to remember where John is in chapter 4, 5, 6. Do you remember? He's in heaven. So, let me remind you, he is already back on earth in chapter 9 because he says, "I beheld an angel descending from heaven," and he was the one that unlocked the bottomless pit and let all those demonic locusts out.

14:4

These are they which were not defiled with women; for they are virgins. These are they which follow the Lamb whithersoever he goeth. These were redeemed from among men, being the firstfruits unto God and to the Lamb. There were three times when a male Jew had to show up at the earthly city of Jerusalem and offer a sacrifice. This tells us why there were so many people in the city when Christ died. He died on what day? Passover. That was one of the times every male Jew had to come to Jerusa- lem to offer sacrifice and then there was one in the Fall known as "Tabernacles." So, the second time is between those. It is known as Pentecost, but back in the day it was known as "Firstfruits." You have Passover, that was the day Christ died. The book of Leviticus says that you go to the first day of the week after Passover and you count 50 and that's when Pentecost takes place (or, "Firstfruits). What would that mean to a famer? The first crop. The farmer would come in and offer an offering to the Lord, the first sign of produce from God. Then in the feast of Booths, they would bring another offering and it was also called the ingathering. So, you had the firstfruits which was a sign of that which was to come known as the ingathering. So, they would sacrifice a portion of the firstfruits in good faith that they would have much more to gather at the ingathering. We find out from Romans 11 that the "ingathering" takes place at the end of the "fullness of the Gentiles." If the Firstfruits is Jews, then it stands to reason that the "ingathering" also speaks to Jews. At the end of the tribulation period, after the "firstfruits", God will save ethnic Israel through a mass revelation of truth.

And in their mouth was found no guile: for they are without fault before the throne of God. Is this the same 144,000 that we had in chapter 7? Both groups of 144,000 have a seal on their foreheads. After both visions preaching that goes out to every kindred, every tribe, every tongue, every nation. In chapter 7:9 you see a group of people of multi-ethnicity after the introduction of the 144,000 and in this passage, you see a gospel preaching that happens from the sky. Now, where does this take place? Before the throne. See it in both chapters. And then what are they doing in both chapters? They're following the Lamb.

Chapter 7 has the 144,000 on earth and here's why: because chapter 7:1 you have a judgment that's about to take place on the earth. And you see an angel saying, "Don't do it yet. We have to seal the 144,000." Remember that the seven trumpets start and the seven trumpets happen in about the last half of the tribulation period. We see from the Hebrews 12 passage above that this occurrence of the 144,000 is in Heaven, not earth.

Is this symbolic of something or are we dealing with something literal? John goes into such detail about these 144,000. First in chapter 7, telling us what tribe they come from. Then he tells us their gender and he tells us their status as unmarried. It's hard for me to believe that these are symbolic of anything. Rather, we really do have 144,000, 12,000 from each tribe, it says in chapter 7.

14:6

And I saw another angel five more angels are found in verses 8, 9, 15, 17, and 18.

fly in the midst of heaven, I wanted to point out to you that this happens three times in the book of Revelation—an angel flying through the heavens saying something. 14:6 is the 2nd one.

> *Revelation 8:13 And I beheld, and heard **an angel flying through the midst of heaven**, saying with a loud voice.*

The third time an angel preaches in the heavens, he is announcing to the birds that they can come and eat at Armageddon (chapter 19).

having the everlasting gospel to preach unto them that dwell on the earth, and to every nation, and kindred, and tongue, and people, What is the everlasting gospel? Are there several different gospels? I don't think so and here's the fact, it's called a lot of different things in the New Testament: it's called the gospel of the kingdom; it's called the gospel of the Lord Jesus Christ; Paul calls it "my gospel." There is a segment of Bible believing Christianity out there that believes that there is a different gospel in the Old Testament than in the New Testament and since the tribulation is known as Daniel's Seventieth Week then they see that it is a continuation of the Old Testament and a reverting back to the Old Testament gospel.

> *John 3:15 That whosoever believeth in him should not perish, but have **eternal life**. 16 For God so loved the world, that he gave his only begot- ten Son, that whosoever believeth in him should not perish, but have **everlasting** life.*

Now, that, with John 3:14, really sounds like a Gospel that has "eternal significance" like the "everlasting Gospel" here in 14:6. By the way, "eternal" in 3:15 and "everlasting" in 3:16 are the same Greek word and they have the idea of "timelessness."

So, this angel is flying through the heavens and he's preaching good news that's timeless, it's eternal, it's everlasting. You can have life that doesn't end. That sounds like the same gospel. Think about this: some people say the gospel changed at the death of Christ. John 3 happens before the crucifixion; that's a conversation that took place probably a year before the crucifixion, maybe more with Nicodemus.

> *Galatians 1:6 I marvel that ye are so soon removed from him that called you into the grace of Christ unto another gospel: Which is not another; but there be some that trouble you, and would pervert the gospel of Christ. But though we, or **an angel from heaven, preach any other gospel** unto you than that which we have preached unto you, let him be accursed.*

What does "accursed" mean? Let them be damned. Let them go to hell. "If an angel from heaven preaches another gospel to you than the one I preached to you, let him go to hell." Do you think that has any relevance to Revelation 14:6? You have an angel from heaven preaching the gospel.

That's amazing. That's God-like for him to put that in two places in the Scripture.

> *Galatians 3:5 He therefore that ministereth to you the Spirit, and wor- keth miracles among you, doeth he it by the works of the law, or by the hearing of faith? 6 Even as Abraham believed God and it was accounted to him for righteousness. Know ye therefore that they which are of faith, the same are the children of Abraham. 8 And the scripture,* **foreseeing that** *God would justify the heathen through faith,* **preached before the gospel unto Abraham, saying, In thee shall all nations be blessed.**

How were all the nations blessed in Abraham? Through the Gospel: Christ died for our sins and rose again. If that was not the Gospel Abraham heard, then he heard, based on Galatians 1:8-9, a false Gospel. If He did hear the Gospel of Christ, then it is indeed the timeless Gospel ("everlasting"/"eternal").

> *Isaiah 52:7 How beautiful upon the* **mountains** *are the feet of him that bringeth* **good tidings**, *that publisheth peace; that bringeth good tidings of good, that publisheth salvation; that saith unto* **Zion**, *Thy God reigneth!*

"Good tidings" is also "Gospel" in various translations. So we have a particular piece of good tidings or gospel that is preached to those on Mount Zion and it is "the Lord reigns."

> *8 Thy watchmen shall lift up the voice; with the voice together shall they sing: for they shall see eye to eye, when the LORD shall* **bring again Zion**.

So we have the Lord coming; we have Zion; and we have this good news that the Lord reigns in Isaiah 52. Don't you think that's just a tad odd? Notice who is the one that is bringing the good tidings in verse 7? It should be us by application but I want to maybe even focus in a little bit more. This is a prophecy of the Christ because in verse 7 it says "the feet of him that bring good news or publish peace and brings good tid- ings of good to Zion," and in verse 8 we find that it's actually the Lord bringing Zion. So, you should know that the feet of him that bring the good news are the same feet that actually come to Zion. That's interesting. Why is that interesting? Look, please, at Zechariah 14.

Jerusalem has three valleys: You had a valley over on the west side of Jerusalem known as the Valley of Hinnom. This is where, at least in the intertestamental period, they took criminals' bodies and trash, and they threw them in this burning area where the refuse of the city was burned. The Greek word is *Gehenna*. Over on the east side of the city, we have another valley that is known as Kidron or Cedron. Across the valley on the east side of Jerusalem (Kidron) is a mountain called the "Mount of Olives."

> *Zechariah 14:1 Behold, the day of the LORD cometh, and thy spoil shall be divided in the midst of thee. For I will gather all nations against Jerusalem to battle; and the city shall be taken…3 Then shall the LORD go forth.*

Remember, Isaiah 52, he was going to bring Zion. Remember that? Zechariah 14, the Lord is going forth. That means he's leaving from some place and going to another place.

> *14:2 He's going forth into captivity and the residue of the people shall not be cut off from the city. 3. Then shall the LORD* ***go forth, and fight*** *against those nations, as when he fought in the day of battle. 4.* ***And his feet shall stand in that day upon the mount of Olives.***

In Acts 1, where was Jesus when he gave the last words to the disciples? Mount of Olives. Acts 1:9, it says he ascended into heaven and a cloud took him out of the sight of the apostles and it said there stood by him two men in white, stood by the 11 two men in white and said, "You men of Galilee, what are you gawking at? What are you staring at? This same Jesus that has been taken from you into heaven

shall so come in like manner." So, he went away visibly from the Mount of Olives with a cloud. You'd better know that when he comes back, he's coming back visibly in a cloud to the Mount of Olives just like Zechariah 14 says. It says his feet will plant on the Mount of Olives, Isaiah 52 says that he's going to bring good tidings to Mount Zion. Remember, Zion is a heavenly reality that will be brought to earth. What did the disciples pray in the Lord's Prayer? "Thy kingdom come, thy will be done on earth as it is in heaven." In Revelation 14, we see that heavenly Zion and in Revelation 19, we're told that the heavenly Zion is brought to earth. Isaiah 52 says that there will be some beautiful feet that bring the good news that "God reigns" over to Mount Zion. There is going to be a walk taken, if you will, that will go from the Mount of Olives to Mount Zion.
Psalm 24, here's what David said about Jesus,

> *Lift up your heads, O ye gates, and be lift up ye everlasting doors for the King of glory shall come in. Who is this king of glory? The Lord strong and mighty.* **The Lord mighty in battle**.

Psalm 24 speaks of a day when Christ will return to earth in battle and that he will come through some gates, and he will conquer foes (Isaiah 52), and he will person- ally and visibly walk across the Kidron Valley onto Mount Zion and sit down on the throne of David. The feet of Christ are going to land on the Mount of Olives. 1st Thessalonians 4 says that on that regal return to earth, we'll go and meet him in the air. Why? Because if he comes down on the Mount of Olives and let's just say I'm in Fayetteville, North Carolina, I'm going to miss out unless there's a mechanism that He uses to help me join His train and that is known as the "rapture."

> *Matthew 24:3 And as he sat upon the **mount of Olives** the disciples came unto him privately, saying, Tell us, when shall these things be? and what shall be the sign of thy coming, and of the end of the world?*

Look where they put the coming of Christ and the end of the world, they put them together and did Jesus correct them? No, it must have been that their question was right in line. His coming will happen at the end of the world.

> *Matthew 24:4 And Jesus answered and said unto them, Take heed that no man deceive you. For many shall come in my name, saying, I am Christ; and shall deceive many. And ye shall hear of wars and rumours of wars: see that ye be not troubled: for all these things must come to pass, but* **the end** *is not yet.*

The end of what? The end of the world (verse 3). Many versions rightly have "end of the age."

> *Matthew 24: 7 For nation shall rise against nation, and kingdom against kingdom…9 Then shall they deliver you up to be afflicted, and shall kill you: and ye shall be hated of all nations for my name's sake. And then shall many be offended, and shall betray one another, and shall hate one another. And many false prophets shall rise, and shall deceive many. And because iniquity shall abound, the love of many shall wax cold. But he that shall endure unto the end, the same shall be saved. 14 And this* **gospel of the kingdom** *shall be preached in all the world for a witness unto all nations; and then shall the end [of the age] come.*

If we're talking about a kingdom, what are we also talking about? A king. And what does a king do? Reigns. It sounds like Isaiah 52 all over again, doesn't it? Good tidings that God reigns.

14:7

Saying with a loud voice, Fear God, and give glory to him, so he's preaching the gospel and commanding the nations to fear God and give glory to him, **for the hour of his judgment is come**. Who is he preaching this to? End of verse 6? **To every nation, kindred, tongue and people.**

*Revelation 13:7 And it was given unto him, to make war with the saints, and to overcome them: and power was given him over all **kindreds, and tongues, and nations**. 8 And all that dwell upon the earth shall worship him, whose names are not written in the book of life of the Lamb slain from the foundation of the world.*

The beast has power over every kindred, tongue, people, nation whose names are not in the book of life, right? Apparently, since you have an angel preaching to every **kindred, tongue, people and nation**, he's going after those who are not yet saved but whose names are in the book of life. Somehow we have a reason for this angel to be preaching. Why is he preaching? Because there are still people who God has identified for himself, whose names are in the book of life, who will not be fooled by the beast and that's who the angel is going after.

It seems like we know the beast's regime goes for the last 3 ½ years of the tribulation period and since he's deceiving the whole world when the prophet makes the image of the beast speak; the false prophet brings fire from heaven; and there's an apparent resurrection from the dead. So you have these three miracles that the beast and the false prophet are able to pull off and they're swaying the whole world except for those who are saved already or are not saved but are with the currently saved in what location? The Lamb's book of life. Your name has been there for sometime, folks. You're going to find out in chapter 17 that it's been there since the foundation of the world. There was not a single time when the Lord was nervous about one of those names being blotted out. All that the Father gives will come. There is not a single name in the Lamb's book of life that doesn't come to the Son; that doesn't get drawn by the Father. Not a single one and because they're drawn by the Father and they come to the Son, the Son does not cast them out. That's right, John 6:37 in concert with Revelation which, by the way, written by the same man.

14:8

And there followed another angel saying Babylon is fallen. Is fallen

that great city, because she made all the nations drink of the wine of wrath of her fornication. When it says **Babylon** we should also think about religion "reaching to the heavens" at the Tower of Babel with its confused languages (Genesis 11). Why were the languages confused? Because God judged them. Why did God judge them? The city Babylon that's mentioned here in these Scriptures, if we look at the evidences of it, it appears to be like this certain city.

That great city "Great city" comes from two words: *megas* and *polis*. Where in the book of Revelation does it talk about a great city?

> *Revelation 11:8 And their dead bodies shall lie in the streets of that **great city** which is spiritually called 'Sodom' and 'Egypt' where also our Lord was crucified.*

Where was Jesus crucified? Jerusalem. Jesus was crucified in Jerusalem, but we could spiritually call Jerusalem "Sodom." Again, they're saying "Sodom" was a great city. They're saying it was like "Egypt," and it was "a great city." Does that mean that this "Babylon" is Jerusalem?

> *Revelation 16:19 And **the great city** was divided into three parts. And the cities of the nations fell and the great **Babylon** came in remembrance before God to give unto her her cup of wine of the fierceness of his wrath.*

> *Revelation 17:18 And the woman which thou sawest is **that great city**, which reigneth over the kings of the earth."*

This Babylon is going to be kind of a powerful city. It will reign over the kings of the earth. In other words, it will be the center of all of rulership, all of political power. This is going to be an important city some day. Now, is there one city on all earth that runs the entire earth today? No, so I don't think that we have this city yet. We don't have a one-world government run from one city, but it does say that it reigns over the entire earth this city, whatever this city is.

*Revelation 18:10 Standing afar off for fear of torment saying, Alas, alas, **the great city Babylon** that mighty city!*

Is "one hour" a figurative way of saying "that moment" or "that day" or "short period of time?"

*Revelation 18:16 And saying Alas, alas **that great city**, that was clothed in fine linen, and purple, and scarlet, and decked with gold, and precious stones, and pearls! 18. And cried when they saw the smoke of her burn- ing, saying, what city is like unto this **great city**! 19 And they cast dust on their heads, and cried, weeping and wailing, Alas, alas, that **great city**, wherein they made rich and all had ships in by the sea. By reason of her costliness, for in one hour she is made desolate." 21 And a mighty angel took up a stone like a great mill stone and cast it into the sea. Thus with violence shall the **great city Babylon** be thrown down and shall be found no more at all.*

*Revelation 21:10 And he carried me away in the spirit and to a great high mountain and showed me **that great city**.*

That great city. Which one? Are we referring to one we've been talking about this whole book of Revelation? Jerusalem? It seems the climactic city has much to do with the first "Great City." Jerusalem" is "that great city." Jerusalem is where his chosen people have come from. Jesus was crucified in Jerusalem. Well, He's got to destroy it; he's got to have judgment upon it. I think that's just some of the evidence that would make me think that this new city, this Jerusalem was indeed referred to as Babylon. A new Babylon.

*Ezekiel 16:26 Thou hast also committed fornication with the Egyptians, thy neighbors great of flesh. And have increased in whoredoms to provoke me to anger. 29. Thou hast moreover multiplied thy fornication **in the land of Canaan**. Yet, thou hast or thou wast not satisfied therewith.*

Revelation 14:8 is just a preview of chapter 17 and 18 and it says, "Fallen, fallen is Babylon the great."

> *Isaiah 21:9 And behold, here cometh the chariot of men with a couple of horsemen. And he answered and said, "**Babylon is fallen, is fallen** and all the graven images of her gods he hath broken unto the ground."*

God judged Babylon, the original historical Babylon. God judges Babylons through- out the ages.

> *Revelation 16:17 And the seventh angel poured out his vial. And there came a great voice out of the temple of heaven from the throne saying, It is done. And there were voices and thunders and lightnings; and there was a great earthquake such as what was not since men were upon the earth, so mighty an earthquake and so megas. And **the great city** was divided into three parts, and the cities of the nations fell; and great Babylon came into remembrance before God, and to give unto her cup of the wine of the fierceness of his wrath.*

"My great city has become a great Babylon," that's what God is saying. "My people have left me." The timing of this destruction is at the end of the great tribula- tion. It's got to be happening near the end, because it's the seventh angel pouring out her seventh vial into the air.

14:9

And the third angel followed them, saying with a loud voice, If any man worship the beast and his image, and receive his mark in his forehead, or in his hand. John just got done saying that if your name is not in the Book of Life from the foundation of the world, you will worship the beast. And if you worship the beast…

14:10

the same shall drink of the wine of the wrath of God, which is poured out without mixture into the cup of his indignation. You have to understand, John wants you to understand that he is very angry. An angry Lamb. That's almost paradoxical, isn't it? The sheep are just stupid and now I understand why we are called them, but the Lamb, who ever thought about an angry lamb? And that's why in chapter 5 he is called the Lion of the Tribe of Judah but he looks like a lamb that's just been slaughtered. It's a paradox and one days he's coming back not as a lamb but as a lion and he is angry.

And they shall be tormented with fire and brimstone, in the presence of the holy angels, and in the presence of the Lamb. In other words, please understand, we need to stop apologizing for God. It is completely appropriate for him to punish sin. God says, "Don't be embarrassed for me. The smoke of their torment will come up before me and the Father forever." This apparently pleases the Lord because when we talk about things happening in the presence of God and of the Lamb, that is something that is pleasing to him.

14:11
And the smoke of their torment ascendeth up for ever and ever: In 8:3 we find the prayers of the saints being offered up as incense before the Lord. Do you understand the parallel that John is drawing here? It is as pleasing to them to observe the torment of the wicked as it is to receive the prayers of the saints. It's really tempting for us to redefine God and re-explain God and apologize for God but we're commanded here to understand and believe and trust an appreciate this aspect of God, that God is somehow pleased in his economy to design eternal fire prepared for the devil and his angels and somehow people are put there and the smoke of their torment arises before God and his Lamb forever.

> *Isaiah 34:8 a day of the LORD'S vengeance, and the year of recompences for the controversy of Zion. Remember Revelation 14:1, we see the Lamb standing on Zion? So, we're seeing some parallels here. The streams thereof shall be turned into pitch, and*

> *the dust thereof into brimstone, and the land thereof shall become burning pitch. It shall not be quenched **night nor day**, and **the smoke thereof shall go up for ever**: from generation to generation it shall lie waste; none shall pass through it for ever and ever.*

Does this prove that the Lake of Fire is forever and ever and ever and ever without end? I'm not sure that you can prove that it last forever out of Isaiah 34. I'm not even sure you can say that it last forever here but this, I can say, in the book of Revelation it does seem to say it. It's not just the smoke of the torment that lasts forever, it is the torment itself.

> *Revelation 19:20, And the beast was taken, and with him the false prophet that wrought miracles before him, with which he deceived them that had received the mark of the beast, and them that worshipped his image. **These both were cast alive into a lake of fire burning with brimstone.***

They are thrown into *gehenna*, the Lake of Fire (Matthew 10:28; 25:31-46; Revelation 20:10).

The beast and false prophet are thrown into the Lake of Fire. Revelation 20:10, you have Satan being cast into the Lake of Fire, a thousand years later, the beast and the false prophet are still in the Lake of Fire. Do you see that? "Well, they should be there forever." I got that, but remember the ramifications of chapter 14, that same fire and brimstone that was prepared for the devil and his angels are where people go when they worship the beast.

> *Revelation 21:8, "But the fearful, and unbelieving, and the abominable, and murderers, and whoremongers, and sorcerers, and idolaters, and all liars, shall have their part in **the lake which burneth with fire and brimstone** which is the second death."*

So, after this thousand years at this Great White Throne of chapter 20, verses 11-15 Satan is cast into the Lake of Fire, the beast and the false prophet are still there after a thousand years and the verses, the last part of chapter 20 and this verse show us that those who are not in the Book of Life are cast into that very same Lake of Fire that Matthew tells us was prepared for the devil and his angels.

They have no rest day or night See Isaiah 28:16-20 for more on this awful reality for those who engage in this Daniel 9 covenant.

Let's just say this two ways: in the day of judgment for many people, they will be like a man on a bed that is too short trying to cover with a sheet that is too narrow. No comfort and no covering in the day of judgment for those who have made a cov- enant with death and hell. Now, this is just an amazing parallel because in Revelation 20, you see death and hell are mentioned in a pair and they are cast into the Lake of Fire and you see that there are judgments and covenants mentioned in the book of Revelation. Well, here he says that there is no rest for those who are involved with that judgment. It could have been so different for them.

> *Revelation 4 He that sat was to look upon like a jasper and a sardine stone. 8 [The four creatures] had each of them, six wings about him and they were full of eyes within and* ***they did not rest day or night. Saying 'Holy, holy, holy, Lord God Almighty, which was, and is, and is to come.'***

14:14-16

And I looked, and behold a white cloud, and upon the cloud one sat like unto the Son of man, having on his head a golden crown, and in his hand a sharp sickle. "The Son of man." Jesus and, of course, we looked at that also in chapter 1 where John is writing about Jesus walking in the midst of the churches and being described as the Son of man. The book of Matthew uses that term for Jesus over 25 times. So precedence would pretty much tell us that whenever we see that term, that's probably who the writer is talking about.

Revelation 1 opens with the reality of the coming of the **Son of Man** (1:7), and then gives us a vision of **the Son of Man** (1:13).

having on His head a golden crown, It is this crown given mockingly by His enemies when He came at first:

> *Matthew 27:29 When they had twisted **a crown of thorns**, they put it on His head, and a reed in His right hand. And they bowed the knee before Him and mocked Him, saying, "Hail, King of the Jews!" 30 Then they spat on Him, and took the reed and struck Him on the head.*

If that crown was one of humiliation intended for a criminal, then it was my crown. If that crown was intended to shame a law breaker to deter offenders, then it was my crown. It was not our Lord's crown.

Stephanos is the Greek word and the meaning is related to the wreath on and around the head of a person "elevated in rank" or the winner of games.[21]

It is that which is worn by elders and given to the Father (Revelation 4:10). It is seen on Jesus' head but one time and it is not when you might think (Revelation 19 contains *diadema*).

and in His hand a sharp sickle. 15 And another angel came out of the temple, The same **temple** we spoke of in 7:17 and in chapters 21 and 22 when discussing the New Jerusalem and its temple-less-ness.

1. The **Son of Man** and life (Revelation 1:18) is the first (and most recent) mention of the Son of Man and the first thing He mentions is that He "was dead." It is this "Son of Man," formerly

---

[21] "G4735 - stephanos - Strong's Greek Lexicon (KJV)." Blue Letter Bible. Web. 8 Mar, 2017.
<https://www.blueletterbible.org//lang/lexicon/lexicon.cfm?Strongs=G4735&t=KJV>.

identified as a "lamb that was slain who has prevailed" (Revelation 5:5-6).
2. <u>The Son of Man gives this crown to His people (Revelation 2:10).</u> (1 Corinthians 9:25; 2 Timothy 4:8; James 1:12; 1 Peter 5:4).

Revelation 2:10 Do not fear any of those things which you are about to suffer. Indeed, the devil is about to throw some of you into prison, that you may be tested, and you will have tribulation ten days. Be faithful until death, and I will give you **the crown of life**.

3. <u>The Son of Man gives rest to His people (14:13).</u> There is no doubt that the reader is to enjoy the aftermath of such well-wishing because there is One Who defeated death sitting on a cloud.

It seems logical, then, that the "resting saints" of verse 13 are awaiting their "reaping" and gathering into an abode separate from those being judged. That is to say, we are careful to note it is the "Son of Man" who gathers the grain (Revelation 14:14-16), and it is an angel that gathers the grapes (14:17-20). We await the Son of Man, primarily. This **is the patience of the saints.** This is the "gathering of the wheat into the barn" (Matthew 13:30).

This also has ramifications to the reality that we are recipients of this same victory over death: though some may lie in the ground, yet they await full redemption. Perhaps Makant, in her work "the Practice of Story" has it said best:

"Redemption is not dependent upon human ability to imagine it so or upon a chink in the armor of suffering, but upon the character of nature and power of God. Redemption depends upon the hope that God is faithful, that the same God who delivered Israel from slavery in Egypt and who raised Jesus from the dead is indeed bringing new life out of suffering."[22]

4. <u>The Son of Man is responsible for reaps His people (14:15-16).</u>
5. <u>The Son of Man will vanquish His enemies (14:17-20).</u> "Pastor Bill, I thought this was the reaping of the believer. It is indeed, but it introduces the rest of the chapter (14:17-20) where we see that some will die. May it also be said that He is risen without the approval of those who have rejected Him (14:9-11).[23]

14:15

And another angel came out of the temple, crying with a loud voice to him that sat on the cloud Thrust in thy sickle, and reap: for the time is come for thee to reap; for the harvest of the earth is ripe. And he that sat on the cloud thrust in his sickle on the earth; and the earth was reaped. The parable of the wheat and the tares (beginning in Matthew 13:24) speaks to this.

While we typically think about at the battle of Armageddon or of the wars of the people coming against Christ at the end time, that it is totally destructive. If we think about this passage in Matthew, though, there are going to be some that will be saved unto eternal life or be taken into God's barn and not burned in destruction. So, there is even a possibility here that this passage could be considered to be both judgment and salvation for those th at have been trusting in the Lord.

14:17

…and gathered the vine of the earth, and cast it into the great winepress of the wrath of God. Obviously, in this passage or in this verse, the gathering or the harvesting, it is specifically only into the winepress of the wrath of God (Isaiah 63:1 and following).

---

[22]Mindy Makant *The Practice of Story-Suffering and the Possibilities of Redemption* (Waco: Baylor University, 2015), 32.

[23]"smoke before God" like the prayers of the saints (8:3); equally as pleasing.

In Revelation, it said that the grapes are going to be gathered and thrown into the winepress of the wrath of God and here we have a similar prophecy where now God is coming against those that are represented by Edom.

14:20

And the winepress was trodden without the city, and blood came out of the wine- press, even unto the horse bridles, by the space of a thousand and six hundred furlongs. This is approximately 200 miles. See Joel 3:11 and following and Zechariah 14:1-5 for a greater backdrop.

We've seen that type of relationship before when we've been looking at the times coming just before the time of Christ's second return when he comes to earth. Take a look also at Revelation 16:12-16 and Revelation 19:11-15.

What you have is setting the stage for the beast and the false prophet and the armies of the beast and the false prophet all coming from all directions. All converging on this area which is the focus of the world at the end of the tribulation. Christ returns and, of course, we've had the beast and the false prophet and the antichrist that have set up their kingdoms and are ruling from this area of the world and now the King of kings and the Lord of lords is descending to the mount and the armies are amassing from all over to come and try to defeat the King of kings and the Lord of lords. The description is "out of his mouth." Just with his mouth, they are going to become the feast for the birds of the field.

> *Revelation 19:20 And the beast was taken, and with him the false prophet that wrought miracles before him, with which he deceived them that had received the mark of the beast, and them that worshipped his image. These both were cast alive into a lake of fire burning with brimstone.*

Interestingly enough, we have human beings "cast into the lake of fire" in Revelation 20:15. It doesn't seem a stretch to suppose that the one "chaining" Satan in 20:1-3 is also the one casting others into the lake of fire. So, probably an angel has done this.

Chapter 15

15:1

And I saw another sign in heaven, great and marvellous, seven angels having the seven last plagues, the word "plague" is also translated as "blow." It's back in chapter 13 where it speaks about the beast having "a deadly wound." So you could say there are seven last wounds. **for in them is filled up the wrath of God.** They are the seven last plagues because the wrath of God is completed in them so what does that imply about all the judgments before that? If these are the seven last plagues where the wrath of God is completed, what should that tell you about the trumpets, the seals, the thunders? What are they full of as well? Wrath. So, just because we don't see the word "wrath" referring to God's wrath occurring before chapter 15 of Revelation, let's not fool ourselves into thinking that the seals, the thunders and the trumpets are all cupcakes. They're not.

15:2-3

3 And they sing the song of Moses the servant of God, and the song of the Lamb, saying, Great and marvellous are thy works, Lord God Almighty; just and true are thy ways, thou King of saints. We find near the end of this tribulation period, God says, "I have seven last plagues I'm going to dump the wrath of God out on people," and some "on the sea of glass" respond by singing a song of Moses. Who are they? Who are these who are singing the songs of Moses? The ones who have victory. Get this: They are singing the response to something; they're singing the response to the fact that the people that were just torturing them on earth are about to get waxed. On the east side of the Gulf of Aqaba of the Red Sea, the children of Israel are singing. The reader of Exodus 15 can undoubtedly see this as a replay.

Are they sitting back and writing poetry about the poor Egyptians that God punished? Singing songs of praise while there were thousands upon thousands upon thousands of Egyptian households that had no father coming home, no husband coming home? No! They were praising God! Why? God delivered his people.

Here they are sitting by a sea. You have people that have been delivered from the wrath of the worldlings, you have people that have been "exodused" out of the planet and they are standing by a sea singing the song of Moses? What about that? Isn't that what happened in Exodus 15? Where are they standing when they sing the song of Moses? By the Red Sea.

> *Luke 9:28 And it came to pass about an eight days after these sayings, he took Peter and John and James, and went up into a mountain to pray. And as he prayed, the fashion of his countenance was altered, and his raiment was white and glistering. And, behold, there talked with [Jesus] two men, which were Moses and Elias: Who appeared in glory, and spake of his **decease** which he should accomplish at Jerusalem.*

Now, the Greek word behind "decease" in Luke 9:31 is *exodus*. Isn't that something? So, what is the exodus of the believer in Revelation 15? Death. How do they overcome the beast, the false prophet, the number? By being killed; by "decease;" that's their exodus.

And I saw as it were a sea of glass mingled with fire: and them that had gotten the victory over the beast, and over his image, and over his mark, and over the number of his name, Some versions have have the word "conquered" instead of "gotten the victory" as it comes from one Greek word. "Overcame" in 12:10 is the same Greek word. Now we want to know what John thought about this "overcoming." If we return to the letters to the seven churches in Revelation 2-3, we'll find bodies of believers. Theoretically, everyone in these seven churches is a follower of Jesus—having been born-again through faith in Christ.

> *Revelation 2:1 Unto the angel of the church of Ephesus…7 He that hath an ear, let him hear what the Spirit saith unto the*

> *churches; To him that **overcometh** will I give to eat of the tree of life, which is in the midst of the paradise of God.*

Right away we know overcomers "overcome the beast, his mark, his number," and they get "to eat of the tree of life, which is in the midst of the paradise of God." Next, Church of Smyrna:

> *Revelation 2:11 He that hath an ear, let him hear what the Spirit saith unto the churches. He that **overcometh** shall not be hurt of the second death.*

Remember chapter 20, "whosoever was not found written in the book of life was cast in the lake of fire. This is the second death." Already we're told overcomers are: over- comers of the beast, image and the number of his name; they get to eat of the tree of life; and they don't have to go to the lake of fire. In the letter to the church at Pergamos, we find "overcomers" receive an invitation to the temple in heaven for overcomers.

> *Revelation 2:18 And unto the angel of the church in Thyatira...26 And **he that overcometh**, and keepeth my works unto the end, to him will I give power over the nations: And he shall rule them with a rod of iron; as the vessels of a potter shall they be broken to shivers: even as I received of my Father.*

So the fourth church is promised rulership over the nations, authority. Again, if you've read chapter 20, we know that overcomers get to help, at least, rule in the millennium.

So far, they overcome the beast, the image, the number. They get the tree of life in the paradise of God; they do not have to partake in the second death; they do get an invite to the temple in heaven; and they get to rule the nations with Jesus. Not a bad description but we're still not getting the answer to our question which was: what do you do to become an overcomer?

> *Revelation 3:1 And unto the angel of the church in Sardis...5 He*

> *that **overcometh**, the same shall be clothed in white raiment; and I will not blot out his name out of the book of life, but I will confess his name before my Father, and before his angels.*

So, if your name is not blotted out of the book of life, what is the opposite for overcomers? Yeah, you get to be in the book of life.

> *Revelation 3:12 Him that **overcometh** will I make a pillar in the temple of my God, and he shall go no more out: and I will write upon him the name of my God, and the name of the city of my God, which is New Jerusalem, which cometh down out of heaven from my God: and I will write upon him my new name.*

> *Revelation 3:14 And unto the angel of the church of the Laodiceans write; These things saith the Amen, the faithful and true witness, the beginning of the creation of God…21 To him that **overcometh** will I grant to sit with me in my throne, even as I also overcame, and am set down with my Father in his throne.*

We have a description so far of what an overcomer is but not necessarily how you overcome so let's keep looking in the book of Revelation.

> *Revelation 12:10 And I heard a loud voice saying in heaven, Now is come salvation, and strength, and the kingdom of our God, and the power of his Christ: for the accuser of our brethren is cast down, which accused them before our God day and night. And **they overcame him** by the blood of the Lamb, and by the word of their testimony; and they loved not their lives unto the death.*

They overcome Satan. We have another description but we also have a "how"? How do they overcome? By the blood of the Lamb. If you overcome by the blood of the Lamb, the follow-up question should be "What do you have to do to get this blood of the Lamb?" If the only way that you're going to not go to the lake of fire and have your name in the book of life and share the throne of Christ and overcome the beast and the image and the dragon is through the blood of the Lamb, the natural question should be: how do you get this blood of the Lamb?

> *Revelation 21:7 He that **overcometh** shall inherit all things; and I will be his God, and he shall be my son. 8 But the fearful, and unbelieving, and the abominable, and murderers, and whoremongers, and sorcerers, and idolaters, and all liars, shall have their part in the lake which burneth with fire and brimstone: which is the second death.*

Given this passage, we understand that to "not overcome" is eternally fatal. Well, if I wanted to know how you become a partaker of the blood of the Lamb so that I can be an overcomer, I can leave the book of Revelation or I can take a wild guess because we already checked this box and we're just not exactly sure yet how one becomes a recipient of the blood of the Lamb. Now, there are many references in the book of Revelation to the blood. There are, for example, 1:5, "Unto him that loved us and washed us from our sins in his own blood." So there is a particular group of people that have been washed from their sins in the blood of Christ and they are overcomers. We've got that so far, the question is: how do you become a part of that class?

What makes you think that you can become a part of a class that inherits all things, overcomes Satan, shares Christ's throne, is a pillar of the temple of God in heaven, is in the book of life, rules the nations, gets the hidden manna and the white stone, does not partake of the second death, and gets to eat of the tree of life, but it's not "church-age believers;" it's "tribulation saints?" That is a false doctrine created by people who wish to have a pretribulation rapture. We need a group of "overcomers" in the seven churches, and we need a "group of "overcomers" that "overcomes" the dragon, beast, and false prophet" to have a pretribulation rapture. So we're in a crowd that is in the future there in chapter 12, 3 ½ years through the tribulation period, but we're not a part of a crew that is there in chapter 15, verse 1?

If Revelation doesn't tell the story about how to "overcome by the blood of the Lamb," what should I be looking towards next in the Bible? Remember, we're trying to get a little bigger in our search for the context here. We check the immediate con- text and what it takes to be an overcomer of the beast, the image and the number. We don't know how you become an overcomer other than you have to be a recipient of the blood of the Lamb which results in "loving not your own life even unto death" (12:11) which is exactly what Christ did in obeying the Father, he loved not his own life even to death.

Where should we look next? How about the other things John wrote? We're going to go to 1 John. Is it possible that it was a good expectation for the believer in John's day that they would be able to overcome Satan but not "the beast?"

> *1 John 2:13 I write unto you, fathers, because ye have known him that is from the beginning. I write unto you, young men, because **ye have overcome the wicked one**. I write unto you, little children, because ye have known the Father. I have written unto you, fathers, because ye have known him that is from the beginning. I have written unto you, young men, because ye are strong, and the word of God abideth in you, and **ye have overcome the wicked one**.*

So we have fathers and young men that overcome Satan.

> *1 John 2:18 Little children, it is the last time. **As ye have heard that antichrist shall come**, even now are there many antichrists; whereby we know that it is the last time. They went out from us, but they were not of us; for if they had been of us, written unto you because ye know not the truth, but because ye know it, and that no lie is of the truth. Who is a liar but he that denieth that Jesus is the Christ? **He is antichrist**, that denieth the Father and the Son.*

Did you all see that? So he's talking about last times; he's talking about antichrist; and he's talking about being an overcomer of the dragon. I think it's fair to say that we're probably going to see this again in 1 John 4:1-4.

Now, you've heard the last part quoted probably a thousand times in your Christian life and you've been saved a decade, right? But did you know that you're an overcomer of the spirit of antichrist? So in chapter 2 he says you're an overcomer of the wicked one, and in chapter 4 he says you're an overcomer of the spirit of antichrist which drives many false spirits, chapter 4, verse 1, that are in the world. So, whatever is driving this antichrist here, the saints of these seven churches were expected to be overcomers of this spirit of antichrist and when John wrote it in 1 John, he also said, "By the way, there is a spirit of antichrist. Here's how you can identify them and he is the one that will inspire the antichrist that comes. You've heard that he's coming," remember he said that, "You've heard that he's coming and he's already working in the world. The spirit of antichrist is already working in the world and oh, by the way, you've overcome him." Apparently John didn't use the term "antichrist" in the book of Revelation because whoever his audience was, which was the seven churches, was aware that that was the antichrist which is to come so when you are an overcomer of the wicked one, you are an overcomer of the spirit of antichrist as well. So it is presumptive to say the least, to say, "Yeah, I'm an overcomer of the spirit of antichrist but the church won't be here." Wait a minute, seven churches, folks, are told that they're going to be overcomers. What is there for them to overcome if they leave before chapter 12 and chapter 15? It doesn't make any doggone contextual sense.

> *1 John 5:1 Whosoever believeth that Jesus is the Christ is born of God…*

So we have a new birth and belief in the same phrase. Are you all with me? Listen to me: don't put there what God didn't put there. Nothing about "asking Jesus into your heart." How do you become born-again? Believe that Jesus is the Christ. "That's not enough." Oh yeah, you're right, John was probably really confused. No.

> *...and every one that loveth him that begat loveth him also that is begot- ten of him. By this we know that we love the children of God, when we love God, and keep his commandments...4 For whatsoever is born of God overcometh the world: and* **this is the victory that overcometh the world, even our faith.**

So, how do you become an overcomer? Faith. Did you get that?

Now let's see if John remembers what he wrote three chapters ago. Do you think he does? You've overcome the world, you've overcome the wicked one, you've overcome the spirit of antichrist. Do you think John remembers that when he wrote this? I mean, for some of us in our Bible reading plans, it's months between 1 John 2 and 1 John 5 but I'm pretty sure that it might have been three bites of a biscuit ago for John. So, if John tells us all these things about overcomers in Revelation <u>and in 1 John</u>: they overcome the beast, the image, the number; they overcome Satan; they inherit all things; they get the tree of life; they don't have to go to the lake of fire; they get the hidden manna and the white stone; they rule all nations; they get their names in the book of life; they are pillars of God in the temple of God; they share Christ's throne; <u>and they are born-again by faith, the faith that Jesus is the Christ.</u>

15:4

Who shall not fear thee, O Lord, and glorify thy name? for thou only art holy: In verse 1, we have the wrath of God mentioned. **for all nations shall come and worship before thee; for thy judgments are made manifest** We ascertain from this when we see God's wrath in verse 1 and we see a reflection of his holiness in verse 4 and judg- ments in verse 4 that God judges wickedness and that he is completely reasonable in doing so. "Holy" is not the word that is typically behind "holy" in the New Testament. This is a word used only of God. It's two different Greek words. They're using a word that applies only to God in this chapter and it's interesting that it's in the context of him being full of wrath.

David actually stole the wife of a man he murdered. Then had the audacity to say in Psalm 50, "I sinned against God and God really alone." Did he sin against Bath-sheba? Yes. Did he sin against Uriah? Yes. Who else did he sin against? How about the wife he already had and the people of Israel? God Almighty, though, is at the top. Romans 11 says, "Behold the goodness and severity of God." We want a good God that will give us eternal forgiveness through a perfect Son who was sacrificed for our sin but we do not want a severe God that will put people in hell forever. We want a good God that will give us the eternal Son of God on the cross but we do not want a severe God that will give us eternal judgment if we forsake that Son, if we reject that Son; so let's first of all understand that our standard is a little different.

all nations shall come and worship before thee; for thy judgments are made manifest.

> *Psalm 86, 1 Bow down thine ear, O LORD, hear me: for I am poor and needy. 2 Preserve my soul; for I am holy: O thou my God, save thy servant that trusteth in thee. 3 Be merciful unto me, O Lord: for I cry unto thee daily. 4 Rejoice the soul of thy servant: for unto thee, O Lord, do I lift up my soul. 5 For thou, Lord, art good, and ready to forgive; and plenteous in mercy unto all them that call upon thee. 6 Give ear, O LORD, unto my prayer; and attend to the voice of my supplications. 7 In the day of my trouble I will call upon thee: for thou wilt answer me. 8 Among the gods there is none like unto thee, O Lord; neither are there any works like unto thy works. 9 **All nations whom thou hast made shall come and worship before thee**, O Lord; and shall glorify thy name. 10 For thou art great, and doest wondrous things: thou art God alone.*

If you didn't have the book of Revelation, you might get away with actually thinking at some point that this is symbolic or allegory, that you might actually get away with thinking, "Okay, this is just picturing a time when everyone will be saved or most everyone will be saved." But when you get to the book of Revelation, you understand, "Okay, this is a literal thing that's going to happen. All nations really are going to come and bow before the Lord."

> *Psalm 66 1 Make a joyful noise unto God, all ye lands. 2 Sing forth the honour of his name: make his praise glorious. Say unto God, How terrible art thou in thy works! 3 Through the greatness of thy power* **shall thine enemies submit themselves unto thee. 4 All the earth shall worship thee,** *and shall sing unto thee; they shall sing to thy name.*
>
> *Psalm 96 O sing unto the LORD a new song: sing unto the LORD, all the earth. Sing unto the LORD, bless his name; shew forth his salvation from day to day.* **Declare his glory among the heathen**, *his wonders among all people. For the LORD is great, and greatly to be praised: he is to be feared above all gods. For all the gods of the nations are idols: but the LORD made the heavens. Honour and majesty are before him: strength and beauty are in his sanctuary. Give unto the LORD, O ye kindreds of the people, give unto the LORD glory and strength. Give unto the LORD the glory due unto his name: bring an offering, and come into his courts. O worship the LORD in the beauty of holiness:* **fear before him, all the earth.** *10* **Say among the heathen that the LORD reigneth:** *the world also shall be established that it shall not be moved. 11 Let the heavens rejoice, and let the earth be glad. 12 Let the field be joyful, and all that is therein: then shall all the trees of the wood rejoice. 13 Before the LORD, for he cometh, for he cometh to judge the earth: he shall judge the world with righteousness, and the people with his truth.*

Think about the slippery slope if you make that allegorical or symbolic. We have a real problem if you do that. He went up physically, literally, in a body, after his resurrection. He says he's coming in like manner. So, these prophesies in Psalm 96, though they might have been poetic primarily to the original reader, this is going to have physical, literally fulfillment.

*Psalm 97 **The LORD reigneth; let the earth rejoice**; let the multitude of isles be glad thereof. Clouds and darkness are round about him: righteousness and judgment are the habitation of his throne. A fire goeth before him, and burneth up his enemies round about. 4. His lightnings enlightened the world: **the earth saw**, and trembled. The hills melted like wax at the presence of the LORD, at the presence of the Lord of the whole earth. 6. The heavens declare his righteousness, and **all the people see his glory**. Confounded be all they that serve graven images, that boast themselves of idols: worship him, all ye gods.*

If all idol worshipers are dead at Armageddon, we have a real issue here because there are people who will be yet living after he comes.

*Psalm 98 O sing unto the LORD a new song; for he hath done marvellous things: his right hand, and his holy arm, hath gotten him the victory. 2. The LORD hath made known his salvation: his righteousness hath he openly shewed **in the sight of the heathen.** He hath remembered his mercy and his truth toward the house of Israel. **All the ends of the earth have seen** the salvation of our God. Make a joyful noise unto the LORD, all the earth: make a loud noise, and rejoice, and sing praise.*

As effective as David and this Psalmist might have been at declaring the works of the God of Israel, they were not able to really effectively, definitely, literally say "the whole earth knows about him." They might have said poetically "everyone knows about Jesus." That's poetic license. We'll allow you to be exaggerative like that and generalizing but a literal fulfillment of this takes place at the Second Coming of Christ we find in the book of Revelation.

Isaiah 6:1 In the year that king Uzziah died I saw also the Lord sitting upon a throne, high and lifted up, and his train filled the temple. Above it, stood the seraphims: each one had six wings; with twain he covered his face, and with twain he covered his *feet, and with twain he did fly. 3. And one cried unto another, and said, Holy, holy, holy, is the LORD of hosts, **the whole earth is full of his glory.***

Poetically true in Isaiah 6? Sure. Literally true in Isaiah 6? Not until the Christ comes. However, this is a forecast. This looks a lot like Revelation 4. This should tell you that Isaiah is seeing a vision of something yet in the future.

*Isaiah 66:18, For I know their works and their thoughts: it shall come, that **I will gather all nations** and tongues; and **they shall come**, and see my glory. 19. And I will set a sign among them, and I will send those that escape of them unto the nations, to Tarshish, Pul, and Lud, that draw the bow, to Tubal, and Javan, to the isles afar off, that have not heard my fame, neither have seen my glory; and **they shall declare my glory among the Gentiles**. 20. **And they shall bring all your brethren** for an offering unto the LORD out of all nations upon horses, and in char- iots, and in litters, and upon mules, and upon swift beasts **to my holy mountain Jerusalem**, saith the LORD, as the children of Israel bring an offering in a clean vessel into the house of the LORD.*

Often, folks have in mind that all the remaining people on the planet are definitely going to be in the Valley of Megiddo. That's going to be difficult. Even if you take a chronological view of Revelation, is it likely that you'll get less than 1 billion people on the globe? Probably not. Are you going to get them into the valley? Probably not. It's not like these men decide, "Let's go fight Jesus in the Valley of Megiddo. Come on, kids, load up. We're going to get in the station wagon and drive over to Israel." There are people all over the planet that are not going to be affected by Armageddon. After Christ returns, evangelism is still taking place with those Jews that are converted at his coming. Why? Because the nations need to hear of his glory.

Micah 4:1 But in the last days it shall come to pass, that the mountain of the house of the LORD shall be established in the top of the mountains, and it shall be exalted above the hills; and people shall flow unto it. And **many nations shall come, and say, Come,** *and let us go up to the mountain of the LORD, and to the house of the God of Jacob; and he will teach us of his ways, and we will walk in his paths: for the law shall go forth of Zion, and the word of the LORD from Jerusalem.*

Zechariah 14:1 Behold, the day of the LORD cometh, and thy spoil shall be divided in the midst of thee. For I will gather all **nations against Jerusalem to battle.** *And the city shall be taken, and the houses rifled, and the women ravished; and half of the city shall go forth into captivity, and the residue of the people shall not be cut off from the city. Then shall the LORD go forth, and fight against those nations, as when he fought in the day of battle. And his feet shall stand in that day upon the mount of Olives, which is before Jerusalem. 5. And ye shall flee to the valley of the mountains; for the valley of the mountains shall reach unto Azal: yea, ye shall flee, like as ye fled from before the earthquake in the days of Uzziah king of Judah. And it shall come to pass in that day, that the light shall not be clear, nor dark:…16. And it shall come to pass,* **that every one that is left of all the nations which came against Jerusalem** *shall even go up from year to year to worship the King, the LORD of hosts, and to keep the feast of tabernacles.*

Malachi 1:11 For from the rising of the sun even unto the going down of the same my name shall be great **among the Gentiles;** *and in every place incense shall be offered unto my name, and a pure offering: for my name shall be great among the heathen, saith the LORD of hosts.*

Why is all of this important? Because if we are resurrected/raptured, like Jesus says "after the tribulation of those days," (Matthew 24:29) we're going to have glori- fied bodies, and we will not be procreating in the Kingdom to come. There is going to be a need for people with natural bodies in the millennial kingdom because we're ruling and reigning with Christ. He has a glorified body and we will have glorified bodies and in the age to come, there is going to be a need for people who don't have glorified bodies because Jesus said in Matthew 23, "In the resurrection they will nei- ther marry nor be given in marriage." In the final analysis, then, Christ will reign over those that enter the kingdom with natural bodies, and this reign will be shared with his glorified people.

> *Revelation 5:9 And they sung a new song, saying, Thou art worthy to take the book, and to open the seals thereof: for thou wast slain, and hast redeemed us to God by thy blood out of every kindred, and tongue, and people, and nation...You have made us unto our God kings and priests: and* **we shall reign on the earth** *....13. And every creature which is in heaven, and on the earth, and under the earth, and such as are in the sea, and all that are in them, heard I saying. Blessing, and honour, and glory, and power, be unto him that sitteth upon the throne, and unto the Lamb forever and ever.*

> *Revelation 11:15. And the seventh angel sounded, and there were great voices in heaven, saying, The kingdoms of this world are become the kingdoms of our Lord, and of his Christ; and* **he shall reign for ever and ever**. *And the four and twenty elders, which sat before God on their seats, fell upon their faces, and worshipped God, Saying, We give thee thanks, O Lord God Almighty, which art, and wast, and art to come; because thou hast taken to thee thy great power, and hast reigned. And* **the nations** *were angry.*

> *Revelation 19:6 And I heard as it were the voice of a great multitude, and as the voice of many waters, and as the voice of mighty thunderings, saying, Alleluia: for the* **Lord God omnipotent reigneth.**

> *Revelation 20:1 And I saw an angel come down from heaven, having the key of the bottomless pit and a great chain in his hand.*

*And he laid hold on the dragon, that old serpent, which is the Devil, and Satan, and bound him a thousand years, and cast him into the bottomless pit, and shut him up, and set a seal upon him, that he should deceive the nations no more, till the thousand years should be fulfilled: and after that he must be loosed a little season. And I saw thrones, and they sat upon them, and judgment was given unto them: and I saw the souls of them that were beheaded for the witness of Jesus, and for the word of God, and which had not wor- shipped the beast, neither his image, neither had received his mark upon their foreheads, or in their hands; and **they lived and reigned with Christ** a thousand years. But the rest of the dead lived not again until the thousand years were finished. This is the first resurrection. Blessed and holy is he that hath part in the first resurrection: on such the second death hath no power, but they shall be priests of God and of Christ, and shall reign with him a thousand years.*

15:8

8 And the temple was filled with smoke from the glory of God, and from his power; and no man was able to enter into the temple, till the seven plagues of the seven angels were fulfilled. Almost 50 weeks after the Exodus, there is glory in the Tabernacle.

> *Exodus 40:34 Then a cloud covered the tent of the congregation, and the glory of the LORD filled the tabernacle.* ***And Moses was not able to enter into the tent of the congregation, because the cloud abode thereon, and the glory of the LORD filled the tabernacle.*** *And when the cloud was taken up from over the tabernacle, the children of Israel went onward in all their journeys: But if the cloud were not taken up, then they journeyed not till the day that it was taken up. For the cloud of the LORD was upon the tabernacle by day, and fire was on it by night, in the sight of all the house of Israel, throughout all their journey.*

So you have this idea that when the tabernacle was set up, the presence of God in the form of a glory cloud was so thick in that tabernacle that Moses couldn't even go inside of it.

Chapter 16

16:1-2

And I heard a great voice out of the temple There was an angel coming out of the temple crying with a loud voice in 14:15. The presence of God filling this temple with smoke as seen in the last verse of chapter 15 is also reminiscent of Isaiah's 6th chapter where there were angelic beings speaking in the temple where smoke also arose. Incidentally, instead of the voice crying out for Isaiah to "Go" and preach we have a voice here crying for the seven angels to **Go your ways, and pour out the vials of the wrath of God upon the earth.** In the absence of specificity in this passage it seems like the voice of God, or at least Christ (given John 12:41), is the voice we are seeing here.

And I heard a great voice out of the temple Where is this temple?

> *Revelation 15:5 And after that I looked, and, behold, **the temple of the tabernacle of the testimony in heaven** was opened: and the seven angels came out of the temple, having the seven plagues, clothed in pure and white linen, and having their breasts girded with golden girdles.*

When Moses was given the pattern for the tabernacle on Mount Sinai, he patterned it after what he saw in heaven.

> *Hebrews 8:1 Now of the things which we have spoken this is the sum: We have such an high priest, who is set on the right hand of the throne of the Majesty **in the heavens**; a minister of the sanctuary, and of **the true tabernacle, which the Lord pitched, and not man.** For every high priest is ordained to offer gifts and sacrifices: wherefore it is of necessity that this man have somewhat also to offer. For if he were on earth, he should not be a priest, seeing that there are priests that offer gifts according to the law: who serve unto the example and shadow of heavenly things, as*

> *Moses was admonished of God when he was about to make the tabernacle: for, See, saith he, that thou make all things according to the pattern shewed to thee in the mount.*

saying to the seven angels, We know that the angels are messengers of God, they are servants of God to do his will.

> *Revelation 15:1 And I saw another sign in heaven, great and marvellous, **seven angels having the seven last plagues**; for in them is filled up the wrath of God.*

So, that's the first time we see these specific seven angels mentioned. There are several other references to seven angels: you have the seven angels of the seven churches which are found in the first three chapters and you also have the seven angels with the seven trumpets. Now, these specific seven angels in 15 and 16 that have the vials of the wrath of God are also mentioned later in Revelation 21:9 one of these angels is showing John the Bride, the Lamb's wife. We don't know if these were all three dif- ferent instances, the seven angels to the seven churches or the seven angels with the trumpets or these with the seven vials are the same group or not but it seems possible.

And the first went, and poured out his vial upon the earth; Why is he pouring out his wrath upon the earth? Christ is worthy of worship and the followers of the beast (most of the earth-dwellers) are worshiping the beast instead.

> *Revelation 14:9-10 And the third angel followed them, saying with a loud voice, **If any man worship the beast and his image, and receive his mark in his forehead, or in his hand, the same shall drink of the wine of the wrath of God.***

Again, in chapter 16:2, the vials being poured out upon those that have the mark of the beast and worship his image, so what the angels were prophesying would happen in Revelation 14:9-10 is now taking place here in chapter 16:2. God is a jealous God and he wants the praise and worship of his people, of his creation and when the praise that is due to him is being given to the beast and He has been rejected, then you could see why the wrath of God would be poured out on the earth on those that have the mark of the beast and worship his image.

From chapters 12 and 13 we know that the beast comes on the scene during the last 3 ½ years of the 7 years of tribulation. So these people are the ones that have received his mark and have worshiped his image, then this is falling in that last 3 ½ year period.

and there fell a noisome and grievous sore upon the men which had the mark of the beast,

> *Revelation 13:16, he says, and this is the second beast that came up, also known as the false prophet, And he causeth all, both small and great, rich and poor, free and bond, to **receive a mark in their right hand, or in their foreheads: and that no man might buy or sell, save he that had the mark, or the name of the beast, or the number of his name**. 18. Here is wisdom. Let him that hath understanding count the number of the beast: for it is the number of a man; and his number is Six hundred threescore and six.*

We see that the second beast is enforcing, that all people on earth are receiving the mark of the beast. Then in chapter 16, we're seeing that God is pouring out his wrath upon all those that have the mark. So you can see that this is talking about this is a worldwide judgment that is being poured out.

a noisome and grievous sore Is God capable of making everybody in the world that had the mark receive the sore and those that did not (those that were elect) to not get the sore? Of course he is. You know, we have the examples in Exodus of the plague of the flies, the plague of the cattle, the plague of the hail and the plague of darkness where it specifically mentions that God was protecting and shielding his people from the plagues and from the judgments of God. It's pretty clear here in verse 2 that it says that this judgment, this vial, is being poured out upon those that have the mark and those that worship his image.

> *Exodus 9:8-12, And the LORD said unto Moses and unto Aaron, Take to you handfuls of ashes of the furnace, and let Moses sprinkle it toward the heaven in the sight of Pharaoh. And it shall become small dust in all the land of Egypt, and shall be a **boil** breaking forth with **blains** upon man, and upon beast, throughout all the land of Egypt. And they took ashes of the furnace, and stood before Pharaoh; and Moses sprinkled it up toward heaven; and it became a boil breaking forth with blains upon man, and upon beast. And the magicians could not stand before Moses because of the **boils**; for the boil was upon the magicians, and upon all the Egyptians. And the LORD hardened the heart of Pharaoh, and he hearkened not unto them; as the LORD had spoken unto Moses.*

The Greek word behind **grevious sore** is *helkos*. It means "a putrefying wound." Job is another example of someone in the Bible that had boils or sores and it says that "he scraped them with a potsherd."

16:3

And the second angel These angels may very well be the same seven angels that have been involved with the book of Revelation all along (to the 7 churches and holding the 7 trumpets).

> *Revelation 17:1 And there came **one of the seven angels which had the seven vials**, and talked with me, saying unto me, Come hither; I will shew unto thee the judgment of the great whore that sitteth upon many waters.*

There is a lot of stuff in that verse that we haven't gotten to yet but what I wanted you to notice is that one of these seven angels shows up again and takes part in commu- nication with John the Apostle.

> *Revelation 21:9 And there came unto me **one of the seven angels which had the seven vials** full of the seven last plagues, and talked with me, saying, Come here, I will shew thee the bride, the Lamb's wife.*

Maybe this is the same angel, maybe it's not—but what is he doing in both situations? "Come with me. I want to show you something," so apparently these angels were revealers as well. So you have little revelaters within the book of Revelation, and they're angels.

poured out his vial upon the sea; and it became as the blood of a dead man: Where have we seen this plague before? The second angel in verse 3 and the third angel in verse 4 are making the water blood. We're just looking at another Exodus, the ulti- mate Exodus. Let's just remind ourselves here that in Exodus 7:14, we have the water becoming blood. Remember, that was the first plague that God did through Moses to Pharaoh and Egypt. We see this three times in the book of Revelation: 16:3; 8:8 (twice) and chapter 11 with the two witnesses. This is the third time water is turned to blood in the book of Revelation. Some people, because the two witnesses occur in the great tribulation (the second 3 ½ years), and since the vial is happening in the great tribulation and it is water into blood, some people think maybe that it's one and the same occurrence. It might be. It might be that the witness is calling it down and the angel is performing it from heaven, I don't know. It might be the same act just described differently.

and every living soul died in the sea. This is not a proof text for some sort of human population in Atlantis or something nor is it a proof text, please hear me well, it is not a proof text that dolphins have a soul like you and I have a soul or whatever. Soul simply means "life force." Let me please show it to you in your King James Bible: Revelation 8:9, "A third part of the creatures which were in the sea and **had life** died." Over here, "the second angel poured out his vial upon the sea; and it became as the blood of a dead man: and every living soul died in the sea." That's the King James version, it's two different translations but the same Greek word and it's talking about every living thing in the sea, everything that had a life force driving it is dead so there is no doctrine there about how your doggie will go to heaven with you because it has a soul. Once I get to Revelation 19 and find white horses coming out of heaven, I have no problem believing there are some dogs running beside them. You say, "Well, I don't believe that." Fine, it's harmless, disagree with me and just laugh with me.

16:4

And the third angel poured out his vial upon the rivers and fountains of waters; and they became blood. There are a lot of similarities between the trumpets and the vials. Compare this chapter with Revelation 8 where we have a bloodying first of the major water in both the third vial and the third trumpet. In the 2nd trumpet and 2nd vials we are also dealing with the main water and in the third and the third it's the fountains and the rivers so it says we're even going to get the water that's inland. It's going to be undrinkable. Now, I don't know what happens to you when you are thirsty and you can't find anything to drink but people do crazy things when that happens. What is the world's population going to do when there is no water to drink?

In the trumpets, the water becomes blood and then the vials, did you see what it says? It becomes as the blood of a dead man so you look everywhere in the waters both in the main waters and in the inland waters and you have coagulated blood in the waters.

Scientifically speaking, humanly speaking, you would say that this happens really close to the end of the tribulation period with no water supply—since we're told the fifth trumpet lasts for five months and it's the stinging demonic scorpion type locust things and that would probably be the last five months of the tribulation period as well. The stench would be something.

16:5

And I heard the angel of the waters say, Thou art righteous, Who is this angel of the waters? This could simply be the angel pouring out the vial? After all, in Revelation 14:18, we have the custodian of the fire that's an angel. In 7:1-2, we have angels that are in charge of wind. So we have angels that are in charge of fire and wind—so maybe we have one that is in charge of water now? This may seem strange, but we do know, based on Ezekiel and Daniel, that there are angels that have geographical responsibilities as well (they're called the Prince of Persia, the Prince of Babylon and others) so there are other angelic responsibilities in the Bible.

> *Ephesians 6:12 We don't wrestle against flesh and blood but against principalities and powers and rulers of the darkness of this world and spiritual wickedness in high places.*

Presumably in the angelic world, there are lanes of responsibility: even wind, fire, and water. There's no problem with me that there is some sort of hierarchy that God uses and delegates to go and handle things which is the whole point of Job 1, they come and present themselves and say, "Here's what I've been doing." There is so much military reference in the Bible.

And I heard the angel of the waters say, Thou art righteous, O Lord, which art, and wast, and shalt be, because thou hast judged thus. We have an angel watching his responsibility basically go away. Here's an angel pouring out the wrath of God on the waters, it turns into blood both in the sea and inland waters and the angel in charge of the waters has this one response.

16:7

And I heard another out of the altar say, Even so, Lord God Almighty, true and righteous are thy judgments. Presumably if context means anything and John is teaching us anything, we say this voice is the martyred saints under the altar (6:9-11) because now they've had their answer to prayer.

16:8-9

And the fourth angel poured out his vial upon the sun; and power was given unto him to scorch men with fire. 9 And men were scorched with great heat, and blasphemed the name of God, which hath power over these plagues: and they repented not to give him glory.

> *Isaiah 13:6 Howl ye; for the day of the LORD is at hand; it shall come as a destruction from the Almighty. Therefore shall all hands be faint, and every man's heart shall melt: And they shall be afraid: pangs and sorrows shall take hold of them; they shall be in pain as a woman that travaileth: they shall be amazed one at another;* **their faces shall be as flames.**

It sounds like lots of sun. So we're going to go right here and say Isaiah 13 and we're going to make us a little table here and we're going to go check, lots of sun. We have a passage about the day of the Lord and there are apparently people suffering from burning.

> *Isaiah 13:9 Behold, the day of the LORD cometh cruel both with wrath and fierce anger, to lay* **the land** *desolate: and he shall destroy the sinners thereof out of it.*

I would like you to please notice that in Isaiah 13 there is an emphasis on the land.

> *Isaiah 13:10 For the stars of heaven and the constellations thereof* **shall not give their light: the sun shall be darkened** *in his going forth, and the moon shall not cause her light to shine.*

What does that look like? Lots of darkness. Who is this supposed to happen to in Isaiah 13:1? Babylon. So, you're faced with wondering a couple of things: The Baby- lon that's forecast in the book of Revelation and somewhat fulfilled in real history as it now stands.

> *Isaiah 13:17 Behold, I will stir up the Medes against them which*

> *shall not regard silver; and as for gold, they shall not delight in it.*

Now, remember the last Babylonian king we find in the book of Daniel is Belteshazzar. Do you remember Darius the Mede? Darius was the Median king and so the Medes and the Persians were next so when we read Isaiah and we find out in chapter 13:17, that the Medes are going to come and punish the Babylonians, we see Isaiah 13 is history.

> *Isaiah 24:1 The Lord makes the earth empty and makes it waste and turns it upside down and scatters abroad the inhabitants thereof....13 When thus it shall be* **in the midst of the land** *among the people, there shall be as the shaking of an olive tree,*

So there's still a focus in the middle of this worldwide thing and it's Jerusalem. We found out in the book of Revelation that Babylon in the Old Testament is always defined or at least the great harlot in the Old Testament is always defined as Jerusalem. We don't have any reason to believe that the Babylon in the book of Revelation is anything but Jerusalem.

> *Isaiah 24:6 Therefore hath the curse devoured the earth, and they that dwell therein are desolate: therefore the inhabitants of the earth are* **burned***…18 And it shall come to pass, that he who fleeth from the noise of the fear shall fall into the pit; and he that cometh up out of the midst of the pit shall be taken in the snare: for the windows from on high are open, and the foundations of the earth do shake. The earth is utterly broken down, the earth is clean dissolved, the earth is moved exceedingly. The earth shall reel to and fro like a drunkard, and shall be removed like a cottage; and the transgression thereof shall be heavy upon it; and it shall fall, and not rise again. And it shall come to pass* **in that day, that the LORD shall punish the host of the high ones that are on high***, and the kings of the earth upon the earth, and they shall be gathered together, as prisoners are gathered in the pit, and shall be shut up in the prison, and after many days*

> *shall they be visited....23 Then the moon shall be confounded, and **the sun ashamed**, when the LORD of hosts shall reign in mount Zion, and in Jerusalem, and before his ancients gloriously.*

In other words it looks like around the time of the Lord's coming there is going to be a period of burning and lots of darkness.

This is a good example of first of all, how some things in the Old Testament are history by the time we're reading it and some of them are prophecy. Now since they use similar language, this is what we need to remember: it did happen a certain way and it was described a certain way so we should probably be careful about reading back into Isaiah 13 what Isaiah 13 should be instructing us instead to read into Revelation.

> *Joel 2:1 Blow ye the trumpet in Zion, and sound an alarm in my holy mountain: let all the inhabitants of the land tremble: for the day of the LORD cometh, for it is nigh at hand; A day of darkness and of gloomi- ness, a day of clouds and of thick darkness, as the morning spread upon the mountains: a great people and a strong; **there hath not been ever the like, neither shall be any more after it.***

What does that sound like? "There has never been a time like this up to this time, there will never be a time like this after this time." It sounds like what Jesus said in the Olivet Discourse: there has never been a time of tribulation like this ever before. It will be a time of great tribulation; it's never happened like this before and it will never happen again. Jesus was using Joel's language. Jesus was using Old Testament material and so what the reader of the New Testament needs to decide is: was this something that was already fulfilled or is this something that has yet to be fulfilled?

> *Joel 2:3 A fire devoureth before them; and behind them a flame burneth.*

That looks like lots of heat; that looks like people are being burned up.

Think about Revelation, the fourth vial. Was that John's perspective…an angel pouring something out on the sun? Can you think of other times in the book of Revelation where John is saying something and it's a matter of his viewpoint? How about chapter 6 of Revelation where he says, "I saw something under something"? The only way it makes sense is if it's a matter of perspective. Was it a matter of, "From my perspective it looks like they're standing below the altar"? He's in the spirit, he was in heaven in chapter 4 and now he's back on earth in chapter 9, 10, 11. It's really hard to tell sometimes where he's standing but let's just say that he's in a localized place known as heaven or we could say that he's on the isle of Patmos in the body seeing visions which is what chapter 1 says. Let's leave a little bit of room here for writer's perspective. We know that you can fit like 10,000 earths in the sun so I don't think that it's improbable that when John looked and saw an angel pouring out his vial on the sun it was an angel standing close to him in the sun's silhouette, perhaps. Remember, he's seeing a vision so we don't know that an angel actually dumps wrath on the sun. It's poetic. It's a vision. It's something he sees. Could I say that the sun got so hot that it burned people? Yes, that's the plain sense of the reading. I do believe what is not poetic is that the sun gets hot. At some time here in the last 3 ½ years of the tribulation, I'm not sure that someone's going to be able to look up from the earth and see an angel pouring out wrath on the sun.

If John were prophesying of a hurricane, he may have said, "I saw an angel pouring wrath out on the Atlantic Ocean and it stirred up and went into the eastern seaboard of the United States."

Revelation 8:12 And the fourth angel sounded, and the third part of the sun was smitten.

Did you notice how the trumpets and the vials go together up until now? You have trumpets 2 and 3 were about bloodying the waters and becoming bitter. Vials 2 and 3, the same thing. Here's trumpet four, vial four: they both affect the sun. Here, a 1/3 of the sun's power is gone.

Revelation 7:9 After this I beheld, and, lo, a great multitude, which no man could number, of all nations, and kindreds, and people, and tongues, stood before the throne, and before the Lamb, clothed with white robes, and palms in their hands; And cried with a loud voice, saying, Salva- tion to our God which sitteth upon the throne, and unto the Lamb. And all the angels stood round about the throne, and about the elders and the four beasts, and fell before the throne on their faces, and worshipped God, Saying, Amen: Blessing, and glory, and wisdom, and thanksgiving, and honour, and power, and might, be unto our God for ever and ever. Amen. And one of the elders answered, saying unto me, What are these which are arrayed in white robes? and whence came they?" Where did they come from? "And I said unto him, Sir," so he said to one of the 24 elders, "Sir, thou knowest. And he said to me, These are they which came out of great tribulation, and have washed their robes, and made them white in the blood of the Lamb.

The first thing I want us to remember: here's the last 3 ½ years of the tribulation period. The sense of the original language is these are they that are "coming out of great tribulation." They are coming out. So little by little, these people are leaving the earth. And how are they doing it? They washed their robes white in the blood of the Lamb, that's usually short term, verse 14, that's usually a way of saying that they died and paid for their faith with their lives. This is why we say that Revelation is another Exodus or the ultimate Exodus because it tells the story of how the people of God leave the earth or are rescued from the Egypt of the world. Now, let's remember something here as we get into verse 15: what were the two things that were described as putting men in torment in the fourth vial? Two elements really? Heat and the sun.

> *Revelation 7:15 Therefore are they before the throne of God, and serve him day and night in his temple: and he that sitteth on the throne shall dwell among them. They shall hunger no more, neither thirst any more,* **neither shall the sun light on them, nor any heat.** *For the Lamb which is in the midst of the throne shall feed them, and shall lead them unto living fountains of waters: and*

God shall wipe away all tears from their eyes.

So little by little, many if not most of the Christians are dying and are leaving the earth, and John wants you to remember this heat and sun later on in chapter 16 occur when there is a significant decrease of Christian activity on the earth at that time. Do you remember in the trumpets it says that the people who had the mark of God on their foreheads were not affected. The question is: is that just 144,000 Jews or is that everyone? Revelation 3:12 and 22:4 seems to say that it is all believers. Of course Christ is branding us because he's the Master, right? So the promise to the church of Philadelphia in 3:10 is not "Now, before I fulfill that promise, I'm going to jerk you out of here." No, there are people in the book of Revelation who have the name of God on them and those who are being tormented by the sun during the fourth vial hate the fact they're being tormented by the sun and there's a group of people that aren't and they just so happen to have the name of God on them and so the others blaspheme that name. The reason people hate us and hate God mostly is because they see that we're in the middle of turmoil, and we're not losing our minds. Let's remember that in the Exodus which is the pre-Revelation (or you could call Revelation the ultimate Exodus) the Israelites were safe from all the plagues in Goshen. They are being sheltered in some supernatural way.

    Even after the 10 plagues on Egypt, the last one being the death of the first born, people and livestock, Pharaoh still changed his mind and pursued the Israelites. Their army, chariots, footmen, whomever stood on the banks of the Red Sea and watched the water part allowing God's people to cross on dry land. They would have had to thought about all of the events that only God could have done in the past several weeks in Egypt, and known that the parting of the sea was not a natural phenomenon. Did they actually believe that if it was God providing a means of escape for His people that He was going to let the Egyptians recapture them? If they did make it across and rounded up the people, who was going to keep the "land bridge" open or re-open it if had closed after them?

You see, people whose heart is "evil and desperately wicked" don't have logical thoughts or follow practical actions much like the blind men of Sodom who still grope for the door. Thus, while the narrative in Revelation 16 doesn't make sense to us—it makes perfect sense based on who men really are; products of their father the Devil.

16:10-11

And the fifth angel poured out his vial upon the seat of the beast; And with that same tongue, isn't it ironic…they blaspheme in verse 11. When you see this fifth vial, do you think of that might have happened earlier in Scripture? The plague of darkness in Egypt back in Exodus, right?

> *Revelation 2:12 And to the angel of the church in Pergamos write; These things saith he which hath the sharp sword with two edges; I know thy works, and where thou dwellest, even **where Satan's seat** is: and thou holdest fast my name, and hast not denied my faith.*

See notes on **2:12**, and know that if a pagan temple in Pergamos is known as "Satan's seat" and if precedence means anything, then when you get to chapter 16, what would you expect the beast's seat to be? A temple of some sort. You say, "Well, that's just a guess." Okay, maybe, but it's a good guess; it's an educated guess; it's an informed guess.

> *2 Thessalonians 2:1 Now we beseech you, brethren, by the coming of our Lord Jesus Christ, and by our gathering together unto him, That ye be not soon shaken in mind, or be troubled, neither by spirit, nor by word, nor by letter as from us, as that the day of Christ is at hand. Let no man deceive you by any means: for that day shall not come, except there come an apostasy first, and that man of sin be revealed, the son of perdition. 4 Who opposeth and exalteth himself above all that is called God, or that is worshipped; so that he as God sitteth **in the temple** of God, shewing himself that he is God.*

So does the beast have a temple? Yes. It looks like this particular plague is poured out, that is it is centralized, I'm not saying it's only in Jerusalem on this temple but I am saying that it is focused there. It says it. I'm just going to believe what I read. Remember now, if you don't care what the reader would have thought when he read the letter of Revelation, you would never know what the people of Pergamos would have thought when they heard "Satan's seat." It's very important that we study what the reader would have thought.

In Pergamos was the seat of Satan. Here it's the seat of the beast so just like the people of Pergamos would have thought a temple ("Temple of Zeus") when they heard "seat of Satan," those same readers probably would have thought the "seat of the beast" in chapter 16 was a temple.

and his kingdom was full of darkness; Consider Exodus 10. There were ten plagues. Here is the 9th.

> *Exodus 10:21 And the LORD said unto Moses, Stretch out thine hand toward heaven, **that there may be darkness** over the land of Egypt, even darkness which may be felt.*

Darkness that can be felt? You might have some idea what blackness that can be felt feels like if you've ever been in a place where there's absolutely no light. I think we were down several hundred feet in Mammoth Caves in Kentucky. The guide said, "Now I'm going to do something some of you have never experienced before in your life. I'm going to turn off the light and you're going to see absolute darkness." It's hard for us to imagine this because even when you turn off the lights in our rooms in our homes, we've got alarm clocks and cellphone chargers, tablets that come on every time there's a sports update, street lights coming through the blinds. In any case, we don't have any idea what this is like but I'm willing to tell you, if you've ever experienced that, there we were and that tour guide turned off their light and, I mean, it was so dark that you'd almost panic.

> *Exodus 10:22 And Moses stretched forth his hand toward heaven; and there was a thick darkness in **all the land of Egypt** three days.*

Folks, it says "all." All the land of Egypt. Please look at the next verse,

> *Exodus 10:23 They saw not one another, neither rose any from his place for three days.*

Again, there's that incapacitation where you're just sitting around thinking, "What in the world can I do? I can't see a thing. Every time I try to light a candle, the match goes out." Nothing works. Look at the next phrase, "but all the children of Israel had light in their dwellings." There is darkness where? "In all the land of Egypt." At this point in the chronology, where are the Israelites? In Egypt; in Goshen which is a part of the land of Egypt.

So How is it possible that both can be true? It must mean "all except the dwellings of the people of God" so when we see in the book of Revelation "all the earth" or "all earth dwellers," the precedent is set in Exodus for us to see "all except the people of God." There it is. There is your precedent. I don't care if you like it. It doesn't matter. It's right there on the page. We've got to be willing to be instructed through the Scripture. It says "all of Egypt was dark," yet the people of God are still in Egypt and they had light so when we see absolute statements in the book of Revelation—I know I'm saying it a second time, I'm doing it for your blood pressure—when we do see in the book of Revelation that all earth dwellers were punished, it means all and since John is writing the ultimate Exodus, it means "all except the people of God who are still on earth." Remember, chapter 7 says "these are they that are coming out of great tribula- tion." As they're being killed by the wicked one, as they're being persecuted, they are conducting the great Exodus to be culminated with what we would call, the rapture, that I believe we proved conclusively under the seventh trumpet in Revelation 11. As absurd as it might be for us to conceive of an idea where the whole world has blood to drink, except believers; all the world is covered with sores, except believers; all the world is being burned by the sun, except believers…that precedence was set in the book of Exodus. If it wasn't hard for us to believe it's an historical fact, we shouldn't have a hard time believing it's future too and that if you have the mark of God upon you, if your name is in the book of life from the foundation of the world (Revelation 13:8 and 17:8) and you don't worship the beast's image or have his mark, then you are sheltered from these plagues. It's not as glamorous, perhaps, as a great escape but I think it brings more honor to God to protect you in the storm. We have people here in the book of Exodus being saved from the wrath of God and they're still in Egypt so it's not necessary to assume that you're snatched out of something to be saved from it, that you can actually be saved in it.

> *Isaiah 26:19 Thy dead men shall live, together with my dead body shall they **arise**. Awake and sing, **ye that dwell in dust**: for thy dew is as the dew of herbs, and the earth shall **cast out the dead**. 20 Come, my people, enter thou into thy chambers, and shut thy doors about thee: hide thyself as it were for a little moment, **until the indignation be overpast**. For, behold, the LORD cometh out of his place to **punish the inhabitants of the earth** for their iniquity: the earth also shall disclose her blood, and shall no more cover her slain. 27:1 In that day the LORD with his sore and great and strong sword **shall punish leviathan the piercing ser- pent**, even leviathan that crooked serpent; and he shall slay **the dragon that is in the sea**.*

What does Revelation say the serpent and the dragon are (see 20:1-3)? They're Satan. So the punishment of Satan happens sometime around when he dumps his indigna- tion upon the earth and he protects his people in the middle of it.

and they gnawed their tongues for pain, 11. And blasphemed the God of heaven because of their pains and their sores, and repented not of their deeds. If you believe man is evil enough, you believe God has to elect some or everyone goes to hell. If you have people who are being punished by God with sores on the top of their heads, the soles of their feet; they're drinking blood; they're scorched by the sun, and now it's so dark they can feel it—while none of the believers who are outside the mark of the beast are experiencing that—you would think that that would cause them to fall on their face before the Lord. But they don't because they hate God. This is a picture of human nature. If you were to go down to hell right now and open the door and say, "All you have to do is believe on Christ," they would curse in your face and slam the door shut. Don't ever forget that. We are not as good as we think we are. Without Christ, we would curse God, stomp on Jesus, do despite to the Holy Spirit and hap- pily go to hell versus repenting towards God and putting faith in Jesus. Bunk on a man-centered theology that says, "No, I would believe on Jesus if I were just..." No, no, you love your sin and you hate God and I do too outside of Christ.

It's not that they're blind to him; it's not that they don't know who's responsible for this. They do know and they're blaspheming him. Who do they resemble in this act of blasphemy? In the context they just take on the personality of the one whom they follow. They start mirroring the antichrist because in chapter 13:6 this is what the antichrist did; that's what the beast did is he blasphemed the God of heaven and so when you take his mark and worship his image, you end up blaspheming the God of heaven.

> *Revelation 11:6 [The two witnesses] have power to shut heaven, that it rain not in the days of their prophecy: and have power over waters to turn them to blood, and to smite the earth with all plagues, as often as they will. And when they shall have finished their testimony, the beast that ascendeth out of the bottomless pit shall make war against them, and shall overcome them, and kill them. And their dead bodies shall lie in the street of the great city, which spiritually is called Sodom and Egypt, where also our Lord was crucified. And they of the people and kindreds and tongues and nations shall see their dead bodies three days and an half, and shall not suffer their dead bodies to be put in graves. And they that dwell upon the earth shall rejoice over them, and make merry, and shall send gifts one to another; because these*

two prophets tormented them that dwelt on the earth. And after three days and an half the Spirit of life from God entered into them, and they stood upon their feet; and great fear fell upon them which saw them. And they heard a great voice from heaven saying unto them, Come up hither. And they ascended up to heaven in a cloud; and their enemies beheld them. And the same hour was there a great earthquake, and the tenth part of the city fell and there were slain of men seven thousand: and ***the remnant were affrighted, and gave glory to the God of heaven.***

So we have people here repenting during that ministry. Some people in the location or the locality or at least the relative nearness of these witnesses are repenting, and they're part of the remnant. They are giving God the glory. They're not profaning God. If, based on 11:14, these two witnesses are bringing plagues upon the earth and these plagues are the plagues of the seven vials, these two groups of people are living at the same time and both "repenting and giving glory to the God of Heaven" and "repenting not and blaspheming the God of Heaven."

I guess the fifth vial takes place with the sixth seal. I am only guessing since during the sixth seal the sun and the moon become dark. It would seem hard to have the sun dark and then so bright it is burning people.

16:12

And the sixth angel poured out his vial upon the great river Euphrates; and the water thereof was dried up, that the way of the kings of the east might be prepared. " The way of the kings of the east. That leaves a lot of room for guessing and you know a lot of empires have changed, but we have seen kings before in the book of Revelation, haven't we? We have known of ten kings. So, we have these kings of the east that are able to get now to what the Old Testament says will be the focus which should be Jerusalem. The location of this war, however, is given in 16:16: "Armageddon." Also, Megiddo which means "crowded hill" is its name. It's where a young king who did great things for God died in a battle. His name was Josiah. Josiah became king at age 8, the second youngest king in the history of Judah. Joash was the youngest at age 7 so Josiah was king at age 8 and he finally died in a town somewhere the valley of Megiddo, the valley of Armageddon. So this is a real place and it's a real place that's not far from Jerusalem. The reader should be prepared to believe that this was fulfilled, in part, when the kingdom of Christ came without observation (Luke 17:30-31). Consider how those who prayed believed Psalm 2:6 was fulfilled in their day (Acts 4).

> *Joel 3:1 For, behold, in those days [after the events of Joel 2 which surround the 6th Seal] and in that time, when I shall bring again the captivity of Judah and Jerusalem, I will also gather all nations, and will bring them down into the valley of Jehoshaphat [meaning "the Lord Jehovah is Judge] 2.* **I will also gather all nations, and will bring them down** *into the valley known as the place where Jehovah judges, and will plead with them there for my people and for my heritage Israel, whom they have scattered among the nations, and parted my land…9 Proclaim ye this among the Gentiles; Prepare war, wake up the mighty men, let all the men of war draw near; let them come up: Beat your plowshares into swords, and your pruninghooks into spears….11. Assemble yourselves, and come, all ye heathen, and* **gather yourselves together round about***: thither cause thy mighty ones to come down, O LORD. Let the heathen be wakened, and come up to the valley of where Jehovah judges, Jehoshaphat: for there will I sit to judge all the heathen round about. Put ye in the sickle, for the harvest is ripe. Get you down; for the press is full, the fats overflow; for their wickedness is great. Multitudes, multitudes in the valley of deci- sion: for the day of the LORD is near in the valley of decision. 15.* **The sun and the moon shall be darkened, and the stars shall withdraw their shining.** *The LORD also shall roar out of Zion, and utter his voice from Jerusalem; and the heavens and the earth shall shake: but the LORD will be the hope of his people, and the strength of the children of Israel. So shall ye know that I am the LORD your God dwelling in Zion, my holy*

mountain: ***then shall Jerusalem be holy, and there shall no strangers pass through her any more.***

16:13

And I saw three unclean spirits like frogs come out of the mouth of the dragon,
We first see the dragon in chapter 12, and he is Satan (12:9).

and out of the mouth of the beast, The first place that we see the beast is in Revelation 13.

and out of the mouth of the false prophet. We see him first in Chapter 13 as well: And I beheld another beast coming up out of the earth; and he had two horns like a lamb, and he spake as a dragon."

16:14

For they are the spirits of devils, these unclean spirits that are coming out of the dragon, the beast and the false prophet are "spirits of devils." Some Bibles have "demons." **working miracles.** 1 Kings 22 tells a story and it involves, believe it or not, Jehoshaphat and not just Jehoshaphat but King Ahab. Together they were kings over the 12 tribes of Israel. It was time for Ahab to die and God had to get Ahab to a particular battle to get him killed. They asked for all the prophets to tell King Ahab what to do and all the prophets who were false prophets, told King Ahab, "Go ahead and go up to that battle and you'll do just fine. You're going to conquer them."

King Jehoshaphat said, "Ahab, there's no way in the world that I think that any of your prophets know God if they met him in the middle of the road and shook his hand," in so many words. That's the Sturm paraphrase. He said, "Isn't there another prophet?" And Ahab says, "There is a prophet. His name is Micaiah but I hate him because he only speaks negative about me." So they went and got Micaiah out of his house. He was never hanging around with the prophets of Ahab, he was at his house, probably making oatmeal or something and he went up to his front door and said, "Ahab wants to talk to you." He said, "Ahab doesn't want to talk to me. He's not going to get any good news out of me." "He wants you to come so shave and get your stuff on and come out to the chariot." He gets in the chariot, they roll on back to the place where, I think, Samaria where Ahab and Jehoshaphat were and Jehoshaphat says, "Please tell us what we're supposed to do about this battle." This is what Micaiah said, "Well, here's what I saw. I saw the Lord in heaven and all the host of heaven were around him and God said, 'What should I do to get Ahab to go up to Ramoth-gilead?' I saw one of the spirits come before God and say, 'I'll go and be a lying spirit in the mouth of his prophets' and God said, 'Sounds like a plan.'"

So, here we have in the valley of Jehoshaphat something happening. Spirit beings are being used to tell lies to get kings to the valley of Jehoshaphat. What an amazing parallel! We have these false spirits of devils working miracles probably working mir- acles through people. They go forth to kings of the earth and of the whole world to gather them to battle, that great day of God Almighty. You have false prophets with the power of false spirits working miracles. You know Jews who love miracles will fall prey to this in the first 3 ½ years. They'll love to have a Messiah figure that does miracles like Moses.

great day of God Almighty. As you look at 1:8 through verse 12, look at who is talking in verse 8: "I am Alpha and Omega, I am the Almighty." It also says in verse 11, "I am Alpha and Omega, the first and the last," so who is saying it in verse 8, who is saying it in verse 11? Verse 12 says, "I turned to see the voice," and who had the voice that said, "I am Alpha and Omega, I am first and the last, I am the Almighty?" The Son of man. Who would you say that is? It is Jesus. Who is claiming to be the "Almighty" in this Scripture but Christ?

So we understand that in chapter 16 when it says to gather them together to the great day of God Almighty it is also the day of Christ, the day of Jesus. Whoa, I don't know if you just caught what we just said: The day of Christ happens in chapter 16 of Revelation.

Philippians 1:6 He that begun a good work in you will perform it until **the day of Jesus Christ**.

What? The Holy Spirit inside of you is going to perform a work and we say until the day of the rapture? The rapture happens during the day of Christ but apparently there's something else that happens around that time period too: the battle of Armageddon. Paul talks about the day of Christ six more times.

16:15

If you have a Bible that has the words of Christ in red, a few people might have those Bibles, you find this verse kind of jumps off the page at you because it's in red. In the ESV rendering, it actually has the verse in a parenthetical sense.

> *(Behold, I am coming like a thief! Blessed is the one who stays awake, keeping his garments on, that he may not go about naked and be seen exposed!)*

The King James rendering is, **Blessed is the one that watches**, I think is how it makes particular reference to it. There's a strategic placement to this verse. What is it doing here? Looking at the surrounding context, If I hear news reports of the Euphrates River drying up and being able to be used as a means of entrance into the Middle East, I know that the coming of Christ is drawing near. I don't have to be caught off guard. I'm not like the master of the house who wasn't watching for the thief and was clueless; I know what the signs are.

With verses 14 and 15 mentioning of Armageddon and then this promise of a coming like a thief, we don't have a pre-trib scenario. Every pre-tribulation rapturist believes that the Battle of Armageddon occurs at the end of the tribulation. This verse is either just incredibly out of place there, or we've got Christ coming very near to the Battle of Armageddon.

Someone say, "Well, this isn't the pre-trib rapture." Agreed, you can't use post- trib lingo that Christ uses in Matthew 24,[4] Paul uses in 1 Thessalonians 5,[5] Peter uses in 2 Peter 3[6] and John uses in Revelation 16 and say that it points to a pre-tribulation rapture just because it says "thief in the night." When one uses that language and quote those verses in support of a pre-tribulation rapture, you are ripping the verses out of their context.

The thief in the night is used in the sense of the coming of Christ: Matthew 24:43; Luke 12:39, those are parallel accounts; 1 Thessalonians 5, it is used twice, in verse 2 and verse 4; Peter's reference to the Day of the Lord, that's 2 Peter 3:10; and then twice in Revelation. The thing I want to bring to the reader's attention is that it's not a good thing that Jesus comes to me as a thief. It means you're not ready. Paul, in Thessalonians, says that he doesn't come to you like a thief, he comes to those in the darkness like a thief. He clearly distinguishes the language.

Jesus compares the time of his coming with the time of Noah. It's not every day you see a boat being built that's 450 feet long. To say that the coming of Christ is like that of the coming of Noah and then to say that it's sign-less is ridiculous. Are you trying to tell me that there were no signs that a flood was happening? How about preaching for 100 years? How about building a boat for close to 100 years? How often do you see animals approaching 2 x 2 and in groups of seven for the clean animals? How often do you see them all coming to a ship. So Jesus says the days before His *parousia*, which Paul says is the same thing as "our gathering together unto him" in 2 Thessalonians 2:1, is just like the days preceding the time of Noah.

Now, this is great: right before the flood starts happening, right before the door is shut, Noah and his family are done building the boat, the animals are in the boat, and seven days passed between the time that the ship was built, the animals were in the ark, everything is ready to go and God waited seven more days before the flood- waters came. Seven days. Isn't that something?

Reconsider 3:5

He that overcometh, the same shall be clothed in white raiment;

and I will not blot out his name out of the book of life, but I will confess his name before my Father, and before his angels.

In each of the seven churches, we're seeing a pattern: he introduces himself, he says here's what I like about you, here's what I don't like about you and here's what you can expect. If you are an overcomer, you can expect white raiment, you can expect your name in the book of life and you can expect to have your name confessed before God and the angels.

So, along with the coming as a thief, I want us to pay special attention as well to the garment talk because when we turn back to 3:5, this is going to look really familiar. He said, "Blessed is he that watcheth and keeps his garments lest they walk naked." So, we're looking for the thief and we're looking for the garment talk.

And to the angel of the church in Sardis write: 'The words of him who has the seven spirits of God and the seven stars. 'I know your works. You have the reputation of being alive, but you are dead. Wake up, and strengthen what remains and is about to die, for I have not found your works complete in the sight of my God. Remember, then, what you received and heard. Keep it, and repent. If you will not wake up, I will come like a thief, and you will not know at what hour I will come against you. 4. You have a few names even in Sardis which have not defiled their garments and they shall walk with me in white for they are worthy. He that overcomes, **the same shall be clothed in white raiment.**

Here is garment talk which goes hand-in- hand with particular reference to "the thief in the night." So, what kind of pre-tribber ever uses Sardis? Never. They jump to Philadelphia, but what about this? Here, He's talking to saints who are going to live in the last half of the tribulation period.

So, if you're in Sardis and the Book of Revelation is to you—six other churches, yes—but to you and you get to chapter 16 of Revelation, are you going to think that Christ is talking about two different groups—one in chapter 3 and another in chapter 16? Of course not.

All seven of these churches are given a promise if they will "overcome." Now, what kind of sense does it make for Jesus through the pen of John to address seven churches, tell each and every one of them that you have a special blessing if you overcome and then remove them before they overcome anything (in view of Revelation 12:10-11 & 15:1-2)? "Blessed are you if you overcome and you'll get this. Blessed are you if you overcome, you'll get this." He does it seven times and then removes them before anyone overcomes anything.

Now, granted, all of these believers are dead now but they were expecting it to shortly come to pass (chapter 1). John said that these things could happen at any moment; that they would start happening. Jesus used the same language in Luke 21, "When you begin to see these things look up."

Remember, this letter concerning Daniel's 70the week is written not to Jews, but to churches. These churches are given a forecast of a time when they would, as saints, need to overcome the dragon and the beast. They are told, "Be ready to overcome," and then they're raptured out before there's even any need to overcome? That's ridiculous. The warnings in the seven letters to the seven churches have absolutely nothing to do with chapters 4-19? No way. It's almost as though there are two books. John says, "I am going to warn you about a tribulation period that you're not going to experience because you're going to be raptured?" No. "We're going to tell you about it, we're going to warn you about it. In fact, we're even going to tell one of the churches, 'If you don't repent, I'm going to cast you into great tribulation.' So, we're going to warn you about it, we're going to tell you about it and then before you ever need to worry about it, we're yanking you out of here. That doesn't make any sense. We go to chapter 4 and, "After this I looked and behold a door." There is nothing that gives us any indication that he's not still writing to the seven churches.

Reconsider 4:1

John, you might notice in verse 2, is not in the body. Well, if he's not in the body, that hardly counts as a rapture of the church because the rapture of the church are people being translated in their bodies. They have bodies; they are glorified bodies. So, if John is a picture of the church at the rapture, it's a lousy picture because he comes back in chapter 9. So, all of a sudden, if he's the church when he goes up in chapter 4, he is the church when he comes down during the trumpets half way through the tribulation period? I don't think so.

There are just so many reasons why it doesn't work but probably the most pro- nounced is that John the Apostle is God's last canonical word and we're supposed to believe that John believed that the next event on the calendar for the church was a pre-tribulation rapture and he didn't even care enough about it to tell us. Think about that. He even says the purpose of this book is to tell you about the unveiling of Christ and he doesn't even mention something that happens seven years before that that is the next event on the calendar?

Reconsider Matthew 24

It's not much different than suggesting that the Olivet Discourse is not for Christians, it's for Jews. Why did we baptize Sunday if it's to the Jews? Matthew 28 is to the same group of disciples minus Judas. So if you have to have those disciples representing two different groups—sometimes they represent Israel and sometimes they represent the church—we have no idea when is when. In Matthew 18, it's the church. We get our passage for church discipline from this very idea, "tell it to the church."

How about when they're giving the Lord's Supper in chapter 26? All of a sudden it's not a church ordinance. You can't be Baptist and be pre-trib. All of a sudden, we're not baptizing and we're not doing the Lord's Supper. It's Jews. So, what you have is this selective application of particular texts to particular groups without any legend to tell me when to do what. That's, in essence, what we're dealing with here. Unless you understand that the seven references to thief in the night in Matthew, Luke, Thessalo- nians, Peter and Revelation are all making reference to the Second Coming of Christ that comes after the tribulation. Once you see that, then it just makes perfect sense. It all falls right in place and you don't have to do gymnastics with the text. And that's what we're trying to achieve here.

I wanted to make sure that you understood that the references to Jesus' coming as the thief in the night are not references to a pre-tribulation rapture but instead are references to the coming of Christ that occurs after the tribulation. That was our main point and we started it in Revelation 16 and we called to your attention the particular location of that verse. Look at it in the context of the seven bowl judgments and the verses placed after number six and just before seven and there's the particular reference to the Battle of Armageddon right there. Think about that before you make a conclusion that thief in the night equals pre-tribulation rapture. That's what we want you to do. Think about that and then study Matthew 24 and study 1 Thessalonians 5 for your- self and see what you come away with, with regard to the thief in the night concept.

Chapter 19

19:1

And after these things I heard a great voice of much people in heaven, saying, Alleluia; "Alleluia" is really a Hebrew word that's found in the New Testament and it means "praise to Jehovah" or "praise the Lord" and it's only used in the New Testa- ment here. I'll say that again: this word in the New Testament is only used here and it's used four times. Then, look at verse 5, the middle of the verse. You have a voice coming out of the throne saying, "Praise our God" so that voice is speaking in Greek. So, really the word is used five times in this passage of Scripture. I would say probably that this is that same group of people as in Revelation 7:9 and following. This is that multitude of which no man can number. These are they that are coming out of great tribulation and they have washed their robes and made them white in the blood of the Lamb.

19:2

For true and righteous are his judgments: for he hath judged the great whore, which did corrupt the earth with her fornication, and hath avenged the blood of his servants at her hand.

> *Revelation 17:1 And there came one of the seven angels which had the seven vials, and talked with me, saying unto me, Come hither; I will shew unto thee the judgment of the great whore that sitteth upon many waters: With whom the kings of the earth have committed* **fornication***, and the inhabitants of the earth have been made drunk with* **the** *wine of her* **fornication***….4 And the woman was arrayed in purple and scarlet colour, and decked with gold and precious stones and pearls, having a golden cup in her hand full of abominations and filthiness of her* **fornication.** *5 And upon her forehead was a name written, Mystery Babylon the Great, the Mother of* **Harlots.**

She is loose and we remember from chapter 14 that we're dealing here with the city of Jerusalem. Let me show you something here. Also, 18:18 calls her a "great city." So you see that in 17:1 one of the seven angels that had bowls of wrath showed John this woman who is known as the whore who is a great city. There are at least 10 examples of how the Great Whore of Babylon is being placed in distinction with the bride of the Lamb. There is clearly a parallel between chapters 17 and 18 description of the great whore and chapter 21 and 22 description of the bride of Christ.

19:3-4

4 And the four and twenty elders and the four beasts fell down and worshipped God that sat on the throne, saying, Amen; Alleluia. Very little has changed. Seven years probably, 15 chapters and God is still on his throne and the 24 elders and the four beasts are still worshiping him.

19:8

And to her was granted that she should be arrayed in fine linen, clean and white: for the fine linen is the righteousness of saints. With all these Genesis-Revelation parallels, one would wonder why there is "clean, fine, white linen" instead of the nakedness Adam and Eve had before the curse.

19:8

And he saith unto me, Write, Blessed are they which are called unto the marriage supper of the Lamb. And he saith unto me, These are the true sayings of God. First I'd like to point out that the marriage supper of the Lamb takes place when Christ comes again as He returns in Revelation 19. This is not some sort of supper that takes place in heaven with believers like pre-tribulation rapturists teach; that it takes place for seven years in heaven during the tribulation period. The first reference to the "Marriage Supper of the Lamb" is in Revelation 19--or if we want to rephrase it we could say "the marriage feast of the Son of

God." It would seem that we should wonder if John the Revelator was party to any conversations that Christ might have led in this whole idea of a marriage supper or a feast.

> *Matthew 8:10 Jesus heard it, he marvelled, Verily I say unto you, I have not found so great faith, no, not in Israel. And he said, many shall come from the east and west, and* **shall sit down** *with Abraham, and Isaac, and Jacob, in the kingdom of heaven.*

There is going to be feasting in the kingdom of heaven. So, right away, if this is the marriage supper of the Lamb, then you understand why it takes place not until the coming of Christ when he comes to set up his kingdom. You say, "Well, he comes before then." Well, actually, Paul told Timothy in 2 Timothy 4:1, "I charge thee before God who will judge the quick and the dead." When? "At his appearing in his kingdom." So, if those two items happen at the same time which is the natural reading of that passage, then that means that he sets up his kingdom when he appears. In other words, he will not appear until it's time to set up his kingdom and when he sets up his kingdom in Matthew 8, he says that'll be the time of sitting down and eating and drinking.

> *Matthew 22:2* **The kingdom of heaven is like unto a certain king, which made a marriage** *for his son, and sent forth his servants to call them that were bidden to the wedding: and they would not come. Again, he sent forth other servants, saying, Tell them which are bidden, Behold, I have prepared* **my dinner**: *my oxen and my fatlings are killed, and all things are ready: come unto the marriage. But they made light of it, and went their ways, one to his farm, another to his merchandise. And the remnant took his servants, and entreated them spitefully, and slew them. But when the king heard thereof, he was wroth: and he sent forth his armies, and destroyed those murderers, and burned up their city. Then saith he to his servants, The wedding is ready, but they which were bidden were not worthy. Go ye therefore into the highways, and as many as ye shall find, bid to the marriage. So those servants went out into the highways, and gathered together*

all as many as they found, both bad and good: and the wedding was furnished with guests. And when the king came in to see the guests, he saw there a man which had not on a wedding garment: And he saith unto him, Friend, how camest thou in hither not having a wedding garment? And he was speechless. Then said the king to the servants, Bind him hand and foot, and take him away, and cast him into outer darkness; there shall be weeping and gnashing of teeth. For many are called, but few are chosen.

Interesting: we have the Son of God and we have a calling to the marriage. Now, that's almost a copy of what is found in Revelation 19 and yet, Jesus said this is what the kingdom is like. So the kingdom is like a wedding feast. Please notice that neither in Revelation 19 do we find the bride being called to a wedding nor do we see a bride here in Matthew 22. No bride here at all. In fact, they are called guests. I think this answers the question as to who populates the millennial kingdom. These are Jews who have not believed on Christ as their Messiah but are coming as guests and, I think, will believe on Christ during the millennial age. Hopefully, early but in any case, they will not have glorified bodies because they are not born-again yet they are invited as guests. "Why Jews and not Gentiles?" Well, I think in this case Jesus is speaking to Jews, contextually. That is certainly not to say that some Gentiles, who like these Jews have not heard of Jesus of Nazareth being the Messiah, will not be "guests" at this wedding.

Some people would say, "Well, the guests are believers from other dispensations." I have a problem with that: I believe that believers of every dispensation are part of the bride. You have two choices according to Paul in 1 Corinthians 15: you're either "in Adam" with his curse or "in Christ" with his life. That's Romans 5 and 1 Corinthians 15. Now, if it's possible to be somewhere in between—neither in Christ nor in Adam—then I could see where you could say there is a third group, those who are saved but not yet in Christ but Romans 5 and 1 Corinthians 15 give us really two choices: in Adam where you die and in Christ where you are made alive.[24] I don't believe you can say that the Old Testament saint of today who is in heaven, is not in Christ nor do I believe that you are going to talk about some future group of special dispensation of tribulation saints that were part of the guests. No, I don't believe these are saints at all. I believe these are people who have come to the wedding feast and came prepared for the kingdom.

How is it that people who are saved and in Christ are guests (Matthew 22)? The reason the bride is not mentioned in Matthew 22 is because the bride was a Pauline mystery at this point and I believe that they were being invited at least as guests or as attendants to the bride.

> *Luke 22:17 Take and divide it among yourselves: For I say unto you, I will not drink of the fruit of the vine,* **until the kingdom of God shall come.**

We're looking for a time when the kingdom comes? You mean, it's not existent in the heavens during a seven year tribulation period? No, you will have to wait until he comes to enjoy the kingdom which is likened to a marriage supper.

Now, is it a literal supper? I believe we'll have suppers there but the parables of Christ tell us that the kingdom itself is the supper, the marriage feast of the Lamb. I don't know how that looks exactly; I don't know all the components; I don't know if everyone who is in the millennium will be able to partake. But I do know this: if you're living now and you go into the millennium because you've been saved or somehow you have been a nation as described in the later part of Matthew 25 there, you'll not see the kingdom at all. The kingdom itself is the marriage feast of the Lamb and that those who are married to him are the saved or those who are invited or "called" to the marriage supper of the Lamb.[25]

---

[24] Which makes the discussion of infant salvation particularly interesting.

[25] Perhaps we see an invitation to the masses upon earth in verse 9 while we await the population of heaven in verse 14?

19:10

And I fell at his feet to worship him. And he said unto me, See thou do it not: I am thy fellowservant, and of thy brethren that have the testimony of Jesus. wor- ship God: for the testimony "Testimony" comes from the word *martyr*. **of Jesus is the spirit of prophecy.** What does it mean to say the spirit of prophecy is the testi- mony of Jesus?" Well, the Spirit of God comes from the word *pneuma*. What word do you see there that we use a lot today? Pneumatic (air powered) tools, right? Well, the Greek word behind "spirit" is *pneuma* and the study of the Holy Spirit is known as pneumatology, therefore, the study of the Holy Spirit is the study of the breath of God, the wind of God. The Holy Spirit is a person who is the embodiment of the breath of God.

> *2 Peter 1:10 Wherefore the rather, brethren, give diligence to make your calling and election sure: for if ye do these things, ye shall never fall: For so an entrance shall be ministered unto you abundantly into the everlasting kingdom of our Lord and Saviour Jesus Christ...15. I will endeavour that ye may be able after my decease to have these things always in remem- brance. For we have not followed cunningly devised fables, when we made known unto you the power and coming of our Lord Jesus Christ, but were eyewitnesses of his majesty. For he received from God the Father honour and glory, when there came such a voice to him from the excellent glory, This is my beloved Son, in whom I am well pleased.18. And this voice which came from heaven we heard, when we were with him in the holy mount. 19. We have also a more sure word of prophecy; whereunto ye do well that ye take heed, as unto a light that shineth in a dark place, until the day dawn, and the day star arise in your hearts: knowing this first, that no prophecy of the scripture is of any private interpretation. 21. For the prophecy came not in old time by the will of man: but holy men of God spake as they were **moved by the Holy Ghost**.*

Prophets spoke prophecy by the Holy Spirit. "Moved along"

there is a nautical term and it has the idea of being moved along like a sailboat when the wind blows through the sail and so Peter says prophets in the old time, you could say that of the Old Testament. Then it might make sense to you when you look at the next verse in the next chapter which starts talking about false prophets so it must be that he's about to tell us about people that don't agree with what he just said.

So, what does it mean when it says "the testimony of Jesus is the spirit of prophecy?" Let's think this through. The witness of Jesus is the spirit of prophecy. Look at chapter 1 of Revelation with me. We're going to do a little comparison here so maybe we can get an idea.

1. What is the martyrdom of Jesus that is the spirit of prophecy?

2. Why would John have fallen down to worship someone who wasn't God?

> *Revelation 1:1 The Revelation of Jesus Christ, which God gave unto him, to shew unto his servants things which must shortly come to pass; and he sent and signified it by his angel unto his servant John. Who bare record of the word of God, and of the **testimony** of Jesus. Blessed is he that rea- deth, and they that hear the words of this prophecy, and keep those things which are written. 4. John to the seven churches which are in Asia, Grace be unto you, and peace, from him which is, and which was, and which is to come; and from the seven Spirits which are before his throne; And from Jesus Christ, who is the faithful witness, and the first begotten of the dead, and the prince of the kings of the earth. Unto him that loved us, and washed us from our sins in his own blood, And hath made us kings and priests unto God and his Father; to him be glory and dominion for ever and ever. Behold, he cometh with clouds; and every eye shall see him, and they also which pierced him: and all kindreds of the earth shall wail because of him. Even so, Amen. I am Alpha and Omega, the beginning and the ending, saith the Lord, which is, and which was, and which is to come, the Almighty. I John, who also am your brother, and companion in tribulation, and in the kingdom and*

> *patience of Jesus Christ, was in the isle that is called Patmos, for the word of God, and for the **testimony** of Jesus Christ. 10. I was in **the Spirit** on the Lord's day.*

We have John writing prophecy in two different places and we're told in two different places it is the spirit of prophecy that is teaching him to do this.

> *Revelation 1:12 And I turned to see the voice that spake with me. And being turned, I saw seven golden candlesticks; And in the midst of the seven candlesticks one like unto **the Son of man** ...18. I am he that liveth, and was dead; and, behold, I am alive for evermore.*

We could say a witness is someone who has seen the resurrected Lord. The apos- tles had to see the resurrected Christ to become apostles (Acts 1; 1 Corinthians 9:1). We understand that being a witness of the testimony of Jesus or having the witness of Jesus is the same. The word "testimony" there is the same word used in Acts 1:8, "For you shall receive power after the Holy Ghost has come upon you and you shall be witnesses." Well, who is in that crowd of 11 that day? John was. John was told in Acts
1:8, "You will be witnesses of the resurrected Christ, and the Spirit of God is going to help you do it." 2 Peter 1:10 & 21 spoke about prophesying of the Christ that should come? The Holy Spirit carried them along as like a wind does a sailboat.

When we say in Revelation 19:10 **the spirit of prophecy is the testimony of Jesus** we're saying that the knowledge of a resurrected Christ drives prophecy. Out of all the things that John could have talked about, he speaks of the 2nd Coming as the whole purpose of the book of Revelation. That Jesus is coming and so if he's coming, that must mean what? That he went away. The fact that he went away must mean what? In order to go away, you have to be here. And if you've already died, don't you have to actually come back from the death?

To say that you believe in the Second Coming of Jesus, when you say, "I believe in a physical, visible, bodily Second Coming of Jesus," you're saying, "He got up from the dead." When we say that the testimony of Jesus or the eye witness accounts of the apostles and 500 brothers, we see what drives the belief into the Second Coming of Christ. If He's alive, that means he's coming back again.

What is prophecy? Telling what's going to happen. Knowledge, then, of a resurrected Christ is the breath behind prophecy. The **spirit of prophecy** is the knowledge of a resurrected Christ. In other words, "if Jesus wasn't alive, you'd have nothing to talk about." Think through that phrase with me: "the testimony of Jesus is the spirit of prophecy" or "the martyrdom of Jesus is the breath of God that drives prophecy" or "the eye witness accounts of a living Christ who was dead is what drives us to talk about a Second Coming."

> *Revelation 14:11. And the smoke of their torment ascendeth up for ever and ever: and they have no rest day nor night, who worship the beast and his image, and whosoever receiveth the mark of his name. 12. Here is the patience of the saints: here are they that keep the commandments of God, and the faith of Jesus. And I heard a voice from heaven saying unto me, Write, Blessed are the dead which die in the Lord from henceforth: Yea, saith **the Spirit**, that they may rest from their labours; and their works do follow them.*

Who does he see immediately after he hears that voice? Verse 14, Son of Man. Reve- lation 19:10: Why do you think John bowed to this being? Think of Revelation 1, of Revelation 14, and Revelation 19. The third time that this sort of scenario happens: why do you think that John bows to this voice? He thought it was the Son of man that was speaking to him. It's only happened two other times and both times he looks up and sees Jesus. So, in 19:10 he has to be told, "No, no, no, no. I am of thy fellowservant, of thy brethren that have the testimony of Jesus."

19:11

13. And he was clothed with a vesture dipped in blood: and his name is called The Word of God. The word of God. That is the word in the Greek, *logos*. It actually has a full range of meaning. It has an idea of "an expression of a thought." One can see that Jesus is being called the "Word of God."

> 1. He is, therefore, the "Living Word." In Luke 1, we see Gabriel showing up to Mary in the town of Nazareth and he says to her basically, you're going to be with child,
>
> *Luke 1:31 You're going to call his name Jesus" 34 [she says] How shall this be, seeing I know not a man? 35 And the angel answered and said unto her,* **The Holy Ghost shall come upon thee**, *and the power of the Highest shall overshadow thee: therefore also that holy thing which shall be born of thee shall be called the Son of God.*

The Spirit overshadowed her. So the one who is called "the Word of God" was wrought or brought forth by the Holy Spirit. What does *logos* mean? It means an expression of a thought and we have Jesus being called the expression of God's mind in Luke 1.

> *John 1:1 In the beginning was the Word, and the Word was with God, and the Word was God. The same was in the beginning with God. All things were made by him; and without him was not anything made that was made...14 And* **the Word was made flesh,** *and dwelt among us, (and we beheld his glory, the glory as of the only begotten of the Father,) full of grace and truth...18 No man hath seen God at any time; the only begotten Son, which is in the bosom of the Father,* **he hath expressed Him**.

The "Word of God," the expression of God, created everything and the expression of God in this context is a person and it is Jesus. He has declared the mind of God. Perhaps you're wondering, "I wish I knew God the Father better." You can know him perfectly through his Word: First and foremost, his Son. See John 14:

> *1 Let not your heart be troubled: ye believe in God, believe also in me. In my Father's house are many mansions: if it were not so, I would have told you...6 Jesus saith unto him, I am the way, the truth, and the life: no man cometh unto the Father, but by me...8 Philip saith unto him, Lord, shew us the Father, and it will satisfy us. 9 Jesus saith unto him, Have I been so long time with you, and yet hast thou not known me, Philip?* **he that hath seen me hath seen the Father;** *and how sayest thou then, Shew us the Father?*

Jesus said, "You want to know about the Father? You want to know what he thinks? Listen to me. You want to know what he looks like in his character? Look at me. If you want to know what God was thinking, you need to listen to my words and do what I say and come through me to get to him." That's pretty audacious, isn't it?

2. The Scripture is the "written Word."

> *2 Timothy 2:15 Study to shew thyself approved unto God, a workman that needeth not to be ashamed, rightly dividing* **the word (logos)** *of truth.*

Is Timothy being told here to study the Christ? It's not a very Paul-like/Pauline usage to use the word *logos* when referring to a person and why do I say that we're probably talking about the written word of God? Look further in this letter to Timothy

> *2 Timothy 3:16 All scripture is given by* **inspiration of God,** *and is profitable for doctrine, for reproof, for correction, for instruction in righteousness:*

That word, *"inspiration of God"* is the "breathing" of God. God breathed his word, His Scripture. Every time you speak you have a puff of air come out of your mouth. It takes wind, it takes breath to speak. Because of the responsibility on a pastor named Timothy to teach his flock out of Scripture, it follows that this is the "Word of truth" found one chapter earlier (2:15). Christ is long gone so what does a pastor teach his people? The "Word of God. So this "written Word/*logos*" is the expression of the mind of God. Do you want to know what God is thinking? You cannot at this time know God's mind through the physical man of Christ, the Living Word. He is gone for now. However you can know what God is thinking through His Word, the Bible. It was given to use, says 2 Timothy 3:16, by His breath; His Spirit. So, just as the Living Word came to us through the Holy Spirit (in Mary), so the Written Word came to us through the Holy Spirit.

> 3. The words of the prophets and apostles, when speaking for God, were the "Spoken Word/*logos*."
>
> *Amos 3:7 Surely the Lord GOD will do nothing, but he revealeth his secret unto his servants **the prophets**.*
>
> *2 Peter 1:19 We have also a more sure **logos/Word of prophecy**; where- unto ye do well that ye take heed…21 The prophecy came not in old time by the will of man: but **holy men of God spake as they were moved by the Holy Ghost.***

This has the idea of a wind blowing against a sail on a sailboat. So if we desire to know the mind of God, we must hear Him speak. We have been allowed, from a Biblical perspective to hear Him speak by way of the Holy Spirit in these three ways.

And I saw heaven opened, We have what's called a bookend, for lack of a better word. We kind of find these in different books of the Bible—a left and right bookend of distinguishing where a topic kind of begins and then where a topic ends. We're at the right bookend where this event here is culminating. A left bookend and we find that in chapter 4:1:

> *After this I looked, and, behold, a door was opened in heaven: and the first voice which I heard was as it were of a trumpet talking with me; which said, Come up hither, and I will shew thee things*

which must be hereafter.

That's God talking to John saying, "Hey, you're done writing the seven letters that I told you to write to the seven churches. Come up here and let me show you what's going to happen hereafter." That's the first bookend here at the beginning of all this information that takes place between the bookends.

and behold a white horse; When you think of white you think of purity and something untainted that finds itself with the marriage idea later in verse 14. The color of white was a symbol for victory; that's fitting too as he's coming in victory at his Second Coming. Yeah, it is important. The only other time that a white horse was mentioned in Revelation was back in chapter 6:2:

> *And I saw, and behold **a white horse**: and he that sat on him had a bow; and a crown was given unto him: and he went forth conquering, and to conquer.*

and he that sat upon him was called Faithful and True, One could draw a compar- ison from the first time the white horse is mentioned in Revelation: it's a false Christ riding on that horse whereas here it is the actual Christ on the white horse coming at his Second Coming.

This "faithful and true" is a name that Christ has used before in Revelation 3:14 when John is addressing the church at Laodicea.

> *And unto the angel of the church of the Laodiceans write; These things saith the Amen, **the faithful and true** witness, the beginning of the creation of God.*

19:12

His eyes were as a flame of fire, This is another way that Christ is described:

*Revelation 1:12-14 And I turned to see the voice that spake with me. And being turned, I saw seven golden candlesticks; And in the midst of the seven candlesticks one like unto the Son of man clothed with a garment down to the foot, and girt about the paps with a golden girdle. His head and his hairs were white like wool, as white as snow; and **his eyes were as a flame of fire.***

There isn't going to be anything that's hid from God's knowing presence or his know- ing about anything that he puts his eyes upon in a figurative sense. He will know everything. He's going to reveal anything about everybody and every instance. I just don't want to get too far into the figurative, but the literal appearance of what John saw concerning Jesus could have some allegorical sense.

and on his head were many crowns; The last crown that Christ wore was the crown of thorns. We need to first distinguish what type of crown this is because there are two types of crowns or words used for crowns in Revelation. The word crown is used six times in Revelation: three times it's used in one sense and then three times it's used in the sense that it is here in verse 12. The first one that is used in Revelation is in chapter 4, verse 4 and again in verse 10 are to describe the crowns that the 24 elders are wearing (it is also used in 9:7 describing locusts). The Greek word for that crown is *stephanos* and that's a type of crown that's described as a wreath or a garland. Sometimes you see the Greeks wearing those, the vegetation that they wore on top of it and sometimes it was maybe in gold to represent the wreath, but it was something given to you for an achievement.

The second type of crown and the one that we're really concerned about in verse 12 is this word in Greek called *diadema*. We see this three times as well in Revelation: once in 12:3 describing the red dragon or Satan. We see it again in chapter 13 describ- ing the ten crowns on the antichrist. The word *diadema* describes the actual crown of a king or the kingly ornament of the head. That's the word here that's being used in verse 12 to describe the many crowns on Christ's head. I kind of thought it was fitting that John would use this *diadema* in particular—a word used for the actual crown of a king. It's fitting that you would have many *diadema* on the head of the one that's called King of kings and Lord of lords.

and he had a name written, that no man knew, but he himself. The only other time that this reference was made to this name that no one knows but he himself is way back right around chapter 2. In chapter 2, John wrote to the church of Pergamos.

> *Revelation 2:17 He that hath an ear, let him hear what the Spirit saith unto the churches; To him that overcometh will I give to eat of the hidden manna, and will give him* **a white stone, and in the stone a new name written, which no man knoweth saving he that receiveth it.**

See the commentary on 2:17.

We have this invitation to a heavenly temple, and I think it's fitting that John put this here in 19:12 because we're getting ready to see the New Jerusalem that's coming down from heaven.

19:13

And he was clothed with a vesture dipped in blood: and his name is called The Word of God. Whose blood is this that's on his vesture? Isaiah 63:1-6 answers this.

19:14

And the armies which were in heaven followed him upon white horses, clothed in fine linen, white and clean. Who makes up the armies which were in heaven? I can answer this question by asking another question: who is in heaven wearing fine white linen that's clean already?

> *Revelation 4:4 And round about the throne were four and twenty*

> *seats: and upon the seats I saw **four and twenty elders sitting, clothed in white raiment;** and they had on their heads crowns of gold.*
>
> *Revelation 6:11 **And white robes were given unto every one of them**; and it was said unto them, that they should rest yet for a little season, until their fellowservants also and their brethren, that should be killed as they were, should be fulfilled.*

Who are we talking about there in 6:11? Those souls under the altar who await vengeance for their martyrdom.

> *Revelation 7:9-14 After this I beheld, and, lo, a great multitude, which no man could number, of all nations, and kindreds, and people, and tongues, stood before the throne, and before the Lamb, **clothed with white robes**, and palms in their hands.*

These are those saints that are coming out of the great tribulation.

And the armies which were in heaven followed him upon white horses, clothed in fine linen, white and clean. And out of his mouth goeth a sharp sword. 2 Thessalonians 2:9 says that he will destroy the wicked one with the spirit of his mouth. The spirit of his mouth, I submit unto you, is that two-edged sword of this Revelation 19.

19:15

And out of his mouth goeth a sharp sword, that with it he should smite the nations: We just identified who could be in the armies of heaven and then they're all gathered here, they're following behind. Let us also remember there is a stern warning to those who may need to fear being on the receiving end of this 2nd coming:

> *Revelation 2:16 Repent or else I will come to you quickly and will fight against them **with the sword of my mouth.***

and he shall rule them with a rod of iron: and he treadeth the winepress of the fierceness and wrath of Almighty God.

> *Revelation 14:9 And the third angel followed them, saying with a loud voice, If any man worship the beast and his image, and receive his mark in his forehead, or in his hand,* ***The same shall drink of the wine of the wrath of God,*** *which is poured out without mixture into the cup of his indignation; and he shall be tormented with fire and brimstone in the presence of the holy angels, and in the presence of the Lamb.*

And out of his mouth goeth a sharp sword, that with it he should smite the nations. He treadeth the winepress of the fierceness and wrath of Almighty God. And he hath on his vesture, and on his thigh a name written, KING OF KINGS, AND LORD OF LORDS. 17 And I saw an angel standing in the sun. That's probably a perspective thing. In other words, if John is on the isle of Patmos, he looks up and he sees heaven opened and he sees this vision of the Christ coming from heaven and then he sees an angel standing in the sun. So, probably it's like a ball player saying, "I can't see the ball. It's in the sun." John is looking up and he sees toward the direction of the sun, he sees an angel much an eclipse of sorts but I believe it's an angel.

And he cried with a loud voice, saying to all the fowls that fly in the midst of heaven, Come and gather yourselves together unto the supper of the great God. Why is that language of a supper interesting in this context? The marriage supper of the Lamb is not mentioned in the book of Revelation until chapter 19. That is signif- icant. It's interesting how John writes here. He comes back and God shows him "now that you've talked about the marriage supper of the Lamb, let's talk about the supper of the great God." Let's see what's served.

16 And he hath on his vesture and on his thigh a name written, KING OF KINGS, AND LORD OF LORDS.

> *Revelation 17:14 These shall make war with the Lamb, and the*

Lamb shall overcome them: **for he is Lord of lords, and King of kings:** *and they that are with him are called, and chosen, and faithful.*

19:18

That ye may eat the flesh of kings, and the flesh of captains, and the flesh of mighty men, and the flesh of horses, and of them that sit on them, and the flesh of all men, both free and bond, both small and great. You see the beginning of a judgment in chapter 20:11 and who is standing at it? The dead small and great. Who is being killed and their flesh eaten in chapter 19:18? The small and great. So we have this idea where John says, "Alright, you might think they're going to be judged right away." But what happens between those two judgments takes place in chapter 20:1-9. What is it? A thousand years, that's right. That's important to see.

19:19

And I saw the beast, and the kings of the earth, and their armies, gathered together to make war against him that sat on the horse, and against his army. And the beast was taken, and with him the false prophet that wrought miracles before him, with which he deceived them that had received the mark of the beast, and them that worshipped his image. These both does not refer to beast, false prophet and the crowd that followed them. **cast alive into the lake of fire burning with brimstone**? There is only two in this crowd that immediately circumvent the Great White Throne Judgment (20:11-15). In the context of "Kill the dragon and get the girl", the antichrist is the counter-Christ—attempting to steal the affections of those who will belong in relationship to Christ (to no avail; Revelation 13:8; 17:8).

Chapter 20

20:1-2

1. And I saw an angel come down from heaven, When it comes to the opening verse of our six-verse section, one must determine the nature of the "binder". The reader finds that it is an angel. It is more than possible that "angel" is symbolic here. That is, the "angel" represents somebody else. Why is this possible? Because we are told Lucifer is "an angel of light" (2 Corinthians 11), but he is called a dragon here. So it is possible that he doesn't appear to be a dragon here, yet that is what he is called. This does not mean that the binding, the chain, the key, and the pit are symbolic necessarily. It could be that "angel" and "dragon" are symbols, but what is realized is that Satan is "bound" for "1,000 years".

If this angel, prior to the "1,000-year reign" is metaphorical, then it stands to reason that the angel in the 5th trumpet (9:1), the angel with 7 thunders (10:1), and the angel as the announcer of Babylon's judgment (18:1) could also be metaphors.

having the key of the bottomless pit and a great chain in his hand. 2 And he laid hold on the dragon, Consider Isaiaih 25:8 and 26:19-27:1 to see to which one John refers.

20:3

And cast him into the bottomless pit, and shut him up, and set a seal upon him, that he should deceive the nations no more, till the thousand years should be fulfilled: and after that he must be loosed a little season. I don't know how long the little season is but we need to see that it's been used before: The fifth seal. We find someone under the altar from the perspective of John. He looks at the altar in heaven and he sees souls under it who have been martyred and he says, "Just hang on for a little season." Well, if John saw that in AD 95 and they're still waiting, I don't have any idea how long this set of time is here after the

1,000 years.

20:4-7a

And I saw thrones, and they sat upon them and judgment was given unto them, and I saw the souls Now, in Genesis 2 we understand that man became a living soul. That word "soul" there means "life force." In other words, so long as you have life in your body, you have a soul. That's just a little bit too simple for some folks. They want to get mystic. There's no need to. We're not talking about disembodied souls sitting on thrones here. Let me give you some scriptural precedent here (with the same Greek word):

> *Revelation 8:8 And the second angel sounded, and as it were a great mountain burning with fire was cast into the sea: and the third part of the sea became blood; And the third part of the creatures which were in the sea, and had **life**, died; and the third part of the ships were destroyed.*
>
> *Revelation 12:11 And they overcame him by the blood of the Lamb, and by the word of their testimony; and they loved not their **lives**...*

What?! "they didn't love their souls even to death?" I thought "the soul that sinneth it shall die!" Are these people dying? Does that mean they're sinners? See how crazy it can get if you start saying that when "soul" is used, the only thing you can see it as is a person who has died and this is their immaterial part? You can see that if you just use the other English word that's used in other places of the book, there is no need to see that these people are still dead on thrones.

In the first chapter of Exodus, it talks about the number of people that migrated from Canaan to Egypt and it said "70 souls." What, they left their bodies in Canaan? Of course not! So we're dealing with a general usage of anyone that has a life. They're a soul. So, any creature that has a life is said to have had a soul. Maybe it's not a problem to say that fish don't go to heaven when they die but maybe we need to reframe our usage of the words a little bit and adapt them to biblical usage because what is true is that fish don't have a spirit that communes with God. You could probably theologically be correct saying that, but I hope you can see that you don't have to have a uniform interpretation of this verse to say, "Oh, here in Revelation 20:4, we're dealing with dead people reigning somewhere."

7 And when the thousand years are expired, Please notice that it is used six times in this passage of Scripture. "Thousand years" is used in other place:

> *Psalm 90:1 Lord, thou hast been our dwelling place in all generations. Before the mountains were brought forth, or ever thou hadst formed the earth and the world, even from everlasting to everlasting, thou art God. Thou turnest man to destruction; and sayest, Return, ye children of men. For **a thousand years in thy sight are but as yesterday** when it is past, and as a watch in the night.*

> *Psalm 50:9 I will take no bullock out of thy house, nor he goats out of thy folds. For every beast of the forest is mine, and the cattle upon a **thousand** hills.*

Now let's talk about other numbers in the book of Revelation. Was the reign of the antichrist really 42 months? One thousand two hundred and threescore days? Was it really that? If it wasn't, then you have to deal with the fact that in Daniel 9, the first 69 weeks are literal and the 70th week is not. Are you ready to do that? Do you really believe he only saw two witnesses? Were there really 24 elders? That's all he saw? And when he doesn't know the number, what does he say? "I can't number them." He says it here in chapter 20, particularly verse 8, the end of the verse, "to gather them together to battle: the number of whom is as the sand of the sea." He doesn't give us a number. In chapter 7, when he sees a multitude of every ethnicity, race, culture, creed, you name it, he says a multitude which? No man can number.

If he said "it lasted for a thousand years," I would say, "Okay, that probably means that it could be a shorthand for forever; after all, in the Old Testament it's used for shorthand for forever." But the problem is that he goes out of his way to say it six times: "thousand years:" figurative. A "thousand years:" probably figurative. A "thousand years:" could be figurative. A "thousand years:" probably not figurative. A "thousand years:" I don't think it's figurative. A "thousand years:" how could this be figurative? That's what the reader should be thinking but I can't make you think that way.

Now, I want to mention this reign of 20:6:

> *Revelation 5:8 And when he had taken the book, the four beasts and four and twenty elders fell down before the Lamb, having every one of them harps, and golden vials full of odours, which are the prayers of saints. And they sung a new song, saying, Thou art worthy to take the book, and to open the seals thereof: for thou wast slain, and hast redeemed us to God by thy blood out of every kindred, and tongue, and people, and nation; And hast made us unto our God kings and priests:* **and we shall reign on the earth.**

One of the possibilities is that they mean the new earth. Now, I would probably believe that if the last time we saw the 24 elders was somewhere in here in chapter 20 but let's look at the last time the 24 elders are seen in the book of Revelation. Look at chapter 19. What happens in verses 11-15? The second coming of Christ. Christ returns and where do we see the 24 elders for the last time in the book? 19:4 And the four and twenty elders and the four beasts fell down and worshipped God that sat on the throne, saying, Amen; Alleluia. What happens next? We see the heavens open in verse 11. Now, the last time we see the 24 elders is here (Revelation 5:8) and then in the chronology (20:4), we see these 24 elders say, "We're going to reign on the earth." Look, there are people who are reigning in chapter 20:4. I have to believe until I can see better proof in another way that this is the same reigning forecasted in chapter 5:10. Why? Because the 24 elders promised it in chapter 5:10 and the 24 elders are seen right before the second coming that brings the reigning in chapter 20:4 and you don't see them again after that. To me, that is a good hint that chapter 5:10 and 20:5 are talking about the same reigning.

Remember: in the chronology, it's before the thousand years, it's before Satan is loosed, it's before the battle of Gog and Magog, it's before the great white throne of Revelation 20, it's before the new heaven and new earth are seen. If the 24 elders reign on the earth during the new heaven and new earth, why are they not seen in Revelation immediately preceding the new heaven and new earth show up in chapter 21? They're seen, rather, immediately before the second coming which is before the millennium in chapter 19. I think that's a strong point for a literal kingdom, at least, on the earth.

5 But the rest of the dead lived not again until the thousand years were finished. This is the first resurrection. Blessed and holy is he that hath part in the first resurrection: on such the second death hath no power, but they shall be priests. Well, what's the second death? We'll see in verse 15. We have a resurrection at the beginning of the 1,000 years and we have a second death at the end of the 1,000 years and John is going to get to it so hang on with me. There are "thrones" and "judgment" for 1000 years.

In 2 Samuel 7:16, God speaks to King David:

> *And thine house and thy kingdom shall be established for ever before thee:* ***thy throne*** *shall be established for ever.*

This is known as the Davidic Covenant. God has promised David and his off- spring that they will always have a king on the throne. Abraham was promised par- ticular land. Abraham was promised the Promised Land. David was promised his line would be the kings of this Israel. We have two promises that are particular to the nation of Israel: Abraham when it comes to land; and David when it comes to who is in charge of the nation.

> *Isaiah 9:6, For unto us a child is born; unto us a son is given: and the **government** shall be upon his shoulder. And his name shall be called Wonderful, Counsellor, The mighty God, The everlasting Father, The Prince of Peace. Of the increase of his **government** and peace there shall be no end, upon **the throne of David, and upon his kingdom**, to order it, and to establish it with judgment and with justice from henceforth even forever.*

Then, when Christ comes, he is coming to sit on the throne of his human father, great, great, great, great, great grandfather David and he's going to be the King of Israel as the son of David.

> *Matthew 21:9 And the multitudes that went before, and that followed, cried, saying, Hosanna **to the Son of David**: Blessed is he that cometh in the name of the Lord; Hosanna in the highest.*

What were they expecting Jesus to do? Set up the reign under the kingdom of David.

> *Jeremiah 31:8-9 Behold, I will bring them from the north country, and gather them from the coasts of the earth, and with them the blind and the lame, the woman with child and her that travaileth with child together: a great company shall return thither. They shall come with weeping, and with supplications will I lead them: I will cause them to walk by the rivers of waters in a straight way, wherein they shall not stumble: for I am a father to Israel, and Ephraim is my firstborn.*

We have God here promising Israel he's not done with them. Do you see that? He's promising to Israel that there's going to come a time when he's going to gather them together and rule over them.

> *31-33 Behold, the days come, saith the LORD, that I will make a **new covenant** with the house of Israel, and with the house of*

> *Judah. Not according to the covenant that I made with their fathers in the day that I took them by the hand to bring them out of the land of Egypt; which my covenant they brake, although I was an husband unto them, saith the LORD: But this shall be the covenant that I will make with the house of Israel. After those days, saith the LORD, I will put my law in their inward parts, and write it in their hearts; and will be their God, and they shall be my people.*

So we have two promises that are joined here. The Jews are expecting King Jesus to come and have a kingdom that is almost solely Jewish here on the earth and they are expecting it to be a Jewish government that goes on and on and on and it's for the nation of Israel. Then in Jeremiah we have the promise of changed hearts that want to obey the commandments of God. A new covenant that promises changed hearts to obey the king of the kingdom. Two promises that were supposed to join at the 1,000 year millennial reign and this is the big deal in Matthew. Listen carefully: we have a kingdom with its subjects having a heart for their king and his commands and we have a physical kingdom on earth with the son of David reigning among the Jewish people. So when we say, "Well, is the kingdom here now or is the kingdom coming?"

> *John 3:3 Except a man be born-again he cannot see the **kingdom of God**.*

First, we have this literal, physical kingdom that is the kingdom that the son of David will reign on the earth in Jerusalem on a literal throne among literal people on a literal earth for 1,000 years. Second, He will have a people that have a heart that is towards the commands of their king.

Remember, the kingdom from the Old Testament perspective is a physical, visible, literal reigning of Christ among physical, visible people on earth. It is also going to be in that time that those people have changed hearts that desire to obey their king. Those people in that kingdom will have changed hearts that will desire to honor their king.

> *Mathew 6:9 After this manner therefore pray ye: Our Father which art in heaven, Hallowed be thy name. 10* **Thy kingdom come**. *Thy will be done in earth, as it is in heaven.*

What are they praying about? The Second Coming. When Christ presented Himself to the Jews as their King (Matthew 3:2) it was supposed to be that the Jews would receive the kingdom and have both the changed hearts that worship the king and the physical, literal, visible kingdom. But because they rejected their king, God offered that new covenant Gentiles as the people of God ("true Israel of God"; Gala- tians 6:16) await the coming kingdom (2 Timothy 4:1).

So when reading the Gospels…the parables in Matthew 13 and Mark 4 and Luke 11, we're dealing with an audience who is expecting a kingdom that was both physical and spiritual but because they rejected their king and crucified him, that same king offered to the Gentiles the spiritual aspects of that new covenant. When He comes again at the end of the tribulation period and sets up his 1,000 year reign, he will save that ethnic nation of Israel (those who remain) and will give them their physical, visible kingdom and will give to them that new covenant that he promised in Jeremiah 31.[7]

5. But the rest of the dead lived not again until the thousand years were finished. This is the first resurrection. Blessed and holy is he that hath part in the first resurrection: on such the second death hath no power, but they shall be priests of God and of Christ, and shall reign with him a thousand years. The resurrection before the thousand years is of all saved people living at that time and saved people who are dead at that time. Now, if we say that the first resurrection is passed already, then are we saying that the unsaved people get a bodily resurrection after the thousand years but saved people do not? In Revelation 20:11, we have people standing before the great white throne so it appears, then, that since you have the sea giving up the dead which are in it, that constitutes a resurrection, the second resurrection. And the second resurrection, Jesus calls the resurrection unto damnation as does Daniel (John 5 and Daniel 12)--at least as it applies to those who are both living in their respective current ages *and* do not take part in the **First Resurrection.**

6. Blessed and holy is he that hath part in the first resurrection: on such the second death hath no power. One thing that is very certain: from the perspective of the beginning of this thousand year reign, if you are not a partaker of the first resurrection, you are a partaker of the second death. The implication is: if you are not a partaker in that resurrection and you died before that point, then the second resurrection is what you take part in and you will take part in the second death. There is nobody who is now living, who will die before the coming of Christ, who dies lost who will not be hurt by the second death. All people who die without Jesus now will be a partaker of the second death and, therefore, a partaker of the second resurrection, second death.

There is a second resurrection that is unto corruption or damnation and that happens, apparently, before this great white throne judgment. I know of no unsaved people that will be resurrected prior to this great white throne judgment when hell gives up the dead which are in it. There are amilleniasts out there, people who do not believe in a literal thousand years and since they think it's perhaps happening now and that it's symbolic of the kingdom that now is, well then, what is this first resurrection? It has to be a spiritual one. We're alive in Christ but not physically? Well then, when do we get our physical resurrection? However, if we see that this thousand year period is literal, then we have a physical resurrection and people sitting on thrones ruling.

Now, think that through with me: that implies that if you are not a partaker of the first resurrection, then you are a partaker of the second death. You have no author- ity to say that you are not a partaker of the lake of fire which is the second death in chapter 20:15 if you are not a part of the first resurrection in chapter 20:5-6. In other words, if you're a part of the first resurrection, you are not a part of the second death. However, if you are a partaker in the second resurrection, then you are probably a partaker of the second death.

It seems this is the biggest issue against a-millennialism. What do we do with the two resurrections if we are now living in the 1000 years of Christ's reigning?

On the one hand we can say the "First resurrection is not physical." By itself, this is not an absurd statement. Twice, Jesus seems to give a first, spiritual resurrection, and a second, general resurrection (John 5:24-29; John 11:23-26).

Additionally, we are not explicitly told that there is a bodily resurrection for the 1st Resurrection. Three alternative views are espoused. Let's inject these three into the text, and see what questions come out the other side:

1. The First Resurrection as the New Birth and the 1000 year reign as the church age. So, if the First Resurrection is the new birth, does this mean that those who are raised after the "church age" are allowed to get saved? It says "they lived not again until the 1000 years were finished." So does that mean they are given the new birth then? All of them? Then, who goes to the Lake of Fire? Isn't this Universalism?

On the other hand, what's the point of "on such the 2nd death hath no power over those who take part in the first resurrection?" Doesn't that mean that if you don't take part in the First Resurrection that you are not guaranteed protection from the 2nd death?" So that rules out "lived again" as the new birth. It does not hold a consistent usage throughout these three verses.

2. The First Resurrection as martyrs or saints who die on earth and come to reign with Christ in Heaven and the 1000 year reign is current and ongoing.

Again, does this not require a universal, "everybody goes to Heaven" view, based on verse 5's promise that at least some will "live again" after the 1000 year reign? If this consistent interpretation is required, then it is also discarded in the 2nd verse, as only those "brought to Heaven" before the 1000 years are safe from the 2nd death (20:6).

Now if this is true, then we have people "coming alive in Heaven" after the 1000 years who are not safe from the "2nd death" because they had no "first resurrection." Imagine a class of people in Heaven who are not safe from the lake of fire!

    3. The First Resurrection as a reconstitution of Israel and the 1000 year reign is ongoing. This is a little lesser known and is seen in view of Ezekiel 37 primarily. This view regards Israel's new life as a nation as a sort of resurrection.

Summary: This 3rd view, along with the first two, minimize the bodily resurrection of the believer. How so? If the First Resurrection participants are the only ones "safe from the 2nd death," then there can be no bodily resurrection for the believer in Revelation 20. If the "rest of the dead" who "live again after the 1000 years" are susceptible to "the 2nd death," that means only those who are doomed to this lake of fire are guaranteed bodily resurrections, and I know of no group other than the Jehovah's Witnesses and a few others who hold to such an absurd view.

20:7

And when the thousand years are expired, Satan shall be loosed out of his prison, We're still at the end of the 1,000 years. The devil got out of the bottomless pit, rounded up a posse of rebels so numerous that they number the sand of the sea.

And shall go out to deceive the nations which are in the four quarters of the earth, Gog and Magog, to gather them together to battle, So right away, if you're reading Revelation and you come upon this verse, who is Gog and Magog? In other words, the Scripture mentioned these.

Does Revelation talk about it? Okay, it doesn't. Then I would look where else had the author written…so the gospel of John, 1, 2, 3 John. If the gospel of John, 1, 2, 3 John don't mention it which are the other books John has written, then I would probably think, "Well, what other books are like Revelation?" and then immediately, based on our study here you'd say, "Well, Isaiah, Ezekiel. Let's go and look there." So you're on the right path if you're thinking that way. I can tell you that Revelation does not mention Gog and Magog again so we look elsewhere in Scripture in this prescribed manner.

You can count on the fact that Ezekiel 38 and 39 are the only other place that mention Gog and Magog as a pair. Genesis 10 mentions them when we talk about all the nations coming from Shem, Ham and Japheth but when it comes down to it, the only person that mention them as a nation that might fight battles is Ezekiel.

20:8-10

10 And the devil that deceived them was cast into the lake of fire and brimstone, where the beast and the false prophet are, and shall be tormented day and night for ever and ever. There are some who would say that the Armageddon of chapter 19 happens and then John rewinds and renames it "Gog and Magog." There are some major differences between the two battles, one of them, of course, is that the archenemy in Armageddon is the beast and the false prophet and they're put in the lake of fire at the end of chapter 19 and then chapter 20:10, the devil is cast into the lake of fire where the beast and the false prophet are by John's chronology, how long? A thousand years later.

> *Revelation 14:19 20 And the winepress was trodden without the city, and blood came out of the winepress, even unto the horse bridles, by the space of a thousand and six hundred furlongs.*
>
> *Revelation 16:12 And the sixth angel poured out his vial upon the great river Euphrates; and the water thereof was dried up, that the way of the kings of the east might be prepared. 13 And I saw*

three unclean spirits like frogs come out of the mouth of the dragon, and out of the mouth of the beast, and out of the mouth of the false prophet. 14 For they are the spirits of devils, working miracles, which go forth unto the kings of the earth and of the whole world, to gather them to the battle of that great day of God Almighty...16 And he gathered them together into a place called in the Hebrew tongue Armageddon...17 And the seventh angel poured out his vial into the air; and there came a great voice out of the temple of heaven, from the throne, saying, It is done. And there were voices, and thunders, and lightnings; and there was a great earthquake, [one that hasn't happened since the world was]...21 And there fell upon men a great hail out of heaven.

Revelation 19:11 And I saw heaven opened, and behold a white horse; and he that sat upon him was called Faithful and True, and in righteousness he doth judge and make war. His eyes were as a flame of fire, and on his head were many crowns; and he had a name written, that no man knew, but he himself...17 And I saw an angel standing in the sun; and he cried with a loud voice, saying to all the fowls that fly in the midst of heaven, Come and gather yourselves together unto the supper of the great God; That ye may eat the flesh of kings, and the flesh of captains, and the flesh of mighty men, and the flesh of horses, and of them that sit on them, and the flesh of all men, both free and bond, both small and great.

We put these three chapters together: 14 is Armageddon; 16 is Armageddon; 19 is Armageddon. And we find out that there is a Son of man who is responsible for the killing of those kings of the east: he drops hail on them, causes an earthquake and calls the birds to supper.

Ezekiel 38-39 deal with the battle of Gog and Magog. There is no question in my mind that John had this in mind when he wrote Revelation 20.

Ezekiel 38:1 And the word of the LORD came unto me, saying, 2

> *Son of man, set thy face against **Gog, the land of Magog**, the chief prince of Meshech and Tubal, and prophesy against him, 3 And say, Thus saith the Lord GOD; Behold, I am against thee, O Gog, the chief prince of Meshech and Tubal. 4 And I will turn thee back, and put hooks into thy jaws, and I will bring thee forth, and all thine army, horses and horsemen, all of them clothed with all sorts of armour, even a great company with bucklers and shields, all of them handling swords: 5 Persia, Ethiopia, and Libya with them; all of them with shield and helmet: 6 Gomer, and all his bands; the house of Togarmah of the north quarters, and all his bands: and many people with thee.*

So we have: south, east, west and north, all involved with this battle of Gog and Magog. This is a chief distinction, really, between the kings of the east of Revelation 19 and the four corners of the earth involved with the battle of Gog and Magog. That is a real distinction between the two. I do believe that Ezekiel 38-39 summarizes **both battles**.

So, what you would want to do right away is say, "well, they're probably the same battle." I don't think the chronology of Revelation allows for it, nor do I think that the distinctions between the two battles in Revelation allow for it. For example, the person who is calling them to battle in Revelation 16 for Armageddon are three unclean spirits from the dragon, the beast, the false prophet. In Revelation 20, the beast and the false prophet are clearly already in the lake of fire. Secondly, Jerusalem is the location of the battle of Gog and Magog in Revelation 20—they surround the camp and the beloved city, Jerusalem. The location of the battle of Armageddon is the valley of Megiddo. Those are 50-60 miles away from each other.

> *Ezekiel 38:9 Thou shalt ascend and come like a storm, thou shalt be **like a cloud to cover the land**, thou, and all thy bands, and many people with thee.*

This has a lot in common with the language of Revelation 20: "They go up over the breadth of the earth around the camp of the saints." See below:

> *Ezekiel 38:10 Thus saith the Lord GOD; It shall also come to pass, that at the same time shall things come into thy mind, and thou shalt think an evil thought: 11 And thou shalt say, I **will go up to the land of unwalled villages.***

That doesn't sound like a city; that sounds like a camp…covering the land like a cloud covers—it sounds a lot like going up over the whole breadth of the earth. This is clearly Revelation 20 language.

> *Ezekiel 38:19 For in my jealousy and in the fire of my wrath have I spoken, Surely in that day there shall be **a great shaking** in the land of Israel. 20 So that the fishes of the sea, and the fowls of the heaven, and the beasts of the field, and all creeping things that creep upon the earth, and all the men that are upon the face of the earth, **shall shake at my presence**, and the mountains shall be thrown down, and the steep places shall fall, and every wall shall fall to the ground.*

There is no question that this is Armageddon talk, but it's also Gog and Magog talk. See here:

> *Ezekiel 39:6 And I will send a fire on Magog, and among them that dwell carelessly in the isles: and they shall know that I am the LORD.*

Is there any talk in the three passages we looked at in Revelation about fire coming down upon those in Armageddon? No, but there is in chapter 20 about Gog and Magog so this is talk here about the consuming of fire: That is really good language of chapter 20 but it's also, because of the earthquake, great language referring to Armageddon.

These are inhabitants of a land known as Magog. They are the nation of Magog so though they have a land, they encompass the beloved city and fire comes down and devours them as they encompass the camp of the saints and the beloved city. They're trying to besiege it so fire devours them as they surround the city and so I see language from both battles here.

"Well, so what? You can have an earthquake and hailstones in two different bat- tles." Yeah, but when I read 39:17-20, I see this is very unique.

> *17 And, thou son of man, thus saith the Lord GOD; Speak unto every feathered fowl, and to every beast of the field, Assemble yourselves, and come; gather yourselves on every side to my sacrifice that I do sacrifice for you, even a great sacrifice upon the mountains of Israel, that ye may eat flesh, and drink blood. 18 **Ye shall eat the flesh of the mighty, and drink the blood of the princes of the earth, of rams, of lambs, and of goats, of bullocks, all of them fatlings of Bashan. 19 And ye shall eat fat till ye be full, and drink blood till ye be drunken, of my sacrifice which I have sacrificed for you.** 20 Thus ye shall be filled at my table with horses and chariots, with mighty men, and with all men of war, saith the Lord GOD.*

That sounds an awful lot like Revelation 19 with language of flesh eating birds being invited to the battle. It really looks like Gog and Magog describe both battles.

Then how could it be that it is two battles separated by 1,000 years? Probably the question on your mind is: what license do you get to take one event and shove 1,000 years in the middle of it? What license do you get to take—listen to this question, this is really important—to take an Old Testament Scripture that looks like one event and you take it and shove 1,000 years into it?

Well, I would say that I have no right unless, of course, Jesus did it.

> *Isaiah 61:1 The Spirit of the Lord GOD is upon me; because the LORD hath anointed me to preach good tidings unto the meek; he*

> *hath sent me to bind up the brokenhearted, to proclaim liberty to the captives, and the opening of the prison to them that are bound. 2 To proclaim the acceptable year of the LORD and the day of vengeance of our God; to comfort all that mourn; To appoint unto them that mourn in Zion…the oil of joy for mourning, the garment of praise for the spirit of heaviness; that they might be called trees of righteousness, the planting of the LORD, that he might be glorified.*

If that is all merely poetic license for what happened during the first coming of Christ, I can't believe anything in Revelation so we're taking a passage in the Old Testament, one apparent event from the perspective of an Old Testament author, and we're shov- ing 2,000 years between it. Watch:

> *Luke 4:16 And [Jesus] came to Nazareth, where he had been brought up: and, as his custom was, he went into the synagogue on the sabbath day, and stood up for to read. And there was delivered unto him the book of the prophet Esaias. And when he had opened the book, he found the place where it was written, The Spirit of the Lord is upon me…*

That's Isaiah 61:1. Now, look at verse 19. This is verse 2a of Isaiah 61:

> *Luke 4:19 To preach the acceptable year of the Lord.*

Do you remember the next phrase of Isaiah 61? "The day of the vengeance of our God," but he doesn't read that far. Look at verse 20:

> *Luke 4:20 And he closed the book, and he gave it again to the minister, and sat down. And the eyes of all them that were in the synagogue were fastened on him. And he began to say unto them, This day is this scripture…*

What Scripture? Isaiah 61:1 and 61:2a.

...is fulfilled in your ears.

Ezekiel 38-39	Revelation 19:11-15	Revelation 20:7-9
Countries from four directions (38:4-6)		"four corners of the earth" (20:8)
"speaking with fire" (38:19; 39:6)		"fire from Heaven" (20:9)
"earthquake" (38:19-20)	"earthquake" in 7th vial (16:20)	
"hailstones" (38:22)	"hailstones" in 7th vial (16:21)	
"son of man" announces dinner for birds (39:17-20)	"son of man" is present; "angel announces the dinner for birds (19:17-18)	

Was 61:2b fulfilled in their ears that day? No. So, we're going to do what Jesus does. We're going to take one event and we're going to put 2,000 years in there. That's what Jesus does. If Jesus is willing to do that, then I'm only half as bodacious as He is and put 1,000 years in Ezekiel 38 and 39 to make it two separate events: Armageddon and Gog/Magog.

If Isaiah were standing here, he would see these two events of Isaiah 61:1-2 as one event. He just doesn't see this 2,000 years in between. It's his perspective. But if Isaiah and Ezekiel were both standing here, they would see these three events as one: First Coming; 2nd Coming; Gog/Magog. But, there is 2,000 years between the first two and 1,000 years between the last two. So I'm not doing anything crazy with that passage. The reason I think Ezekiel 38 and 39 relates to both of them is because it is both of them.

William the Conqueror and the Crusades: We would talk about maybe some things that happened 1,000 years ago. Do you think there might be any loyalists that are upset about something that happened way back then? Do you think that if they had a chance they would make it right? I think they're called Muslims. So, if you have people existing through this period of a thousand years (since the Crusades), and there is still an offspring; and they are interested in settling the score…it's not far-fetched to say it's the same ethnicity involved with both wars. Remember, we talked about it in Revelation 15 that some people will live into the millennium. Nations that survive the tribulation period will make it into the millennium and populate the millennium.

20:10

The devil that deceived them was cast into the lake of fire and brimstone, where the beast and the false prophet are, And I should say "and have been for 1,000 years" because at the end of the tribulation, the beast and the false prophet are thrown in the Lake of Fire directly at the end of the tribulation period. When you take the time to look at Isaiah 25:8 and 26:19-27:1, there should be no doubt in your mind that Old Testament prophets rejoiced to visualize the defeat of the "old dragon."

Daniel 7	Revelation 19	Revelation 20
God is white on a throne (9)		"Great White Throne" (11)
"the books were opened" (10)		"the books were opened" (12)
Beast to the flame (11; 26)	"beast cast into lake of fire" (20)	
"There was given to the Son of Man a Kingdom"	"Blessed are they who are called to the	They lived and reigned with

…and shall be tormented day and night for ever and ever. 11. And I saw a great white throne, Why does it look like a great white throne? Because there is someone sitting on it whose appearance is very, very white (Revelation 1:14). **and him that sat on it, from whose face the earth and the heaven fled away; and there was found no place for them.** Old creation, the creation that now is. Remember Genesis 1:1? "In the beginning God created the heaven and the earth." Here, they just disappear. Hebrews 1 says they're folded up like a piece of clothing and put away in a drawer somewhere. All of creation. Let your mind run on the deep end on that one. That is amazing. The end of Revelation is nothing but "take two" Garden of Eden. This time not with a man named Adam who can sin but with a whole race of Adam's race redeemed by Christ Jesus who cannot sin. We have a new heaven and earth that is the same phraseology used in Genesis 1:1. We have a new creation; a whole realm of creation.

But notice, there is no creation existing at this judgment…other than perhaps "the Lake of Fire." God in nothingness judging people: that should make some people shake and quake.

20:11-15

The prophets were continually merging prophecies of what we would now call the first and second comings of Christ. That is, to them it looks like one mountain instead of a mountain range with unseen valleys representing many potential years between two events. The events look like the same event from his perspective. For example, you have a 2,000 year valley between the two "Comings." Then we talked about how you have a second and a third mountain, and the third mountain is after the thousand year millennial reign. Again, he looks off, the prophet looks off and he sees the first coming, the second coming and then the new heaven and the new earth and they all look like really the same thing.

Let me just give you a couple of chapters of the Bible to think about: Isaiah 65 and 66 are a lot along this line. If you read Isaiah 65 and 66, you're going to see where Isaiah, it seems like the first coming of Christ, the second coming of Christ and the new heaven and new earth all look like they're at the same time period. It's really amazing and so there was a time, really, where the New Testament writers even played to that. I won't even say that they were trying to be deceptive but they called it "this age and the world to come" because they were living, obviously, at a particular time and then they looked off into the future and they see a coming of Christ and a new heaven and a new earth. Now, I will even tell you this: I think even biblical authors developed in understanding of prophecy. I'm going to show you that. Because even though to us it's all new and it's all revelation to us, it was that way to them as well.

Death is the word for "grave" and hell is the word *Hades* and so you have bodies coming up out of the sea and the earthly graves and then you have souls coming up out of Hades or hell so you see it is an inaccurate statement to say that sinners who die go to hell forever. You see it right here, they're coming up out of hell**.**

Even though Revelation 20 speaks of 1,000 years separating Christ's second coming, the binding of Satan, and the final judgment of the lost, I'm going to show you that Daniel saw these things as happening moreover at the same time. It's all about perspective. Remember Ezekiel 38 and 39 and the battle of Gog and Magog. Remember that there were certain apparent fulfillments in Revelation 19 and certain apparent fulfillments a thousand years later in Revelation 20 and we talked about how that was possible.

Daniel believed that the events of Revelation 19-20 happened at the same time because Daniel did not have Revelation 20.

Daniel 7:9 I beheld till the thrones were cast down.

In the context, we're talking about preceding kingdoms to the kingdom of Christ.

and the Ancient of days did sit, **whose garment was white as snow;** *the hair of his head like the pure wool; his throne was like the fiery flame, and his wheels as burning fire.*

I want you to notice that we have God sitting on a throne, he has white garments, white hair. In Revelation 20, we see there's a great white throne. I would say the reason it looks white is because of the person sitting on it. If the one sitting on it is so radiant that it looks like nothing but a glorious white, you're going to call it a "white throne," aren't you?

> *Daniel 7:10 A fiery stream issued and came forth from before him: thou- sand thousands ministered unto him. And ten thousand times ten thousand* **stood before him. The judgment was set, and the books were opened.**

It is not hard for me to understand why there are some people who do not believe in a millennium and do believe in a general resurrection of the dead. It's not hard for me to understand why they believe that, in other words, the first and second resurrections happen right on top of each other. However, when I read in Revelation 20 that there's a thousand years between the two events.

Then we see what happens to the rest of the dead that in resurrection are brought up to judgment in the great white throne. We're told that that doesn't happen until Satan is thrown into the lake of fire.

> *Revelation 5:11 I saw a throne and angels about them, ten thousand times ten thousand angels surrounded the throne.*

So in Revelation, we find out that Daniel was talking about those "many angels around the throne." Think this through with me for just a moment: Daniel 7:9 and Revela- tion 5:11 are very, very similar passages of Scripture. I want you to see how absolutely inundated John was with Daniel's teaching. John was dominated by the prophetic authors of the Old Testament. You cannot read Revelation and know what was on John's mind if you don't at least understand that everything he writes is from the Old Testament and here's another example.

> *Daniel 7:11 I beheld then because of the voice of the great words which the horn spake: I beheld even till* **the beast was slain, and his body destroyed, and given to the burning flame.**

If you look at Revelation 19, what is the event where the antichrist is captured and thrown into the lake of fire? The Lord comes for the battle of Armageddon. We have another comparison, but notice that Daniel 7 is now talking about two events that are a thousand years apart in the same passage: the throne scene with the books open and the burning of the beast. You say, "Well, isn't that incorrect of him." No, it's just not as developed as the later authors of Scripture. Time and again you see where God reveals things to his people little by little and by the time you get to Revelation, you find out there's a thousand years between these two events.

Now, I wouldn't write on John's stuff today and say, "Hey, I've got increased revelation on John." Why? Because I'm not an apostle and I'm not a prophet. We shouldn't be amazed, though, that there are still religions out there today that continue to write new material. The Mormons are still writing new material. Why? Because they think that they have apostles and prophets. So what keeps you from writing more Scripture if you still have apostles and prophets? That's why the Bible is not "it" with many reli- gions and cults. Why? Because they still say that they have apostles and prophets and that's who is responsible for Scripture. Look, there are liberties that New Testament authors take that I would never take. They take things out of context like crazy. The New Testament takes stuff out of the Old Testament like crazy but I will give them that license. Why? Because they're a prophet or they're an apostle.

> *Daniel 7:13 I saw in the night visions, and, behold, one **like the Son of man came with the clouds of heaven** and came to the Ancient of days.*

Where does that take place? Revelation 14 which is a sneak peek of Revelation 19. So we have him talking about it like it's one event with Revelation 20, and the very first person who tells us that there's a thousand years between these two events is John. Up until Revelation 20 is written, I would think they were right on top of each other. Why? Because that's all the revelation I had.

> *Daniel 7:14 And there was given [the Son of Man] dominion, and glory, and a kingdom that all people, nations, and languages, should serve him: his dominion is an everlasting dominion, which*

> *shall not pass away, and his kingdom that which shall not be destroyed. 15 I Daniel was grieved in my spirit in the midst of my body, and the visions of my head troubled me. I came near unto one of them that stood by, and asked him the truth of all this. So he told me, and made me know the interpretation of the things. These great beasts, which are four, are four kings, which shall arise out of the earth. 18 But the saints of the most High shall take the kingdom, and possess the kingdom **for ever, even for ever and ever**.*

Revelation 20 tells us how long they possess the kingdom. How long? A thousand years. You say, "I thought forever and ever means forever and ever?" "Ever and ever" means "for ages and ages." That's why if someone said to you they believe it is an absolutely literal thousand years to the tick of the tock, I'm not that rigid. Just like when Elijah was told there are 7,000 in Jerusalem who have not yet bowed the knee to Baal, I don't think it was 7,000 and no more and no less. I don't think it was 7,003 but I am literal enough to believe it wasn't 8,000. Do you know what I'm saying? There is rigid and then there is, "okay, I can work with that." For example, I could say that the thousand year millennial reign was 1,050, I could say it was 950 years but there's a difference between saying I'm literal enough to believe it happens 990-1010 and saying "a thousand means without end" or saying "a thousand means 6,000."

If "ages and ages" is the meaning of "forever and ever," does that mean that those who worship the beast in Revelation 14:10-11 are tormented only for "ages and ages" and not necessarily "without end"— as if "ages and ages" and "only" belong together?

What about Satan in Revelation 20:10? Is there an end to his torment in the lake of fire? If it means without end, I don't believe that it is consistent to say that it means without end and use this Scripture to say so. I did not say that there's a way out of the lake of fire. I want us to be consistent and honest with ourselves about how we interpret Scripture. I cannot prove from these verses that there won't be an eventual annihilation of Satan and those in the Lake of Fire. If that makes me a liberal and you think that's treason, call your Senator. What is clear is that they are there for an awful long time.

> *Daniel 7:21 I beheld, and the same horn **made war with the saints, and prevailed against them**.*

That sounds like Revelation 13, doesn't it? The beast was given the saints to conquer and he did so for 42 months.

> *Daniel 7:22 Until the Ancient of days came, and judgment was given to the saints, and the time came that the saints possessed the kingdom…24 And **the ten horns** out of this kingdom are **ten kings** that shall arise.*

Haven't we seen these ten horns on this beast before? Revelation 13: You need to see that John is bent on quoting Daniel time after time after time. Revelation is not just referring to Daniel, it's quoting Daniel. That's why I am very quick to say that what Daniel says happens, the two events happen right on each other's heels. John says they're a thousand years apart.

> *Daniel 12:1 And at that time shall Michael stand up, the great prince which standeth for the children of thy people: and there shall be a time of trouble, such as never was since there was a nation even to that same time: and at that time thy people shall be delivered every one that shall be found **written in the book**.*

So there are books that are opened, Daniel 7, and there is one book that determines resurrection to life and resurrection unto death in Daniel 12. Both these "books" (Daniel 7) and the "book" (Daniel 12) are found in Revelation 20:11-15.

> *Daniel 12:2 And many of them that sleep in the dust of the earth shall awake, some to everlasting life, <u>and</u> some to shame and everlasting contempt.*

It looks like those three items are right on top of each other, doesn't it? Resurrection to life, resurrection to death and the book of life. It looks like those three things are right on top of each other.

> *John 5:24 Verily, verily, I say unto you, He that heareth my word, and believeth on him that sent me, hath everlasting life, and shall not come into condemnation; but is passed from death unto life...28 Marvel not at this: for the hour is coming, in the which all that are in the graves shall hear his voice, And shall come forth; they that have done good, unto the **resurrection of life**; and they that have done evil, unto **the resurrection of damnation**.*

It looks like these things happen right on top of each other, doesn't it, as in Daniel 12? Daniel 12 says the determining factor is the book of life. It looks like those three things happen right on top of each other: book of life, resurrection of the just, resurrection to damnation. Revelation 20 clears it up.

> *Revelation 20:4 And I saw thrones, and they sat upon them, and judgment was given unto them: and I saw the souls of them that were beheaded for the witness of Jesus, and for the word of God, and which had not worshipped the beast, neither his image, neither had received his mark upon their foreheads, or in their hands; and they lived and reigned with Christ a thousand years. But the rest of the dead lived not again **until the thousand years were finished**. This is the first resurrection.*

Seeing people sit on thrones, reigning for a thousand years, that was the first resurrec- tion. That was the resurrection of the just. The rest, how long do they have to wait? They have to wait a thousand years. John 5 doesn't have that information, it wasn't written yet, Revelation 20 wasn't written in John 5. Revelation 20 wasn't written in Daniel 12. Revelation 20 wasn't written in Ezekiel 38. Revelation 20 is the last word from God.

> *Revelation 20:6 Blessed and holy is he that hath part in the first*

> *resurrection: on such the second death hath no power.*

So, the implication is: if you are not a partaker of the first resurrection, you are a partaker the second death.

> *…but they shall be priests of God and of Christ, and shall reign with him a thousand years.*

Then you say, "Well then, where is the second resurrection that leads to the second death?" See verse 11.

Do we believers have any part in the great white throne judgment? I say "no way" and "maybe." The "no way" part of it is: we do definitely not have any part as those being judged at the great white throne. Why? Because we are raised at the first resurrection. However, we do have a part if you mean a part of the tribunal.

> *1 Corinthians 6 Don't go to law before the unbelievers. Don't sue a fellow believer. If the world will be judged by you, are you unworthy to be judged by the smallest matters?* **Don't you know that we'll judge angels?** *How much more things that pertain to this life?*

Paul's argument is: what are you doing taking people to law when you're going to rule and sort of have a reigning part in a future court where you're even going to judge angels? Well, my contention is that since Satan is thrown into the lake of fire before the great white throne and after the thousand years in Revelation 20:10, it makes good sense to me to say that the fallen angels will also be judged at this time. Since that will be when they are judged by my guesstimation, then 1 Corinthians 6, Paul seems to let us in on the fact that we're also going to judge these angels. We're going to judge them probably at this great white throne.

If you are now a saved man or woman and you die in Christ before the coming of Christ, you will be raised at the first resurrection, you will have a glorified body during the thousand year reign with

Christ on earth and then you will sit as part of the tribunal at the great white throne judgment.

12 And I saw the dead, small and great, stand before God; and the books were opened: and another book was opened, which is the book of life: and the dead were judged out of those things which were written in the books, according to their works. It does not say "every man was judged according to their works and placed in the proper destination based on those works." It says you were put in the lake of fire because your name was not written in the book of life (see verse 15). **13. And the sea gave up the dead which were in it; and death and hell delivered up the dead which were in them.** At the end of the 1,000 year reign, everyone who has ever gone to hell will come up out of it. Get that? So, the preaching, the music, the Bible studies that all say that you're going to go to hell and be there forever…sort of, but not really. At the end of the 1,000 year reign with Christ with saints on the earth, all those souls in hell will come up out of hell for this judgment in the middle of nothingness. Notice that the new heaven and the earth is not until the very next chapter, verse 1, right? So there's no new creation just yet, and the old creation has just been punted. So, this judgment is in nothingness. It's just God and you if you're at this judgment. Believers seem to be spectators (1 Corinthians 6).

There is one qualification for going to the lake of fire or staying out of it: One's name in the book of life. See verse 15. So while I understand there are books there that are judging every person according to their works, there is only one requirement for staying out of the Lake of Fire.

The sea gave up the dead which were in it… That's the bodies… **and death and hell delivered up the dead which were in them,** That's the souls…

and they were judged every man according to their works. 14. And death and hell were cast into the lake of fire. This is the second death. Hell is an English word. You won't find the word "hell" in the

New Testament's original Greek. Hell is not a Greek word. It's not found in the Hebrew Old Testament either. Hell is not a Hebrew word. Interestingly enough, in our New Testament there are 3 Greek words that are translated "hell." So in a way, sinners don't go to hell forever." This, of course, takes place after the thousand years which is covered in the first 9 verses, and after Satan is thrown into the lake of fire.

Hades: A good proof text for Hades is Luke 16:23 where it talks about a particular rich man that died and "in Hades he lifted up his eyes, being in torments." In most translations today, Hell is not found in this passage, but rather the transliteration of hades. Hades is a place where lost people go right now when they die. It is typically what we mean when we say that "if you die without Jesus you will go to hell."

Gehenna: *Matthew 10:28 [Jesus says], I will tell you who you should not fear. Fear not him who can kill this body but cannot kill the soul. Fear him who can kill both body and soul in Gehenna.*

Body and soul get destroyed in gehenna. They go and burn in a place called gehenna. Gehenna is also translated "hell" in the New Testament. In other words, if you take your King James version of the Bible, you will find that in 2 Peter 2:4, in Matthew 10:28, in Luke 16:23...you will find the English word "hell," but the Greek word in each place is different.

If you tell people, "If you don't get saved, you will go to hell forever," that is simply not true. If they die without Jesus, they go to a place called Hades and then they are brought up into the great white throne judgment and then body and soul, you see the sea gave up the dead which were in it, bodies coming up to this judgment. Hell gave up the dead which were in it, (souls coming up to this judgment). Bodies and souls coming from their place of rest or lack thereof, into this judgment described here.

After the great white throne when bodies and souls are met together, people who are judged worthy of the lake of fire are put body and soul into *gehenna*.

15. And whosoever was not found written in the book of life was cast into the lake of fire. First of all, please notice that there are books and then there is a book of life. You're judged according to your works out of the books but what is the determination about whether or not someone goes to the Lake of Fire? It's not "the books;" It's the Book of Life, names in the Book of Life. The books that judge you according to your works are peripherals, they are secondary. It's important that you see that. You don't get into heaven because of your works; you don't miss the Lake of Fire because of your works. The determiner is whether your name is in the Book of Life.

"During the 1,000 year reign there is going to be peace on the earth, does that mean that God takes away the sin?"

Consider the sheep nations and the goat nations in Matthew 25:31-46. Perhaps those "sheep nations" are people that are not dead and they will be the ones who bring the first human babies into the millennium. You have to have humans to have humans. So, if you've got us with glorified bodies, we remember from Jesus saying "in the res- urrection they neither marry nor are given in marriage but are as the angels" and so we're not having children. When we descend with Jesus at the end of the tribulation period, we're going to have glorified bodies that cannot procreate and so someone has to be able to put new children on the planet.

So…*Will sin be still on the earth?* You'll still have human beings that are cursed by Adam's curse, right? You will have people born of Adam's race through the sheep nations, the people that are allowed into the millennium, the 1,000 year reign, because of how they treated the Jews during the tribulation period. There's where your children will come from who will still be, apparently, sinful. However, we know from other portions of Scripture that Jesus will not allow any outward rebellion whatsoever. There is a verse in Isaiah 65:20 which gives the idea of death during this period:

There shall be no more thence an infant of days, nor an old man that hath not filled his days: for **the child shall die an hundred years old; but the sinner being an hundred years old shall be accursed**.

Those children that are born during the millennium are going to die because they don't have glorified bodies. They have to be judged somewhere. I was under the impression that only unsaved folks go to the Great White Throne Judgment. Chris- tians who die during the millennium still apparently need a judgment (Hebrews 9:27). There will be people whose names are in the Book of Life that are at this judgment because they have to be judged at some point. It's not explicit, but it seems like there's going to be people from both groups at this judgment.

15 Whosoever was not found written in the book of life was cast into the lake of fire. Will there be any saved people being judged in Revelation 20? I've got to leave the door open for there being believers present at this judgment. If it says there are those who are not in the book of life, why would there not be people who are in the book of life at this judgment? By the way, if you are a believer in a natural body in the millennium, then whose to say that you're not going to die in that millennium? Now, you might die at a ripe old age just like Adam did at 930 before the world got more and more in bondage to the penalty of sin found in the curse on creation, but there is no indication that believers who have natural bodies won't die natural deaths.

Isaiah Passage	Found in Revelation
27:1; 65:17	21:1
12:6	21:3
25:8; 30:19; 60:20; 65:18-19	21:4
43:19	21:5
41:4; 44:6; 48:12; 55:1	21:6
52:11-12; 65:8-9	18:4; 21:7

If they do die natural deaths, when will they be raised? My contention is that they will be partakers of the second resurrection and probably stand at this judgment and be judged first of all, whether or not their names are in the book of life. And since they, indeed, will have their names in the book of life, they will not be thrown into the lake of fire. 20:15.

If your name is not in the book of life, you will go to the same lake of fire that Satan goes to. Matthew 25:41, Jesus says the day will come when he will say, "Depart from me into everlasting fire, prepared for the devil and his angels."

Chapter 21

21:1

1 And I saw a new heaven and a new earth: for the first heaven and the first earth were passed away

> *Revelation 20:11 And I saw a great white throne, and him that sat on it, from whose face* **the earth and the heaven fled away; and there was found no place for them.**

We see the disappearing act of the first heaven and the first earth. When is the first time those are mentioned?

> *Genesis 1:1 In the beginning, God created the heavens and the earth.*

Hebrews 1:10-12 could go in your margin next to Revelation 20:11. It says that, "Lord, you continue forever. The earth that is now, you will fold up like a garment and basically stick it in a drawer," is basically what he's going to do with the creation that is now. You could also make note of Matthew 24 where Jesus said "Heaven and earth will pass away but my words will not pass away." So when does this take place? In Revelation 20:11.

In chapter 21:1, you should see this as a brand new beginning. The best I can tell there is nothing except the lake of fire and a throne and someone sitting on it and people before the judgment and books. If Genesis 1:1 is the heaven and earth being created and a lot of people think, well then, there's just outer space. No, that's not true. Outer space is the firmament. Remember, we find out from Genesis that the firmament is low enough for birds to fly in and high enough for the sun, moon and stars to be in. Somehow until creation week, there wasn't even this thing called "outer space" so there is nothing.

and there was no more sea. Out of all the things John could've said to describe what a new heaven and a new earth look like, he says "there is no more sea." Why? Where did the beast come out of in Revelation 13? The sea. That's interesting so it could be that John is just telling us no more antichrist.

> *Isaiah 27:1 In that day the LORD with his sore and great and strong sword shall punish* **leviathan the piercing serpent,** *even leviathan that crooked serpent; and he shall slay* **the dragon** *that is* **in the sea.**

Alright, well, let's connect some dots here.

> *Revelation 20:1 And I saw an angel come down from heaven, having the key of the bottomless pit and a great chain in his hand. And he laid hold on* **the dragon,** *that* **old serpent,** *which is the Devil, and Satan, and bound him a thousand years.*

This is a big deal to you because that means that Revelation is a reworking of the Old Testament prophet. Remember, in the New Testament, it's translated from the word "abyss" and the word "abyss" is translated into the English a number of ways—one of which is "sea." That word "bottomless pit" there in chapter 20, verse 1, is one Greek word and the Greek word is "abyss." So, where is the devil going to be bound for a thousand years? In the sea; in the deep; in the abyss. What is he trying to get us to notice here? He's trying to get us to notice Isaiah's fulfillment. That's it. I've showed you this with Exodus, I've showed you this with Genesis and now I'm going to show you with Isaiah that John just wants you to know that this is the fulfillment of every- thing the Old Testament prophets foretold.

> *Genesis 1:1 In the beginning God created the heaven and the earth. And darkness was upon the face of* **the deep,** *and the Spirit of God moved upon the face of the* **waters.**

So the old earth when it was created had this formless water covering. What day of creation does that change as far as the planet earth is concerned? The third day. What comes out on the third day out of the sea? Dry land. So here comes dry land out of the sea on the third day of creation.

2 Corinthians 4:1 talks about Christ being the fulfillment of Creation week. 2 Corinthians 4 says that the first day of creation was a picture of Christ. It says, "For the light that shines in darkness is shined in your hearts," is what it says in 2 Corinthians 4. Christ is the ultimate fulfillment of the first day of creation so we have no problem believing with that pattern, that there are spiritual lessons, not just history and good history and accurate history of the six days of creation, but actual spiritual lessons out of this creation week. Well, what would be a good lesson if you find chaos, void, formless and the only thing, the only one that's paying any attention to it is verse 2, The Spirit of God is moving over this void, formless, chaotic sort of entity known as planet earth and there is no life. The Holy Spirit moves upon the face of the waters and on day three, we have dry land coming out of it and what does it do? It brings forth life: herb and yielding seed and greenery. Think about that: there is chaos, there is lifelessness, the Holy Spirit moves over it and up comes dry land and green life. What a wonderful, wonderful picture of what happens to an unconverted person when Christ finds them! The chaos subsides. So, there is no amount of formlessness or void anymore in the life of someone who the light has shined upon and the Holy Spirit has moved over. Remember, God said "let there be light," that is when a person who is in darkness and is absolutely undiscerning to the world of God: the light is turned on for him but there's no life until the Holy Spirit moves over that person and then, eventually, life comes out and they bring forth fruit.

So, if the first thing that Moses talks about in Genesis 1 concerning the old earth is that it was covered with water. Well then, why do you think that in Revelation 21:1, the first thing he uses to describe the new earth is "no water?" No chaos. No disor- der. No ambiguity. No lifelessness. No fruitlessness. New. Think about that. So, of all the ways

John could have described a new heaven and a new earth, I like the way he described it. No more sea. That doesn't mean you have to pack away your Jet Ski, I don't think that's the point.

21:2

3 And I heard a great voice out of heaven saying, Behold, the tabernacle of God is with men, and he will dwell with them, and they shall be his people, and God himself shall be with them, and be their God.

> *Isaiah 65:18 But be ye glad and rejoice for ever in that which I create: for, behold,* ***I create Jerusalem***.

He's not talking about the old Jerusalem that's sitting on some piece of land in Pales- tine. God is far more impressed with the New Jerusalem He's creating.

> *Ezekiel 37 I will set my sanctuary **in the midst of them**. My tabernacle also shall be with them. I will be their God and they shall be my people.*

> *Ezekiel 43 I will dwell **in the midst** of the children of Israel forever.*

> *Jeremiah 31 **I will be their God** and they shall be my people.*

So, why does the book of Revelation introduce the Son of man in chapter 1 as one who walks among the candlesticks? The candlesticks are the churches so we have now, all of a sudden, this fantastic fulfillment in my estimation where John is telling us that the church is absolutely going to experience the fulfillment of what was promised to Israel.

There is a reason why John said that Christ walks among the candlesticks. So when Jesus Christ is in our midst, "where 2-3 are gathered in my name, there I am in the midst of them," don't you hear the fulfillment of the promise of Leviticus? Christ is saying, "I will be in the midst of you. Moses and the Israelites, they had hearts that were made after Adam their father and they were never able to let me live among them because they kept sinning in my face but here I am, I'm converting you, I'm giving you new hearts. You want to honor and so I want to be among you. If you don't honor me, I'll remove your candlestick. I will no longer dwell among my people." In a very physical manifestation, a very physical way, we have in a future time when God in the body will dwell among us fulfilling the ultimate shadow.

If you see Revelation as nothing but statement of "The church now is the fulfillment of all prophecy." Well, good heavens, all you are is a Jehovah's Witness because the Jehovah's Witnesses teach that if you're part of the 144,000, you're immediately transferred and you get this "spiritual body" resurrection and you go and reign with God in heaven forever. Well, when did the people that stayed down here on paradise earth get to live in the presence of God? They don't. So, what kind of fulfillment do you get in the Scripture if you are just saying, "Hey, Isaiah, that's just picturing the future time of the church?" No, it's the future time of the church in the eternal age when God himself walks among his people. I'm talking about in the body like the Garden of Eden. You see, it starts in Genesis and ends in Revelation and if everything here pictures something that already happened or is happening now, then what is your hope?

21:4

And God will wipe away every tear from their eyes; there shall be no more death, nor sorrow, nor crying. There shall be no more pain, for the former things have passed away." It seems like this refers back to Revelation 20:11 where the "first Heaven and first earth passed away."

> *Isaiah 25:8 He'll wipe away death in victory and the **Lord will wipe away tears from off their faces**…19 and **the voice of weeping shall be no more heard in her, nor the voice of crying**. The days of thy mourning shall be ended.*

John is not writing new material. Hey, he wants the churches to whom he is writing to be encouraged; but the first thing he's trying to get you to see is that this is a fulfillment of Isaiah the prophet. What you're going to see in the future is a fulfillment of what Isaiah has always told the people of God.

21:5

And he that sat upon the throne said, Behold, I make all things new.

> *Isaiah 43:19 I'll do a new thing.*

You have Jesus Christ the word recreating the world. Who is it that recreates the new earth? Jesus does. We weren't there to see the first creation but I think it would be great to be there for the next one and do you know what? He could've, in Genesis 1, just said, "Earth," and everything is as it is today, right? But he didn't do it. Now, I don't know all the reasons why he built it as a process but there's no need to believe that he's going to do it any differently with the second earth, the new heaven, the new earth. And we're all going to be there to watch him craft that new thing? You say, "I wish I was there at creation."

21:7

He that overcometh shall inherit all things;

> *Isaiah 65:9 I will bring forth a seed out of Jacob and out of Judah an inheritor of my mountains and mine elect shall inherit it and my servants shall dwell there.*

The purpose of the book was fulfilled in chapter 19 because the title of the book is "The Revelation of Jesus Christ" and that occurs in 19:11. John is trying to show us is that he's the one who begins everything again because what we don't see in Isaiah is we don't see Christ named. If you were to sum up the Old Testament in one way, it's the New

Testament without "Jesus." That is phenomenal. When you think about the fact that Revelation is Daniel, Ezekiel, Hosea, Zechariah, Malachi, Isaiah, except with Jesus. Jesus returns and makes all things new. He returns and gives us everything. Isaiah 25:9 should also be considered here.

21:10 -13

And he carried me away in the Spirit to a great and high mountain, and showed me the great city, the holy Jerusalem, descending out of heaven from God, 11 having the glory of God. Her light was like a most precious stone, like a jasper stone, clear as crystal. 12 Also she had a great and high wall I mean, if you are a bleeding heart that thinks everybody should be let in, "City life may not be for you." You'd have a problem with the mayor of the city. You'd have a problem with the laws of the city. Since Jesus prepared this place, and it has walls, you may not like Jesus. You may not like the city. You may not even like the citizens. As a matter of fact, you may just be a treasoner at heart. We look in this Scripture and find that Jesus Christ, when found in Scripture building a city, he has a tall wall.

with twelve gates, and twelve angels at the gates, and names written on them, which are the names of the twelve tribes of the children of Israel:13 three gates on the east, three gates on the north, three gates on the south, and three gates on the west. God and the Lamb are interested in visitors. This is not a God Who begrudges guests, but they must come through the gates.

> *Revelation 21:24-26 And the nations of those who are saved shall walk in its light, and **the kings of the earth bring their glory and honor into it.** 25. Its gates shall not be shut at all by day (there shall be no night there). 26 And they shall bring the glory and the honor of the nations into it.*

> *Isaiah 60:24 And the **nations of them which are saved shall walk in the light of it.** The Gentiles shall come to thy light.*

John wants you to know the book of Isaiah is being fulfilled right here in these verses. Shadows of fulfillment in the first coming of Christ? Yes. Ultimate fulfillment in the events that surround the second coming of Christ? Yes. We could give this up to the Holy Spirit's perfect recall of Isaiah. This is not hard at all for us to conceive as John has been staring into Heaven for chapters.

Here are some other reasons to consider the idea of the New Jerusalem descending before or during the millennium:

1. We have kings bringing honor to the city in 21:24. What is the point of talking about kings of the earth bringing their glory and honor into a New Jerusalem if we're talking about kings of the earth of a future heaven and earth that hasn't been created yet?
2. Why would Christ prepare such a place for His people to be in for little or no time before they are away from it for 1,000 years?
3. Why would nations need to be healed? There are trees, or at least a tree, within the city for this purpose (22:2). Is there really a curse in the New Heaven and New Earth, already forecasted? It seems better to say that these are the nations who have survived the Great Tribulation and are granted access to the millennium, prior to the New Heaven and New Earth.
4. Gog and Magog surround the New Jerusalem at the end of the millennium (20:9). How could this happen if the city has not yet descended?

So that is why I'm putting forth the idea that there is room in the text to believe that just like John can't write about two things at once, he wrote about something and then started talking about something that took place in what he wrote. It's a lot like Genesis 1. Genesis 1 talks about the first six days of creation and then in Genesis 2 he talks about the sixth day of creation again where he made man and made him a wife and named the animals.

Revelation 21:27 But there shall by no means enter it anything *that defiles, or causes an abomination or a lie, but only those who are written **in the Lamb's Book of Life**.*

The Lamb's Book of Life is the registry of the residents to the holy city, to the New Jerusalem; all who belong in the city have their names in the book of life.

So, as long as you're ok with walls, around which nobody goes without proper citizenship and through which nobody goes without going through particular gates, maybe city life is for you. On one hand, be sure you're a citizen of the New Jerusalem.

It should be noted that you don't want everybody in your city.

Revelation 22:14-15 Blessed are those who do His commandments, that they may have the right to the tree of life, and may enter through the gates into the city. 15 But outside are dogs and sorcerers and sexually immoral and murderers and idolaters, and whoever loves and practices a lie.

There are walls around this city. If you can't stand the idea of heavily vetting those who come inside your wall…then you may actually have a problem with God.

21:15

And he that talked with me had a golden reed to measure the city. Well, if you go to the rod definition it is equivalent of six cubits or if you convert cubits to feet, it would be nine feet so his rod is a nine foot rod.

21:16

And the city lieth foursquare, and the length is as large as the breadth: and he measured the city with the reed, twelve thousand

furlongs. When you convert that to the inch system, it comes out to be 1,500 miles approximately. Well, to give you an idea of 1,500 miles, if you go on, it says,

The length and the breadth and the height of it are equal. Some would say that it is a square city, but also I'm wondering if it could be a pyramid because you can have the breadth and the width and then the height of the city can still be the same height as the width but it isn't square.

21:17

And he measured the wall thereof, an hundred and forty and four cubits, that would be 216 feet.

21:19

In Exodus 28:15 and following, it lists the stones that were garnishing the breastplate of the high priest which each of the stones represented one of the twelve tribes. So we have the twelve apostles and we have the twelve tribes represented in the foundations and in the stones. If you try to go to Exodus and get a comparison between the stones of Exodus and the stone of Revelation, they don't match word-for-word. There's probably a half a dozen of the stones that match word-for-word but it could be just the difference between old Hebrew words for a stone and the Greek words for a stone. They might be the same. The point here is that: the priest's ephod with the twelve stones representative of the twelve tribes of Israel are now going to be merged with the twelve apostles in the New Jerusalem as far as a representation of these people of God in the New Jerusalem.

21:21

And the twelve gates were twelve pearls. If you've ever traveled in Europe and seen some of the castles with the gates at the castles and the cities and so forth, the reason they had gates was to at night keep out or during times of war keep out the marauder- ing thieves or the people they didn't want in during the night-time and so they would shut the gates but for the most times, the gates would be opened. The gate in the city is the opening while the door is the apparatus which is closed. Perhaps the big arched area over the opening is made of pearl.

21:22

But I saw no temple in it, for the Lord God Almighty and the Lamb are its temple. "Temples" are not evil or bad or even unnecessary. They had a purpose. They have a purpose in Heaven. They have no purpose in the New Jerusalem. Out from this temple came "lightening and thundering and earthquakes and voices and hail" (11:19); out from this temple came angels crying for judgment (14:15-17); out from the temple came plagues of wrath (15:5-6). When you know that the temple told stories of turmoil, judgment, and wrath, it makes the existence of a temple in the New Jerusalem bring unpleasantness and grief into the city.

So instead of the turmoil and terror and fear of bloodshed as in the temples of heaven and earth, there is simply the chief offerer, **the Almighty**, and the chief offering, **the Lamb**. Instead of the forms of dead animals—as is the typical image that comes to mind when we think of a temple—we have the last sacrifice of **the Almighty** Who is **the Lamb.** This is, without a doubt, a reminder of Genesis 22:8 and the first promise of God's Lamb.

Some of us are so attached to the way things remind us of feelings in our lives and we mistake it for the presence of God. What is this really, but a sort of idolatry?

> *Revelation 22:9 -11 Then he said to me, "See that you do not do that. For I am your fellow servant, and of your brethren the*

prophets, and of those who keep the words of this book. **Worship God.**"[26]

Apparently, John the Revelator loved angels and fell at their feet, and the angel says, "Nobody here worships anybody but Jesus."

Revelation 19:10 I am thy fellowservant, and of thy brethren that have the testimony of Jesus,

Now, think about that. If these angels are prophets, who are they? As stated previously, I believe that the angel that rebukes John in chapter 19 is actually the Prophet Ezekiel returning to us.

---

[26] I know it's not an identical reaction from this second angel of the last seven but it is a reaction that is much like—both of them say basically, "I'm just like you."

Chapter 22

22:1

And he shewed me a pure river of water of life who did? Verse 9 of chapter 21, "And there came unto me one of the seven angels which had the seven vials full of the seven last plagues." He's being given a tour of the city, the holy Jerusalem, the New Jerusalem and so the two are continuous. **clear as crystal, proceeding out of the throne of God and of the Lamb.** The differences between that millennial temple described in Ezekiel 47 and the city of Revelation 22, the New Jerusalem, are stark, actually. For example, in Ezekiel you have water coming out from underneath an altar and it goes into the Dead Sea.

22:2

In the midst of the street of it, and on either side of the river, was there the tree of life You might notice that there is one street. **which bare twelve manner of fruits, and yielded her fruit every month:** You might have two trees or you have lots of trees and they're all called the "tree of life" as a particular species of tree. Have you seen the banyan trees where you have several different trunk-looking things. Someone might say, "How can we calculate months because there is no moon or sun?" What if there is still moon or sun outside the city? If it comes down during the millennium and there's a moon or sun somewhere to lighten the earth, then this would be outside the city and we would still have a way to calculate months. In Isaiah 66, it says, "From Sabbath day to Sabbath day, they will come and offer sacrifices before the Lord."

and the leaves of the tree were for the healing of the nations. Those in the millennium are still Adam's descendants, even if they're in the millennium and if they didn't die at Armageddon and if they weren't saved and resurrected at the millennium or raptured at the dawning of the millennium, then they will die or at least they would die if they did not have the tree of life.

22:3

And there shall be no more curse, but the throne of God and of the Lamb shall be in it, and His servants shall serve Him. Well, that's not new. We found in chapter 7 that you have a multitude of which no man could number of every kindred, tribe, people and nation and they are serving God in the temple. What is new is that there is no temple in the New Jerusalem so they're serving God directly. We spoke about this in that passage.

22:4

And they shall see his face; Man was ashamed to see God in Genesis 3:9. He sins and then God has to come looking for him, "Adam, where are you?" Well, here there is none of that. Why? The curse has been removed, there is no shame of sin anymore. You see how all these themes that began in Genesis end in Revelation? Before you know it, believers are in the world that he created but with the last Adam.

and his name shall be in their foreheads. We know the mark of the beast can be located either on the forehead or the hand, the back of the hand so that they can use it. Here is a good opportunity to mention that although there is contextual reason to see the 144,000 here (chapters 7 and 14), the mark of God appears on all those who belong in the New Jerusalem—not just 144,000 Jewish, male virgins.

Cain killed Abel and because he did that, he had to be punished and when he was punished or was given his sentence he said to God, "My punishment is too great." He knew very well that people were going to be upset with what he did and they would probably hunt him down and kill him. So in his mind, he was asking for God's protection, "God, protect me because I know people will kill me. I'm sure of it." I don't know if he actually had a moment in his life where he actually felt remorse.

Genesis 4:15 And the LORD said unto him, Therefore whosoever *slayeth Cain, vengeance shall be taken on him sevenfold. And the LORD **set a mark** upon Cain, lest any finding him should kill him.*

Revelation 3:12 Him that overcometh will I make a pillar in the temple of my God, and he shall go no more out: and I will write upon him the name of my God, and the name of the city of my God, which is new Jerusalem, which cometh down out of heaven from my God: ***and I will write upon him my new name****.*

22:5

There shall be no night there: We already saw this in 21:26. This must be a big deal. **They need no lamp nor light of the sun, for the Lord God gives them light.** The source of light is given in Genesis 1:14 and then you see that it's removed here. When God is everywhere, there is no place for light not to be. There isn't a need for a source. Because God is everywhere, the light is everywhere. Incidentally, there was light on day one before the sun and moon and stars were given on day 4. It's in reverse here. The light is coming from those bodies, and then there is light after those bodies. **and they shall reign forever and ever.** See also Revelation 21:23 and compare it with Isaiah 60:19.

Again, if you read back to the bowls of wrath in the book of Revelation, you will find a darkness so thick it can be cut, and that it was "poured out on the seat of the Beast" (Revelation 16). For the reader to hear there is no threat in the New Jerusalem to feel the pain of being on the wrong side of things ever again, is a wonderful, wonderful thing. This is the major difference between being in the image of "Adam" versus the image of "the Last Adam": "being able to not sin" versus "not able to sin". Our lives our characterized by darkness before Christ, and they are burdened by darkness in our trials after Christ, but the darkness that plagues us when it is a burden to go to bed and a burden to awaken will be gone, gone, gone.

In a land with no shadows, where every corner and every place on every street is well-lit, what will you do when there are no movies to view in dark rooms and no theaters where they take God's name in vain, joke about disgusting things, and display murder after murder on the big screen.

22:6

And he said unto me, These sayings are faithful and true: and the Lord God of the holy prophets sent his angel to shew unto his servants the things which must shortly be done. And you can see that that's how the book of Revelation started in 1:1-3.

Behold, I come quickly: blessed is he that keepeth the sayings of the prophecy of this book. And I John saw these things, and heard them. We have kind of a change of scenery altogether. Up until verse 6, he's describing the city that he's walk- ing around in with this angel, and now from verse 7 to the end of the book, it's like closing comments. The tour is over and now Jesus is talking to the churches again. For example, if you'll look in verse 16, "I have sent mine angel to testify unto you these things in the churches." Well, he started out the book talking to the churches and now he's closing the book talking to the churches. And you might notice that he gives a warning of who belongs in the city and who will not be allowed in it. The chronology of the prophecy is done, now they're back on the island real time and he's getting a closing word from the Lord through his angel.

22:8

And when I had heard and seen, I fell down to worship before the feet of the angel which shewed me these things. This is the second time in four chapters that John wants to worship an angel (see also 19:10). **Then saith he unto me, See thou do it not: for I am thy fellowservant, and of thy brethren the prophets, and of them which keep the sayings of this book: worship God.** I know it's not an identical reaction from this second angel of the last seven but it is a reaction that is much like—both of them say basically, "I'm just like you." For example, you might notice in chapter 19:10, "I am thy fellowservant, and of thy brethren that have the testimony of Jesus," whereas in chapter 22:9, he says, "I am thy fellowservant, and of thy brethren the prophets." Now, think about that. If these angels are prophets, who are they? As stated previously, I believe that the angel that rebukes John in chapter 19 is actually the Prophet Ezekiel returning to us.

22:10

And he this angel that told John, "Do not worship me. Worship God." **saith unto me, Seal not the sayings of the prophecy of this book: for the time is at hand.** Where else do we have this idea of sealing a book and time of the end?

> *Daniel 12 But thou, O Daniel, shut up the words and **seal the book even to the time of the end**.*

Well, if Daniel was told to seal the book and you have a guy here in the end saying, "Hey, it's the end. It's time to unseal the book," and this guy says that he's a prophet like John, I'm just leaning in the direction that this is Daniel. You don't have to agree with me but he says he's a prophet and he's talking just like Daniel or talking like someone who talked to Daniel.

When we see the word "angel" we think "brilliantly lighted being from the heavens," but "angel" comes from a Greek word, *angelos*, so angel is not really an English word at all, it's a transliteration. It just means "messenger." When it says that he looked like a messenger, I can live with that. I think that it has come to mean "heavenly messenger." The word "angel" at one time simply meant messenger and because we usually use it to refer to people that are from heaven, we have taken it to mean then that that's what angel means but that's not how the word started out meaning.

If in the resurrection glorified people are like angels in that "they are neither married nor given in marriage" (Matthew 22), I'm okay with saying that when we die, in some ways before the resurrection, we resemble angels. You might remember that at the house of Rhoda in the city of Jerusalem in Acts 12, Peter is let out of prison and they're having a prayer meeting that he'll get let out of prison. He does get let of prison, he goes and knocks on the door of the house where they're having a prayer meeting for him and they say, "Oh, it's his angel. It's not him." So, here they are praying for his release, he's released before their prayer meeting is over and they think, "Oh, we were too late. He was beheaded and now he's an angel." It was theology then that a person takes on the form of an angel or at least there's an angel that takes on his likeness after he's dead. So, I don't have a problem when you have two dead prophets, Ezekiel and Daniel, showing up looking like angels to John in AD 95. I think there's a reason why they are saying, "Hey, we're prophets like you."

22:12

And, behold, I come quickly; and my reward is with me, to give every man according as his work shall be.[27]

> *Isaiah 40:10 Behold, **the Lord GOD will come** with strong hand, and his arm shall rule for him: behold, **his reward is with him**, and his work before him.*

> *Revelation 2:5 Remember therefore from whence thou art fallen, and repent, and do the first works; or else **I will come unto thee quickly,** and will remove thy candlestick out of his place, except thou repent.*

> *Revelation 2:16 Repent; or else **I will come unto thee quickly**, and will fight against them with the sword of my mouth.*

---

[27] With all the Old Testament backdrop on this verse, it seems hard to fit this and verse 20 in some sort of "private" meeting with the believers of this dispensation as said by the Pre-tribulational rapture folks purport. Furthermore, we shouldn't assume these two texts—so close together—are speaking of two different events separated by 7 years. I appreciate this pointed out to me by my friend and former boss, Pastor Sean Harris of Fayetteville, NC.

> *Revelation 3:11 Behold, **I come quickly**: hold that fast which thou hast, that no man take thy crown.*

22:13

I am Alpha and Omega, the beginning and the end, the first and the last.

> *Isaiah 44:6 Thus saith the LORD the King of Israel, and his redeemer the LORD of hosts; **I am the first, and I am the last;** and beside me there is no God.*

I don't know if you have noticed or not, but Isaiah 40:10 and Isaiah 44:6 are clearly references to "God" while Christ applies both of them to Himself. So to say that "Jesus never claimed to be equal with God" is plain nonsense.

22:14

Blessed are they that do his commandments, that they may have right to the tree of life, and may enter in through the gates into the city. In order to determine which "tree" we're talking about, look at the beginning of the chapter. We are therefore talking about the same city as we did in 21:2.

22:15

For without are dogs, "Dogs" was a term for the Gentiles back then.

22:16

I Jesus have sent mine angel to testify unto you these things in the churches.

> *Revelation 1:11 Saying, I am Alpha and Omega, the first and the last:*

*and, What thou seest, write in a book, and **send it unto the seven churches which are in Asia**; unto Ephesus, and unto Smyrna, and unto Pergamos, and unto Thyatira, and unto Sardis, and unto Philadelphia, and unto Laodicea.*

These are the seven churches that it addresses in the beginning of the book. We also understand it's talking about people who are in any church that claims to be a church of Christ.

I am the root and the offspring of David, and the bright and morning star. When somebody says they're going to get to the root of a problem what do they mean? They mean to get to the source. The offspring is the fruit. So Jesus Christ just said for the fourth time, "I am the first and the last:" I am "the root and the fruit."

22:17

And the Spirit In chapters 2:7, 2:11, 2:17, 2:29, 3:6 and 3:13 it says "He that hath an ear, let him hear what the Spirit saith unto the churches." The "Spirit" is the author of this letter to the churches. Thought it may be hard to understand, it can be said that "the Spirit is saying all of this," somehow.

and the bride say, Come. And let him that heareth say, Come. The bride, within the context of chapters 21 and 22, "the holy city, new Jerusalem, coming down from God out of heaven, prepared as a bride adorned for her husband." We have talked about the registry of the city being the book of life.

So the Holy Spirit and a city are saying "Come?" I'm going to draw an analogy for you: if I say the city of Fayetteville, "You know, the city of Fayetteville, North Carolina is a pretty good place, pretty nice place. The people are nice. Fayetteville is a good place to live. The people are nice. The people are helpful." Or the opposite, "Fayetteville is horrible. Fayetteville is dirty." What do I mean by that? Well, let's see: the people are murderers, the people are idolaters, they're rude, they're obnoxious, they're unthankful, they're unholy. So, here in this context, the bride saying "Come" is the inhabitants of the city saying "Come." Furthermore, since the ones that "hear" are the ones addressed in the chapters 2 & 3 references above, we see we are talking about real believers in churches who make up the real bride of Christ as inhibiters of the Holy City.

And let him that heareth say, Come.

> *Revelation 1:3 Blessed is he that readeth, and they that **hear** the words of this prophecy, and keep those things which are written therein: for the time is at hand.*
> *Revelation 2:7 to the angel at the church at Ephesus he says, 'He that hath an ear, let him **hear**.' Revelation 2:11 He that hath an ear, let him **hear**.*
> *Revelation 2:17 He that hath an ear to hear, let him **hear**.*
> *Revelation 2:29 He that hath an ear, let him **hear**.*
> *Revelation 3:6 He that hath an ear, let him **hear**.*
> *Revelation 3:13 He that hath an ear, let him **hear**.*
> *Revelation 3:22 He that hath an ear, let him **hear**.*
> *Revelation 13:9 If any man have an ear, let him **hear**.*

What is that doing right there in the middle of that chapter? What's it doing in the middle of the book? It doesn't appear before chapter 22 and it doesn't appear after the letters to the churches. Why is it right here? Why is it right here if the church members in those seven churches didn't need what was in chapter 13? Why is the church that's not going to be here concerned about what happens during Daniels' 70th week. It doesn't make any sense. A whole book written to them about stuff that they don't need to worry about?

Seven churches full of Christians are being told when they read chapter 13 to make sure they're listening well. Why do they need to worry about it if they're not going to be here? Why do they need promises that the overcomer gets this, this, this and this if they're not going to be here? What's there to overcome? The book has nothing to do with those seven churches if they're not here. What's there to overcome? They have an understanding that the New Jerusalem is a reality for the overcomer and because they have heard, they can contextually say "Come."

And let him that is athirst come. And whosoever will, let him take the water of life freely. Where is this water of life? At the very beginning of this chapter we're told "And he shewed me a pure river of water of life, clear as crystal, proceeding out of the throne of God and of the Lamb."

> *Isaiah 55:1 Ho, every one that thirsteth,* ***come ye to the waters****, and he that hath no money; come ye, buy, and eat; yea, come, buy wine and milk* ***without money and without price****.*

These are words spoken from the Holy City which reaffirms there will be nations that need healing (see end of chapter 21) and this seems to imply that the Holy City will be present during the millennium as there will be nations getting saved.[28]

22:18

For I testify unto every man that heareth the words of the prophecy of this book, What would that tell you about this book? It's supposed to be read aloud to the seven churches. Now, think that through: we have the seven churches listed in order and we saw in chapters 2 and 3, they're listed in the order of travel as to how the messenger would have

---

[28] Now then, just as verses 1-9 come from Ezekiel and verses 10 and 11 come from Daniel, it seems like much of verses 12-17 come from the book of Isaiah. We have Ezekiel, Daniel, Isaiah and Christ says "I'm the Alpha and the Omega, the beginning and the end, the first and the last. I am the root and the offspring of David." Does this not seem like it's wrapping up every Old Testament prophecy? Everything that Ezekiel spoke of—done; Everything that Daniel spoke of, Daniel's 70th week and Jeremiah's "time of Jacob's trouble"—done; The book of Isaiah—done. All these Old Testament prophecies that have been talking about the day of the Lord, the kingdom of heaven, it is all coming to an end here in this last chapter of Revelation. Ultimately, however, all that begun in perfect paradise in Genesis has returned to a peaceful, God-intended state.

delivered them beginning with Ephesus on the southwest of Turkey and continuing on until you get to Laodicea in the southeast of that travel route. So all seven of those churches were to hear this book read. Now, think that through: they meet on the Lord's Day, probably not a Saturday. Not because they thought that Saturday was sinful but because many of them already still went to synagogue and there are some of them getting out of that habit. So, they meet on the first day of the week we find in the book of Acts and they have the entire book read to them.

If any man shall add unto these things, God shall add unto him the plagues that are written in this book: Probably, if you have heard why there's not supposed to be a book of Mormon for example; why there is not supposed to be prophecies given in churches that label themselves as charismatic, we say it's because "Revelation says 'don't add to or take away'," but that is not an honest usage of that verse. Now, you might be able to walk away saying you really stymied them in an argument but it's not honest because the Scripture is very clear when you look at chapter 22:18 that John talking about the Revelation. So please be honest. He's talking about here don't add Revelation 23. That's exactly what he's saying but if you want to say he's saying don't add Revelation Part 2, that is not what he's saying. Do I think that we can have more books of the Bible written today? No, but it is dishonest to use this verse to prove that.

God shall add unto him the plagues that are written in this book:

> *Revelation 9:20 And the rest of the men which were not killed by these **plagues** yet repented not of the works of their hands, that they should not worship devils, and idols of gold, and silver, and brass, and stone, and of wood: which neither can see, nor hear.*

> *Revelation 11:6 These have power to shut heaven, that it rain not in the days of their prophecy: and have power over waters to turn them to blood, and to smite the earth with all **plagues**, as often as they will.*

*Revelation 15:1 And I saw another sign in heaven, great and marvellous, seven angels having the seven last **plagues**; for in them is filled up the wrath of God.*

*Revelation 18:4 And I heard another voice from heaven, saying, Come out of her, my people, that ye be not partakers of her sins, and that ye receive not of her **plagues**.*

So whatever the plagues are, it involves the last day's judgment of Jerusalem, it involves the trumpets, the vials and the ministry of the two witnesses. And you have a promise if you want to claim a promise, you can write a hymn on this one: add to the book of Revelation and you get all the plagues that are in it. He promises those people in those seven churches that if there's anyone in your church that wants to add to this book, they get to stay and be a full partaker. They get to be a full partaker of the plagues written in the book.

22:19

And if any man shall take away from the words of the book of this prophecy, God shall take away his part out of the book of life, and out of the holy city, and from the things which are written in this book. Why do the Bibles read differently? Some say "tree of life" and some say "book of life." There are essentially three main families of Greek manuscripts that traveled down through the early church and the reason our Bibles read differently quite honestly, is not because you have dishonest people sitting in broom closets somewhere trying to mess up God's people. The reason is because some Greek texts read differently than others.

There are three main Greek texts. The Bible was not originally written in 1769 Oxford English and I hope you're not one of those people, bless your heart, that says "I have a 1611 King James Bible in my hand." No you don't. If you have a King James version, like I do, like I read out of every day, if you have a King James version, you do not have a 1611 you have a 1769 Oxford edition. The English you have is 245 years old now. So, don't get your feelings hurt. That's just a fact. You have never been to a church service where they preach out of the 1611 King James version of the Bible.

Between these three different families of Greek texts, there is approximately 93% agreement. 93% agreement between one and two and between one and three there is a 98% agreement. Now, if there are 170,000+ words in the Greek New Testament, then you need to understand that 1.4% disagreement between one and three, 98% agreement, you need to know that that comes to quite a bit less than 4,000 words in the entire New Testament and that's words that are not always different completely, sometimes they're just different in their tense, prefix and suffix. Really, that's just about it.

Now, why does the King James version have "book of life" and not "tree of life?" By the way, "the book of life" is fine because the book of life is the registry of all the people who belong in the holy city and the tree of life is in the holy city so it doesn't change the message but let's just be honest here for a second and here it is: they're not the same. They might both be true but they're not both the correct version of the Word of God. Maybe both are wrong, but they cannot both be right in that they are not both the Word of God as God gave it in this Scripture verse.

In the late 1400s, this guy by the name of Erasmus was making a Greek text. He had about a dozen Greek manuscripts to take from to make his Greek text which later in 1633 to be exact, became known as the *Textus Receptus*; we call it the "received text." It was called that after the King James translation was made but it was always essentially the same thing that Erasmus developed earlier. So, here's Erasmus, a Cath- olic, making a Greek text out of 12 existing manuscripts. It's later used by King James translators to make their King James translation but it's not the only thing the King James translators used. Erasmus had one Greek manuscript representing the book of Revelation. The last leaf of it comprised of the last six verses of Revelation was so faded he couldn't read it. Therefore, Erasmus took the Latin Vulgate and translated it into

Greek for the last six verses of his Greek manuscript. Erasmus did not have a Greek text bearing the last six verses of the book of Revelation. He made one.

Now, that tells me that there is no Greek evidence for "book of life" in this verse. It doesn't make the translation untrue, but in my opinion it makes it incorrect and there is a difference.

Appendices

Appendix 1: The Case for the Post-tribulational Rapture
Appendix 2: JW's & the 144,000

APPENDIX 1: THE POST-TRIBULATIONAL RAPTURE[29]

Introduction

Jesus Christ will return following Daniel's 70th Week. That is a bold statement which requires much substantiation—especially in a day where there are those who even question a future "70th Week of Daniel." However, a more modern doctrine has surfaced which supposes certain dispensational uniquities, and therefore requires a snatching away of gentile believers prior to this week. There are a plethora of godly men who love the Scriptures and argue well for their perspective of the end times as it relates to the church or Israel. There are a number of considerations which ultimately contrast one view from another. There are a number of topical approaches to this subject along, but it seems incumbent upon the Bible believer to do a thorough survey of the pertinent texts to determine God's intent—whether He will remove His people from the earth before the tribulation period or not.

Historical Perspective

The Posttribulation rapture is the most Scripturally-explicit, futurist, pre-millennial perspective of the rapture of the church. That restatement of the thesis, were it coming from somebody of the posttribulation perspective, would be suspicious. However, one of the foremost defenders of pretribulation rapture view says that post-tribulationalism is the "majority view of the church as a whole." Think about that. The church, made up of professing Christendom, holds a view that is majority for close to 1900 years of church history and there is still a segment insisting that "the next event on God's calendar is a pretribulational rapture?" Even doctoral theses from well-known schools would say that there is a "resurgence of a more historic posttrib- ulation type." If it is true that the historic, majority view is a particular stance, why is it being rejected by so many of the popular evangelical writers of

---

[29]Originally written for THEO 630, Eschatology (Liberty Baptist Theological Seminary)
in the Winter of 2014 in pursuit of the ThM.

today?

      Jones cites both the Apostles' Creed of the 2nd century A.D. and the Council of Nicea of the 4th century A.D. to state the essentials of which all believers through- out the church age have held. He states them as Christ's eventual coming; the resurrection of the dead; and a final judgment. The entirety of this view is most simply summarized in a posttribulational rapture perspective. That is to say, there must have been a body of Scripture which led the early church to believe these things occurred together. It is furthermore understood that the early church widely held a posttribulation viewpoint until around the middle ages when a more allegorical perspective on all things prophetic took a hold on professing Christendom. Darbyism, known well by its dogmatic pretribulationalism then took a prominent place in the 19th century until an apparent resurgence made its way into prevalent evangelicalism through the writings of George Ladd and Robert Gundry.

Definitions

Tribulation

      This is that period of time which is identified in Jeremiah 30:7 as "Jacob's time of trouble" and in Daniel 9 as the "Seventieth Week." "Pretribulation rapture" refers to the catching away of believers prior to the period known as the "tribulation." It is, however, usually proposed by those who are known as "dispensationalists"—recognized by those who see clear distinction between Israel and the body of Christ.

Great Tribulation

      This is that period of time identified by Jesus in Matthew 24:15-21 as having begun after the "abomination desolation." 2 Thessalonians 2:3-4 gives this as the stark indicator that the "man of sin" has been "revealed."

Day of the LORD

      Suffice to say that this term is different among the perspectives of eschatology in its starting point, chiefly. The various persectives would all agree that the "wrath of God" is at least related to the Day of the LORD and that these two elements are related to the coming of Christ for His saints as they find close proximity in 1 Thessalonians' 4th and 5th chapters.

There is a second note of interest here: The "Day of the LORD" as described in Acts 2 which quote Joel 2 does not occur until after a certain sign:

> *Acts 2:17-20 And it shall come to pass in the last days, saith God, I will pour out of my Spirit upon all flesh: and your sons and your daughters shall prophesy, and your young men shall see visions, and your old men shall dream dreams: 18 And on my servants and on my handmaidens I will pour out in those days of my Spirit; and they shall prophesy: 19 And I will shew wonders in heaven above, and signs in the earth beneath; blood, and fire, and vapour of smoke: 20 The sun shall be turned into darkness, and the moon into blood, **before that great and notable day of the Lord come:***

The sign described in verse 20 seems easily described in the following two passages:

> *Matthew 24:29 Immediately after the tribulation of those days shall **the sun be darkened, and the moon shall not give her light, and the stars shall fall from heaven, and the powers of the heavens shall be shaken.***

> *Revelation 6:12 And I beheld when he had opened the sixth seal, and, lo, there was a great earthquake; and **the sun became black as sackcloth of hair, and the moon became as blood; 13 And the stars of heaven fell unto the earth, even as a fig tree casteth her untimely figs,** when she is shaken of a mighty wind..*

One can see from the preceding three verses that the "Day of the LORD" occurs after the sign described in those verses (Acts 2:20), and that sign occurs "after the tribulation" (Matthew 24:29). Therefore, the "Day of the LORD" occurs after the "Great Tribulation."

Ecclesiological Conception

Major conflict arises between major views of this doctrine around "what makes up the body of Christ?" One might assume that those saved during the tribulation period are not known as the body of Christ, the church. Otherwise, it would be hard to imagine Christ took the church without leaving any of her behind only to spawn new members of the Christ's body.

Then there is the absence of ekklesia in Revelation 4-19. This produces a lot of consternation on the side of the pretribulationist who believes that after numerous mentions of ekklesia in Revelation 1-3, it would also be widely used in the remaining chapters of the book if, in fact, church age believers were present. That is a strict guideline given the usage of ekklesia by John the apostle to local congregations alone in Revelation 1-3. The question is whether the writer of Revelation was looking specifically at particular localities in Revelation 4-19 necessitating the mention of local ekklesias. Since John never used the word to refer to the worldwide believing body in Revelation 1-3, it stands to reason that it would also not be used when describing general, earthdwelling saints in Revelation 4-19.

Scriptural Consideration

The real problem with saying there are "systems" of interpretation oversight— given the term "systematic theology is that the Bible was not written to be systemized. There are absurd amounts of "takes" and "perspectives" on how certain Scripture patterns ought to be recognized and treated. Since this anomaly occurs even among conservative evangelicals, it is important to approach from a Scripture-only view and to be careful to allow the system to be changed by Scripture and not the other way around. For example, some hermeneutical perspectives say there is a definite difference between Israel and the church while others say there is no need to promote such a distinction. For this cause, a straightforward weighing of the salient Scriptures is appropriate.

Furthermore, although it is tempting to discuss what is not in a passage— rebutting opposing views—the discussion will focus on what is present. Consequently, the view that is lacking Scriptural support should get the least amount of mentioning in this type of project. It is tempting to speak against "secret" this or that as they are glaringly absent, yet what is present speaks much louder than what is absent.

Matthew 24

The "gathering of the elect" (24:31) which follows the "great tribulation" (24:21,29) has an accompanying trumpet which presumably signals assembly as it does in Joel 2:15. Certainly there is a reference to a "last trump" in 1 Corinthians 15:51 where those who are yet living will be "changed" and those that are dead will be "raised incorruptible." One can understand the concept of a "last trump" if this trumpet occurs during Matthew 24's post-tribulation trumpet where one finds the "elect" being "gathered." However, if one sees a "last trump" seven years earlier, one might ask what makes the "last trumpet" (1 Corinthians 15:51) "last" (if there is one to follow seven years later for the gathering of, from the perspective of the pretribu- lational rapturist, another group of "elect"). If, however, it is contended that it was "last" for the believer taking part in the pretribulational rapture, then it should follow that there was some preceding trumpets. However, there no preceding trumpets from this perspective.

Certainly, there are those who would say that the disciples are representatives of ethnic Israel, but that is hard to accept without reservation when Ephesians 2:20 finds Paul naming them as the beginning of what he later identifies in Ephesians 3 as a mystery hidden from the foundation of the world and what he even later identifies in Ephesians 5 as the church. Unfortunately, there has been, for far too long, a flip- pant, by the way, party line about this body of Scripture being directed at Israel rather than the foundation of the church which happened to be, by and large, Jews living in and around Jerusalem. After all, by the time of the Olivet Discourse, Christ has promised to remove, for the time being, the kingdom from the Jewish nation and has begun the turn to a Gentile composition of His Messianic kingdom as is seen in the progression of Matthew leading up to the Olivet Discourse. Of course, the question that should follow is how the church can be in view in Matthew 18 regarding church discipline, in Matthew 26 regarding the Lord's Supper, and in Matthew 28 regarding the Great Commission, yet the church is not in view during the Olivet Discourse. Or, more profound—how the Olivet Discourse can have one audience as Israel and the Lord's Supper, two days later, can have another audience, composed of the same men, as the church.

Luke 21:36

Here is a Scripture that deals, in great detail, with many of the issues sur- rounding the Great Tribulation as described by Matthew 24. Here Jesus seems to introduce the idea that one could escape these things and, instead, find themselves standing before the Lord. One might find this counterintuitive as there is no clear cut "salvation by grace/once-saved-always-saved" perspective here. Certainly Walvoord, a Dallas Theological Seminary Professor at the time, would have that soteriological stance, yet there is mention here of "pray that you will be found worthy to escape." At worse, this is a salvation that is works-based. At best, it is salvation that must be maintained through a state of mind. Perhaps more acceptable is that this supposed "rapture" is a partial rapture that has nothing to do with "who is saved," but rather "which saved people are ready for the coming of Christ?" Perhaps some light from Psalm 1 would be helpful here. "Chaff" is driven away by wind and what remains is what "stands in the congregation of the righteous" (Psalm 1:4-5). More plainly, the wicked are carried away in judgment while the saint remains to rejoice in the glory of the Lord. This is certainly the feel of 2 Thessalonians 1:6-10.

1 Thessalonians 4:16-5:9

Verse 17 speaks of those who are living at the time of the coming of Jesus "meeting" Christ in the air. This is typically thought of as a time when there is a "meet- ing in the air" with the idea that this meeting takes place for the sake of "meeting" in today's sense. However, there is a unique idea with this idea of "meeting" that speaks of a royal delegation going to meet a dignitary and escorting him or her to the place of purpose or objective. The reason the posttribulation view will stand the test of time is because it does not assume a multiphase 2nd Coming of Christ. There are not two events separated by a period of time.

2 Thessalonians 1:6-10

There is no indication of a supposed "great escape" from the time of judgment described in verses 8-9. As a matter of fact, there is certain flavor of Matthew 25:31 and Hebrews 10:28-29. There is a waiting for judgment and the assumption that believers who have been "troubled" are to rest until Christ's return to carry out this judgment. There is no leaving of the planet prior to this judgment but rather a waiting for the Lord beside, or aside from, this judgment. As a matter of fact, this is a close parallel to the Day of the Lord feel of Matthew 24:29-31 which follows the "tribulation of those days."

2 Thessalonians 2:1-3

Surely some would say that this letter was written to correct the notion that the "Day of the LORD" had already begun. Understanding that the "Day of the LORD" does not begin until after the Great Tribulation would also mean that these Thessalonian believers had somehow feared missing the coming of Christ that occurs simultaneously with or in close succession with that "Day of the LORD."

Meanwhile the "coming of the Lord and our gathering unto Him" is certainly a two-for-one in that there appears to be an event where two things occur: 1. Christ's coming, and 2. Gathering saints around the Christ Who has come. Contextual flow requires Christ's coming and "our gathering" of verse 1 to be the 2nd Coming when the focus of the preceding (1:6-10) and succeeding passages (2:3-7) are taken into consideration. It is, then, most natural to see "His coming" and "our gathering" occurring at the same time. If then, they occur at the same time from 2:1, then these two events contextually connect with the "Day of the LORD" that immediately succeeds them and the vengeance in fire that precedes them. All of these are proceded, then, by the Great Tribulation.

2:2 introduces the idea that there were false letters and teachers claiming to be from Paul which were troubling them. Why were they troubled? Because they feared they missed the "coming of the Lord." This was unnecessary though since Paul had already taught them what was true in a previous exchange (2:5).

Regarding 2:3, there is some discussion of whether the "falling away" and "revelation of the man of sin" are placed in order by the word "first" or whether this word merely speaks of the "Day of the LORD" coming 2nd to these two things. Again, the flow of thought makes little sense if both do not take place prior to the "Day of the LORD" since there is no need to mention either of these components if they do not both precede the "Day of the LORD" as that is the topic Paul has described in this passage: "Has the Day of the LORD come and gone?"

It should also be noted that if the Day of the Lord was to be preceded by the rapture, not only would Paul be superfluous in describing two non-rapture events such as the "falling away" and the "revelation of the man of sin" (2 Thessalonians 2:3-4), but his notion that believers could be overtaken by the Day of the Lord—albeit not as thief (1 Thessalonians 5:1-4)—would be pointless as well.

Revelation 2-3

The reader quickly remembers that there are seven letters to separate churches in these two chatpers. Some have said that there are six warnings to six of the seven churches in clear reference to the Second Coming of Jesus. Certainly, the reader can ascertain at least four from these.

To the Church at Pergamos, Jesus said, "Repent; or else **I will come unto thee** quickly, and will fight against them with the sword of my mouth" (Revelation 2:16). Certainly one would look a little further than the immediate context to see that this is a reference to Revelation 19. Nowhere else in Revelation's narrative does the reader find Jesus with a sword in His mouth. This is most certainly a warning to the church of the Revelation 19 Second Coming. It is wresting the Scripture out of its original, narrative to state otherwise. There are numerous other ways to describe Jesus so the Pergamosian reader does not associate the proposed "coming" with the "sword of the mouth" coming of Revelation 19, but would rather associate it with a preceding coming.

To the church at Thyatira, said Jesus, "But that which ye have already hold fast **till I come**" (Revelation 2:25). Given there is a mention of "Great Tribulation" to those who are not acting the part of those who believe (in counterdistinction to those who are promised deliverance because they have "kept the word of Christ's patience", Revelation 3:10), it should be pointed out that there is only one other mention of "Great Tribulation" in Revelation, and it is found to be a period of time out of which certain 'are coming' (ESV; Revelation 7:14). Furthermore, since

Jesus places this period of time after the Abomination of Desolation (Matthew 24:15-16), there is a connection made: those who are a part of the church of Thyatira had a relevant threat of this Great Tribulation. This would have been pointless, then, had there been a "coming of Christ" that was three and one half years prior to this Great Tribulation. No, the "coming" of Revelation 2:25 must have some connection to the threat of "Great Tribulation" and, therefore, occurred close to this period of time. Jesus already placed a "coming" directly after this "Great Tribulation" (Matthew 24:31) and, therefore, Jesus must be speaking of the same sequence in this prophecy to the church. It does not seem to make sense to assume this is an imminent coming. There are no contextual, explicit statements to that end.

To the church as Sardis, Jesus said, "Remember therefore how thou hast received and heard, and hold fast, and repent. If therefore thou shalt not watch, I will come on thee as a thief, and thou shalt not know what hour **I will come upon thee**" (Revelation 3:3). There are no indications in the immediate context, much like Revelation 2:25. However, much like Revelation 2:25, there are other Revelation-relevant, contextual clues. There is a warning that sounds much like this same verse in Revelation 16:15 and they are found around the time of the 6th vial and the Battle of Armigeddon. Now, if author's intent and contextual flow means anything, it should mean that this tells the reader the approximate timing of this "coming as a thief." In this case it is close to the great battle at the end of the tribulation also spoken of in Revelation 19.

To the Church at Philadelphiam Jesus said, "Behold, **I come quickly**: hold that fast which thou hast, that no man take thy crown" (Revelation 3:11). One would seek to know what this means in relation to the "keeping from" the hour of temptation those who "keep [Christ's] words" can embrace and enjoy (3:10). Certainly, the pretribulationist connects this promise to the coming and, therefore interpret His coming as the "keeping out" mechanism. In other words, they would hold that there is a physical removal of these saints from the earth. Another way to interpret this, however, is that the "quck coming" of 3:11 is that which consummates the "keeping out of the hour of temptation" the saints. Does this not have the same flow to it as

2 Thessalonians 1:6-10? Even more amazing, perhaps, is that the only other time this phraseology is used is in John 17:15 when Jesus' prayer was not that "[the Father] should remove them from the world, but that [He] should keep them from the evil [one]." John records this prayer in His gospel and then records this same phraseology as Christs's words in his Book of the Revelation. Certainly this is no happenstance.

Conclusion

Certainly, no sane believer would ask for tribulation, let alone a trib- ulation aforetime unknown to the world. However, the reader must say with Grudem that this was not a "decision which was ours to make." Does this move the believer to be intimidated or frightened at the prospect of persecution? Perhaps, it does, but should it? Is not the Christ Who designed all things in accordance with His Father's will able also to apportion special grace which was hitherto unknown for this very same "Great Tribulation?" A God Who cannot deem it so is presumably unworthy of the trust of millions for the salvation of their souls.

What Scripture provides us is the understanding that believers are anticipating a "gathering together around Christ at His coming" that occurs with the "Day of the LORD" that does not occur until after the "Great Tribulation."

APPENDIX 2: JEHOVAH'S WITNESSES & THE 144,000

Here are some distinguishing characteristics about these 144,000 in Revelation 7:3-8 and 14:1-5):

    1. They are the same group in both passages.
    2. They are Jewish (7:4-8).
    3. They are male (14:4).
    4. They are virgins (14:4)
    5. They are in heaven. They are with the Lamb. They follow wherever he goes (14:1; 4).

> *Who and how many are able to enter the kingdom?* ***The revelation limits to 144,000 the number that become a part of the kingdom*** *in saying....*[30]

What do they have to be? Male, virgin Jews.

> ***Only a little flock of 144,000 go to heaven*** *and rule with Christ. The 144,000 are born again as spiritual sons of God.*[31]

In Revelation 7, you have two visions. Please notice chapter 7:1-8: It involves ethnicity—the Jews. Then in 7:7-17, we have a vision involving "The great multitude which no man could number of all nations and kindred people." So the first vision in chapter 7 of Revelation deals with Jews and the second vision in that chapter deals with everyone else. So, the Jehovah's Witnesses have to make the Jews of the first eight verses Gentiles if their interpretation is going to carry forth.

---

[30] _____ *Let God Be True* (Brooklyn: Watchtower Bible and Tract Society, Inc., 1952), 136.
[31] Ravi Zecharias *Kingdom of the Cults* (2003), 133.

They have to make it allegory. It has to mean something other than what it says on the page. So somehow, you have to turn a Jehovah's Witness and every Jehovah's Witness into a male virgin Jew. What is wrong with making the Jews of the first vision symbolic? You have two Gentile visions when one is said to be Jewish.

Not only this, but what do the tribes picture? Like the tribe of Asher, verse 6, who does that symbolize? What part of the Jehovah's Witnesses does that symbolize?

You have the first vision is picturesque of Gentiles who are washed in the blood of the Lamb and the second vision is a vision of Gentiles who are washed in the blood of the Lamb. What's the point of that? So there's a real issue. You have to do a lot of gymnastics.

> *As pointed out in chapter 7, the Apostle John was given a vision in which he saw the Lamb standing upon Mount Sion **with him with him 144,000**. John's himself tells us that these are the ones that keep following the Lamb no matter where he goes.*[32]

Alright, so if that's literal then why not the sentence before it? These are virgins, right? That's figurative and somehow the part after that is literal.

> *Yes, they are faithful followers of Jesus Christ specially chosen to rule in heaven with him. After being raised out of death to heavenly life, they rule as kings over the earth. Since the days of the apostles, God has been selecting **faithful Christians to complete the number 144,000.***

How many will there be? 144,000.

> *To arrange for Jesus and **the 144,000** to rule mankind is very*

---

[32] *What Does the Bible Really Teach?* (Brooklyn: Watch Tower Bible Tract Society of New York, Inc., 2005), 85.

loving. For one thing, Jesus knows what it's like to be human and to suffer. Paul said that Jesus is not one who cannot sympathize with our weaknesses.[33] His co-rulers too have suffered and endured as humans.

*God's kingdom is a heavenly government where Jesus Christ is King and from among mankind, **144,000 are taken** to rule with him. The kingdom started to rule in 1914 and since then Satan has been cast out of heaven down to earth. Rest assured, Satan is no longer in heaven. He has been cast out since 1914.[34]*

*The red wine represents Jesus' blood. That blood makes valid the new covenant. Jesus said that his blood was poured out for forgiveness of sins. Humans can thus become clean in God's eyes and can enter into the new covenant with Jehovah. This new covenant or contract <u>makes it possible</u> for **144,000 faithful Christians to go to heaven**. There they will serve as kings and priests for the blessing of all mankind.[35]*

So, what if you're not going to be able to be a part of that 144,000? Then what? Well, the most you can hope for is to be worthy of the resurrection. Until you are raised in the resurrection, you are asleep in the dust of the earth and you know nothing. It's a dreamless sleep, they say and in the morning of the resurrection, you will wake up and you will live in a new body here on earth in paradise.

---

[33] It's interesting, he says Paul said it and it's in Hebrews. So we don't really know that Paul wrote Hebrews.
[34] Ibid., 85.
[35] Ibid., 207.

Made in the USA
Middletown, DE
14 April 2018